In Harm's Way

October 1991

To Dan W.

With Best wishes,

Harlan IIII

In Harm's Way

American Seapower and the 21st Century

Harlan K. Ullman

Center for Naval Analyses

Bartleby Press

Silver Spring, Maryland

Cover Photograph: U.S. Navy photograph by PH1 Terry Cosgrove, USN

Printed in the United States of America

Published by:

Bartleby Press
11141 Georgia Avenue
Silver Spring, Maryland 20902

Library of Congress Cataloging-in-Publication Data

Ullman, Harlan.
    In harm's way: American seapower and the 21st century / Harlan K.
    Ullman.
        p. cm.
    Includes bibliographical references.
    ISBN 0-910155-18-6
    1. Sea-power—United States. 2. United States. Navy. I. Title.
VA50.U49   1991
359'.03'0973—dc20   91-23128
                                                                 CIP

Contents

Illustrations

Tables

Preface

Timing is often everything, both good and bad. I began writing this book a few months after that grand and momentous day in November 1989 when the Berlin Wall came crashing down. With the Wall's political and physical demise, nearly 45 years of Cold War was about to pass into the mists of history. At that point in early 1990, the purpose of this book was to argue that the United States had entered a unique and defining period in its history that would require dramatic, innovative, and perhaps even daring policy responses if the nation was to deal successfully and safely with the unprecedented changes and transformations symbolized by the ending of the Cold War. These findings were to be applied to national security policy and to the process of defining the rationale and shape of future American seapower.

The major consequences for U.S. policy, at least in the first stages of refinement, flowed from the visibly profound changes in the political and military threats posed by the USSR and Warsaw Pact. If and as the magnitude or plausibility of those long-standing threats dissipated, the strategic centroid and public support around which the United States based most of its post-war national security policy would likewise shrink. This contraction would obviously pose profound consequences for the long-standing strategic rationale and military force structure necessitated by this Cold War. However, two requirements remained. First, other threats that had to be dealt with still existed, even if these threats were less precise, ill-defined, more ambiguous, and of less absolute danger than that posed by a belligerent USSR. And, second, the West needed to retain sufficient force and resolve as safeguards against a resurgent USSR and perhaps as instruments to stimulate a further positive transition in that long-standing Soviet threat.

Under these conditions, the test for the United States would be to realign its future security and military policies from the USSR as principal danger to these less clear-cut threats, all the while maintaining sufficient insurance and resilience to protect against even a small prospect of a regenerated Soviet adversary. Thus, for the first time since 1945, the military services would have to understand and identify what level of military capability the nation would support if and as the Soviet threat continued to recede and as other threats, admittedly diffuse and ill-defined, were perceived by the public in importance and danger. Additionally, as the strategic rationale for maintaining U.S. forces shifts, it is not axiomatic that a force structure designed to deter or fight the USSR is, *ipso facto*, the right force for this future world. Recognizing and responding to this condition will therefore become high-priority items.

During the year it took to write this book, the Germanys united, the Warsaw Pact dissolved, and Saddam Hussein attempted to annex Kuwait. Twenty-eight nations joined together under 12 United Nations Security Council resolutions to liberate Kuwait, and the operation called Desert Shield began in August 1990. On January 16, 1991, Desert Shield became Desert Storm, and six weeks later the allies had inflicted a devastating military defeat on Saddam Hussein at virtually no cost to themselves. Throughout those months, the domestic condition within the USSR deteriorated, leading some in the West to wonder whether the Cold War was really over.

Because of these and other events, the purposes of the book were validated and reinforced (at least in the author's view) as the principal regions for 45 years of Western security planning—Europe and the Middle East—were fundamentally changed and reshaped. To be sure, the USSR may remain a rival, and domestic crises there could challenge the world at large. These fearsome events, however, should they arise, will be of a fundamentally different character than the schisms that provoked the Cold War. In addition, as dazzling as the military victory in the sands of Kuwait was, the politics of the Gulf have been profoundly altered, and the future difficulties of building a modicum of peace and stability should not be understated.

This shift in long-term American strategic interests and needs, along with other realities, principally the clash of U.S. domestic priorities with a spartan fiscal environment, will compel us to adopt a new security framework either through careful planning or by simple default. No matter how relevant our forces and force structures were to prevailing in the Cold War, one conclusion is clear. A change is inevitable. Although we apply lip service to recognizing this condition, as a nation, we have yet to take any substantive action on what to do next. Action is needed now. I hope the arguments that follow support this new call to arms and help to make the case for shaping American seapower in this extraordinary future.

I have striven to write this book as a long essay rather than a purely academic tome. Any faults and shortcomings that follow are mine alone. I do owe enormous gratitude to many friends, colleagues, and supporters—the list would be longer than the book. I single out only three: Dr. Phil E. DePoy, until recently, President of the Center for Naval Analyses (CNA) and now a Senior Fellow there, who was the guiding force behind this project and whose broader contribution to the Navy and to the nation requires special recognition and tribute; Mrs. Marty Weaver, of CNA, who valiantly struggled with my illegible writing to turn out the manuscript; and Ms. Louise Hernon who tried to reconcile my prose with the English language.

Washington, D.C.   Harlan K. Ullman
June 1991

Introduction

*Give me a fast ship for I intend
to sail in harm's way.*[1]

John Paul Jones

Whether in the age of Napoleon or in the age of nuclear weapons, the phrase *in harm's way* has encapsulated the fighting spirit of the United States Navy and Marine Corps, forged many of their aspirations, and set much of the ethos for the sea services. Now, even as we sail into the 21st century, this heritage is no less a major philosophical and spiritual determinant in defining the case for maritime power than in the past. However, as profound changes continue to alter our world, the theme of harm's way that has served us so well must be modified to conform to the realities of today and the uncertainties of tomorrow.

Before the nuclear attacks on Hiroshima and Nagasaki that immutably would redefine Clausewitz' enduring relationship between war and politics, harm's way sprung from the same system of metaphysics as Douglas McArthur's dictum that, in war, there is no substitute for victory. Harm's way, at least before the nuclear era, was conceptually and operationally indivisible both in peacetime and in wartime. Despite the fog, chance, and friction inherent in war that created agonizing uncertainties about outcome, preparations, training, and intentions in peace were ascribed to the absolute need for winning in war.

1. For the purist, according to Samuel Eliot Morison in *John Paul Jones: A Sailor's Biography* (Boston: Little Brown and Company, 1959, p. 182), the full quote was: "I wish to have no Connection with any Ship that does not sail *fast*, for I intend *to go in harm's way. . . .*"

During all these centuries, the ultimate purpose of navies was to support and affect the campaign or war fought ashore. Armies, amphibious forces, and, later, tactical airpower won or lost control of the critical landmass. Navies battled other navies, convoyed unarmed ships, landed forces ashore, block-aded coasts, and hurled shot and fire against fixed and moving targets on the ground. This projection of power, however, was invariably in support of broader objectives ashore, and winning command of the sea, as Mahan noted, was not an end in itself.

The dawning of the nuclear age and, most significantly, the invention and deployment of society-threatening ther-monuclear weapons of mass destruction blurred traditional, clear-cut distinctions between potential winners and losers in war. Preparations and intent in peacetime could no longer ex-clusively or wisely rest only on winning a war against the USSR. Deterrence of the USSR and avoidance of nuclear Armageddon were to become the overriding objectives and re-sults of policy in this age. As we will see, the traditional mis-sion of supporting the campaign ashore was to shift as direct-ing retaliatory strikes against an enemy's homeland assumed greater importance. The splitting of the atom, therefore, had the side effect of splitting the meaning and intent of harm's way. Now, four decades later, the ending of the Cold War will no doubt lead to even further mutation and complexity of the meaning.

Although there can be little doubt that the Cold War as we knew it is over, there is considerable doubt whether the world of tomorrow will be either as peaceful or as safe as the world of today. While there is great doubt as to how the USSR will re-solve the vast internal problems it faces, few of us can be un-aware of the fundamental, dramatic, and, in some cases, extraordinary forces that have forever changed the global system that has been in place since the end of World War II. Absolute reversals in Soviet international and domestic policy that were inconceivable only a few years ago became routine and ordinary. Although the USSR at the moment may be aban-doning its reformist track, few believe there is much possibility of rekindling an East-West military rivalry remotely similar to that of the Cold War. The perseverance and prevalence of the

North Atlantic Treaty Organization (NATO) and the dismantlement of the Warsaw Pact as a fighting force are no less remarkable than the explosion of all forms of power across the globe. This diffusion of power has challenged and limited the scope and authority of the two superpowers despite the strength of their military arsenals. The Cold War was an accurate shorthand descriptor of the era that followed the end of the 1939-1945 war and of the U.S.-Soviet rivalry, but that era is now part of history.

For reasons perhaps coincidental, during this century the month of August has been significant in defining and setting much of the course of history. August 1914 and the Great or First World War created a new order and international system on the ashes and devastation of four years of conflict and defined the foundation for most of the next three decades. August 1945 ushered in the nuclear age, ushered out the Second World War, and ultimately led to the Cold War, in which former enemies became allies and former friends became foes. August 1964, the date of the Tonkin Gulf incident and the subsequent Congressional resolution, legitimized and escalated America's involvement in Vietnam, which would ultimately divide the nation in, arguably, its most bitter period since the Civil War.

The events of August 1990, the occupation of Kuwait by Iraq, and the subsequent overwhelming victory of the allied coalition in liberating Kuwait may well prove to be the catalyst and demarcation point that conclusively ended the Cold War. Although post-war events in the Gulf will not play out perhaps for years, the Gulf War provides a useful reference point in assessing the recent and remarkable changes that have occurred to put the 45 years of Cold War history behind us. What comes next in this post-Cold War world, the relevance of harm's way in this new era, and the significance for American seapower are the central questions addressed by this book.

Before August 1990, the great debate on whether the Cold War was over or when it would end had no legitimate and indisputable resolution. Impelled by Mikhail Gorbachev, the United States and the Soviet Union were moving to some form of entente or partnership, and the prospect of a unified Germany was about to reshape the geopolitical and perhaps even the economic structure of Europe. The post-war security system, anchored in military alliances that reflected the fundamental differences between the superpowers and buttressed by nuclear weapons, was being further diluted and partly replaced with a hierarchy that rested in larger measure on economics and on a new or at least more influential international order.

During the six months that Iraq occupied Kuwait, the particles composing the Cold War's molecular structure were fired through and accelerated by a political cyclotron. Europe and the Middle East had long been the centerpieces in our security planning. Now, both regions had changed. Although the consequences and mutations wrought by the "Saddam Hussein effect" will take time to settle out, striking pieces of evidence demonstrate that the Cold War is behind us.

For the first time in its life, the United Nations (UN) had become a formidable and perhaps decisive body in international politics. Its actions to condemn and compel Saddam Hussein to withdraw from Kuwait, first through the weight of economic sanctions and blockade and ultimately through the highly decisive allied offensive, were unprecedented.[1] Although it is far too early to presume that the UN could provide an alternative mechanism for ensuring collective security, the unanimity demonstrated in this crisis was a fundamental departure from the past and a cause as well as an effect of the Cold War's demise.

Perhaps more surprising, even after careful analysis of individual motivations, is the extraordinary coalition of 28 Arab and non-Arab states that sent forces to Saudi Arabia, first to defend the Royal Kingdom and then to evict Saddam Hussein from Kuwait. The presence of Arab states, particularly Syria and Egypt, alongside U.S., British, French, and other forces against a fellow Arab state suggests the degree to which politics have been turned around. The Soviet Union had closely aligned itself with the United States against its former Iraqi

---

1. In 1950, had the USSR not been boycotting the UN Security Council, of which it was and is a permanent member, the action to send forces under the UN flag to counter North Korea's invasion of the south most surely would have been vetoed.

ally and supported the authorization to use force. Although there was dissonance in the ranks over the means for obtaining a peaceful settlement and U.S.-Soviet relations were not helped by the allied ground offensive into Kuwait, no fundamental break in the Moscow-Washington relationship resulted.

In Europe, the unification of Germany is politically and legally complete. The new Germany is a member of NATO, and Soviet troops are now withdrawing from what used to be the German Democratic Republic and will be out of "Eastern Europe" by 1994. Furthermore, a 20-year nonaggression and friendship treaty between Germany and the USSR has been signed, and major arms reductions have begun through the Conventional Forces in Europe (CFE) Treaty signed in November 1990. Although there is irrefutable evidence that the Soviets have not complied with CFE, this violation is unlikely to have lasting consequences given the demise of the Warsaw Pact, although this Soviet action is a useful reminder that the United States and the USSR are not yet full and complete allies. Perhaps the final proof of how much it is really "over, over there" was the redeployment of about half the U.S. Army's strength in Germany to the Persian Gulf, in this case, two tank divisions and an armored cavalry regiment. It is unlikely that those forces will all return to Germany now that the Gulf Crisis is over.

For the Department of Defense (DOD) and the military services that are charged with planning for this nation's security, this unraveling of the Cold War will create many new uncertainties and differences of opinion about the future size, shape, and composition of the forces. This planning exercise may be complicated by perceptions of what lessons, if any, should be drawn from the Gulf War and applied to resolving these issues over future force structure. Before August 2, 1990, the immediate strategic and fiscal challenges facing DOD were intrinsically related to the fiscal year (FY) 1991 budget process. Caught between the pincers of the Gramm-Rudman-Hollings Deficit Reduction Law, a budget deficit then projected at $120 to 140 billion for FY 1991, and automatic spending cuts that would go into effect when the deficit exceeded $64 billion,

DOD faced a Damoclean sword that would amputate major limbs and huge pieces of military bone and muscle.

Ironically, Saddam Hussein provided a brief stay of execution for DOD, because, as long as the Gulf Crisis persisted, the U.S. Congress would not take draconian measures against defense. Now that the war is over, however, budget reality will settle in, and, despite the extraordinary credit the military rightfully earned from defeating Iraq, little of this public good will is likely to be translated into fiscal largesse. This situation poses a double problem. First, DOD must absorb the cuts that have already been mandated by law but deferred during Operations Desert Shield/Storm. The effects of these cuts will be magnified by the increases in spending and in serving personnel (including the Reserves) made for the Gulf War that now must be drawn down. Second, DOD still will have to deal with the broader and long-term budget problems that inevitably must force defense spending lower and lower.

The economic picture within the United States remains uncertain and the federal deficit, despite the so-called historic deficit-reduction package for 1991, continues to soar. In FY 1990, the deficit grew to $220 billion, nearly double the forecast. This figure does not include so-called off-budget expenditures that do not count against the deficit, such as the costs of covering the savings and loan crisis or the Social Security surplus (which is collected by the Treasury now and borrowed against the deficit even though these Social Security funds must be paid out later). The Gramm-Rudman targets have been reset at astronomical new limits to meet likely deficits with some degree of realism. In FY 1991, Gramm-Rudman sequestration was to have been triggered at $64 billion; this deficit ceiling has now been raised to nearly $330 billion. In FY 1992, this ceiling was to have been $28 billion; it is now $317 billion. All in all, this updated and now neutered Gramm-Rudman Law permits an increase in total deficits accumulated for FYs 1991 through 1993 from nearly zero to over $1 trillion. Clearly, now that Operation Desert Storm has been concluded, fiscal reality must set in. Not only will the defense budget become a principal recipient of cuts, it could become an endangered species.

With the war over, the civilian and military leadership in DOD will have to come to grips with redefining the basis and structure for U.S. fighting power. This redefinition could come with lightning speed and, at the outside, is unlikely to be deferred for more than a year or two because of economic pressure caused by growing deficits. One means of beginning this redefinition process is to resolve four sets of fundamental questions that pertain to strategic, domestic, infrastructure, and operational challenges and issues. Ironically, despite the great changes under way, fundamental questions and problems have a timelessness of their own.

During the transition of Chiefs of Naval Operations (CNOs) into and out of office, the Vice Chief (VCNO) usually supervises preparation of the turnover material for the incoming service chief. In the spring of 1982, amidst the large Navy buildup to 600 ships and a maritime high-water mark of sorts, the VCNO's cover letter to the newly-selected CNO was short, direct, and concerned. The letter made three points.[1]

First, it argued that, despite the hooplah surrounding the Navy's expansion, the strategy underwriting this growth was neither sufficiently defined nor articulated to satisfy growing questions from Congress and the media. Restating and publicizing the rationale and strategy for the Navy were recommended as the top priority.

Second, the letter forecast that, unless major changes in improving the efficiency and effectiveness of the acquisition process were implemented, the 600-ship Navy would not be affordable. Driving down prices and costs, therefore, should be high priorities, especially when the positive rate of funding for the Navy began to reverse direction.

Third, better integration of operations to include cross-service as well as cross-fleet requirements was identified as an important priority. These three priorities exist today with even greater relevance and intensity, especially as the size and shape of the future Navy spirals downward. Further, the addition of a

---

1. Letter from VCNO Admiral William N. Small, USN (Ret.), to CNO-designate Admiral James D. Watkins, USN (Ret.), 10 May 1982.

fourth category—domestic—is essential in coping with these changing times and conditions.

The fundamental questions that arise from these current strategic challenges and issues relate to threat and to response. With the Soviet empire in tatters and the dissolution of the Warsaw Pact a reality, the nature of the principal threat to Western security has fundamentally changed. Regarding other potential adversaries, including the remnants of Iraq's army, no plausible or likely threat will materialize for a long time to come that is capable of provoking a Western response remotely close to what treasure and resolve went into waging the Cold War. For the time being, the United States has responded tactically to these events by beginning to downsize its military force structure, but has not acted strategically to alter its basic security assumptions and rationale. In taking the next step, at least four strategic questions must be answered.

First, how can and should the United States deal with this transition in threats so that it ensures prudence and safety vis-à-vis the USSR and keeps enough powder dry to deal with other crises (such as the Gulf War) and threats that menace U.S. interests and security? Will the decline of a large, powerful maritime adversary change the basis for future U.S. seapower needs and how might U.S. strategy respond if there is no longer a big, single navy against which to measure American naval power?

Second, can and should U.S. military power in general and the inevitable builddown in forces in particular be used strategically to induce the USSR to assume a more benign (from the U.S. perspective) military posture? Can naval arms control discussions and agreements be useful instruments in achieving this outcome?

Third, as the threat spectrum expands to include more nontraditional concerns such as drugs and terrorism, how should these challenges be incorporated into future national security frameworks? How far should this accommodation go to cover nontraditional missions and should social and educational functions similar to those performed by the services in the 1930s be seriously considered as part of this new environment?

Finally, can we use the opportunities created by this transition in threats to review our strategic use of technology and possibly to redefine the balance, pace, and urgency of improving capabilities through either product upgrades or "leap ahead" new systems? Indeed, is it possible that we have greatly overestimated Soviet technological proficiency and underestimated our own technical prowess and, if so, can such a technological lead be put to better strategic use?

The domestic issues raise crucial questions about the state of the nation, the degree of interest and support of the public for defense, and the ability of our political process to govern. If there were no Soviet threat, is there some minimum level of military capability the nation would intrinsically demand? How is public mood changing in its attitudes towards national security and what does this suggest for determining and maintaining future support for defense? Has the ability of the political process to govern effectively reached the point where it may harm rather than help in "providing for the common defense"?

The infrastructure that supports defense poses the third set of questions and challenges that must be addressed. Infrastructure is defined to include the defense-industrial base, the basing and logistics facilities, the manpower base, the intelligence base, and the process for acquiring the goods and services for war. In the past, this infrastructure was assumed to be an inexhaustible resource available at our beck and call. That assumption is no longer valid. We need to know what the consequences of the compression in the defense industrial base will be and what should be done, if anything. Can we afford the increasing inefficiency of the acquisition process, in which procuring goods and services in timely, affordable ways is increasingly more difficult? How should we respond to the new demands in personnel and manning mandated by moving from a larger to a smaller force, and, hence, shifting emphasis from recruiting and retaining volunteers to separating and screening those who can no longer serve or who will not be selected to serve? Given the politics of base closings, how do we avoid the pitfalls of a bloated shore structure and an anemic fleet?

Answers to these questions must include analysis and forecast of the trends in each category as this entire infrastructure is transformed, and these answers must ensure that what is maintained is what is needed. Furthermore, because much of the defense infrastructure is inseparable from social and economic issues of domestic political importance, removing the political dimension from future deliberations will be exceedingly difficult.

The final set of questions concerns operational issues. In the past, the Soviet threat simplified and streamlined our planning. Forces that were required to fight and defeat Soviet forces had to be highly capable, ready, well sustained, and well trained. These forces, therefore, could deal with all lesser threats. Emphasis was placed on the capability to strike deeply into the Soviet Union, to reinforce our allies, to defend against attack into Europe, and, later, to safeguard Persian Gulf oil from Soviet aggression. For the Navy, this needed capability translated into systems for conducting (1) deep-water, open-ocean antisubmarine warfare (ASW) against advanced, quiet, Soviet nuclear submarines, (2) long-range, standoff antiair warfare (AAW) to destroy Soviet bombers and missiles well before they could attack key U.S. units, and (3) the demands of combat of the highest intensity against a powerful naval adversary. If that naval adversary disappears, traditional operational planning to defeat that navy must be replaced with other plausible rationale.

In this case, there may be no shortage of non-Soviet threats that might have to be countered, but they will not be in the form of big, ocean-going navies. Thus, operations in the future may likely occur in regions of shallow water, in conditions where close-in combat will take place, under circumstances of no warning, and against relatively small but powerful enemy navies armed with advanced weapons. In addition, the nature of combined operations must now include working with forces as diverse as the Saudis, Syrians, and, possibly, the Soviets. Joint and combined operations had once been defined in terms of integrating the four U.S. services and key allies such as those in NATO. This definition is no longer sufficient.

Even greater demands could be placed on old operational doctrine. For example, the U.S. Navy rarely planned for using and never trained with more than three or four carrier battle groups (CVBGs), and, in those cases, the carriers were arrayed against the USSR. In the Gulf Crisis, however, six CVBGs were ordered to the Persian Gulf region, and four CVBGs operated inside that restricted waterway—a condition beyond the expectations of most analysts.

In this highly uncertain future world, these extraordinary changes and the questions that stem from these changes will require fundamental reassessment and realignment of many of the most basic assumptions, propositions, and policies that have served this nation's security so well since the end of the Second World War. Such a reassessment must extend from the loftiest of strategic perspectives to the details of buying goods and services for defense.

Policy reassessments are inevitable and often frequent tasks of government. Far rarer are significant and actual policy realignments based on these reassessments. In 1969, the newly installed Nixon administration fervently believed that the most fundamental pressures at home and abroad gave the United States no alternative but to alter many of its most basic policies. Perhaps the most publicized result was the rapprochement with China that ultimately would help in ending the Cold War; however, other policy changes had vast strategic, economic, and political impact. These changes were not lost on the U.S. Navy.

In 1970, the new CNO, Admiral Elmo R. Zumwalt, recognized that the Navy was at one of its most critical junctures. A variety of changes—the war in Vietnam that had become a national cancer, the Nixon decision to slash defense spending, and a powerful, modern, ocean-going Soviet adversary with strategic nuclear systems rivaling those of the United States—demanded response by an American Navy that was living largely off an obsolete force that had been designed for and used in World War II. Its 950 ships, many of which were old, obsolete, or both, would be halved in number, and the fleet would be postured on the basis of a smaller, far more modern force capable of responding to domestic priorities and international threats. It should also be noted that none of this was without controversy, some of it still extant.

Twenty years later, the end of the Cold War and the passing of the Soviet military threat provide similar and powerful reasons for reassessment and response. It cannot and must not be assumed that a navy designed to deter or defeat Soviet maritime power is automatically and precisely what is necessary in a world of different threats. Nor can the principle of deterrence based on striking with nuclear and conventional weapons deeply and directly into an enemy's homeland automatically be applied as the best guarantor of peace and stability in the post-Cold War world. Ironically, lessons from the pre-nuclear days, when the ethos of harm's way could be kept indivisible in peace and war, may help identify future strategic objectives and rationale for the Navy.

That the services will have to deal with these pressing issues does not imply that all this can or will be done in a vacuum. Indeed, broader social, political, economic, and governmental realities will dominate the American agenda and subsume the military debate, consigning it to an inferior position. All that may best suit the nation at large. It may not best suit the nation's interests.

Some final nits: First, nowhere in this book is an attempt made to answer the provocative question of whether the United States is and should be a maritime power. As far into the future as most people can see, this country will remain vitally dependent on the oceans for trade, transport, and resources, and no doubt will retain the ability to project its power over, on, and under water. Therefore, ascertaining whether we are, in fact, a maritime power is eccentric to this study.

A corollary point is definitional. The term *seapower* is used in the classical Mahanian sense to include both commercial and naval strength, even though the dramatic decline in the U.S. commercial maritime sector has lessened America's standing in that regard. *Maritime forces* refers primarily to the Navy and Marine Corps, although the contributions of the other services and the Coast Guard are not ignored. These contributions are covered generally in the chapter on alternative force structures. Lengthier analyses showing how the other services could assume greater maritime roles have been left for future efforts.

Second, the argument and strategic rationale made in support of the U.S. Navy is neither at the expense nor denegration of the other services. For the foreseeable future, the United States will require powerful and ready land and air forces; however, as the military, political, and strategic requirements for these types of forces in Europe and Korea diminish and after the Gulf peace arrangement is resolved, there clearly will be reductions. Whether these reductions will lead to a change of a few percent in the Navy's share of a smaller future defense budget depends on how applicable the Navy's posture is perceived to be to other regions compared with heavy ground and air forces.

Third, because the Goldwater-Nichols Defense Reorganization Law of 1986 properly stresses military jointness, the term *joint* is not repeated as a military mantra throughout the text. Clearly, joint operations are essential where they make sense. Land forces, however, are not known for their prowess in hunting submarines, and naval and air forces are not paramount in their ability to seize and hold territory ashore, particularly far inland. Similarly, the Navy has little experience in buying tanks (the Army is the responsible procurement agency for U.S. Marine Corps needs), and the Air Force is not well versed in ship procurement. Understanding these distinctions is as important as avoiding the trap of exercising military jointness only for the sake of jointness.

Fourth, technology has not been singled out as a separate subject. Of course the Navy and Marine Corps will require innovative, ongoing, and imaginative uses of technology. That goes without saying. However, in my view, the appropriate way to view technology is as an instrument to achieve some end and not an end in itself. That bias is reflected in this book.

Last, my pragmatic judgment has led me to the conclusion that future defense budgets are likely to decline in a substantial way. I refer those who are skeptical and would welcome supporting evidence of my prescience, to a report I wrote in 1985:

> The impact of constrained resources on future U.S. force structure and military capability will be profound. Using the study's budget assumptions, which are by no means worse case, U.S. conventional military capability could contract by a quarter to a third and as early as 1990.[1]

In writing this book, the breadth and extent of changing circumstances and the likely consequences for the services became obvious. Given the enormous uncertainties likely to arise from this time of great transition and turbulence, additional intellectual tools and instruments to help the Navy's leadership make decisions will be tremendously important. To abuse a maritime metaphor, a strategic compass and strategic chart for setting a safe course in this highly uncertain and uncharted new ocean are essential for the prudent mariner. Although my days as a mariner are long over, perhaps the accompanying compass and chart may help those in command to find a safe harbor.

1. Harlan K. Ullman. *U.S. Conventional Force Structure at a Crossroads*. Washington D.C.: The Center for Strategic and International Studies (CSIS), 1985, pp. 2 and 43.

1

Four Battle Ensigns

Another year, another dreadful blow!
Another mighty empire overthrown!
And soon we shall or will be left alone!

William Wordsworth

For nearly 45 years, the national security of the United States was irreversibly and inescapably intertwined with containing the Soviet threat and arresting the Cold War fractures and cleavages caused by the seemingly intractable differences between East and West over politics, culture, ideology, and value systems. The passing of the Warsaw Pact and the ending of the Cold War are so stunning that it is not a simple matter to determine what this will mean for redefining and responding to future national security needs. Furthermore, the war in the Gulf has had fundamental if not immediate impact on that critical region. Regarding these events, we are at neither their beginning nor their end, but, as Churchill observed, most likely we are at the point that can best be termed the "end of the beginning." Although the near certain elimination of apocalyptic war against the USSR constitutes a decisive and highly positive condition (as did Iraq's eviction from Kuwait), all other dangers and threats to national security are not also automatically voided.

One seemingly predictable outcome of this extraordinary change in the international order for the United States and its allies, even with the enormous uncertainties that lie ahead, should be a fundamental reassessment, redefinition, and restructuring of the meaning of threat and its overall implications for safeguarding future interests and well-being. However, one should not assume any automaticity in the political process responding as analytical judgment may suggest. Furthermore, any reassessment of threat will be complicated for the West for the short term because of the uncertainties that arise from the disconnect between (1) the initial reforms and relaxations sweeping through the Soviet Union and its former empire that are stark evidence of the end of the Cold War, (2) the remaining still large and very powerful Soviet military that is symbolic of the old threat, and (3) the legitimate worry that all this could be reversed, especially as reform appears to falter. A collision is inevitable between those Americans advocating significant reductions in Western forces now, based on these changes, and those who still counsel caution before taking more striking unilateral action in making military cuts. This collision will be intensified by the crucible of the domestic political process of the United States and the huge budget deficits that cannot be deferred for too many years longer, especially as the nation faces economic recession in 1991.

There are, however, larger and longer-term issues that must be addressed as part of ensuring our national security for the future. Within these shores, the political limitations and realities of our representative system of government and its basis in checks and balances have never been more exposed short of grave national crisis. To put it bluntly, governance is breaking down, and the ship of state is adrift in a wild and tumultuous political sea of economic, social, and physical deficits. This sea is both rising and raging, and, if we are neither determined nor skillful enough, it could capsize us.

Much of this heavy weather comes from the veritable collapse of the Soviet and Warsaw Pact threat. In the past, many of the centrifugal properties as well as the sins of government were contained by this threat. A national rallying point was established, and bipartisan political support was obtainable on grounds of national defense. Now, from another quadrant, comes a battering caused by the reverberations of a changing international order.

Concurrent with the ebbing of the Soviet threat, the continuing and accelerating spread of all forms of power across the globe has checked the authority and reduced the influence of the superpowers. Future grounds for conflict, disharmony, or cooperation are shifting from strategic and military relationships rooted in the Cold War to political and economic interactions. Productivity, balance of payments, interest rates, and stock markets may easily constitute the next generation of "weapons" if the national security environment continues along the current path.

This spread of power, however, does not necessarily signify a safer or more stable world. The nature and identification of legitimate threats to national security have become more difficult to define and certainly less absolute in their danger. Fashioning responses, especially to nontraditional threats for which military force alone will not suffice, will therefore require greater patience, intellect, and skill. Terrorism and drugs are the most frequently advertised of these "gray-area" threats to national security, but there are others. In addition, Saddam Hussein and other would-be villains of one type or another are bound to arise in this uncertain future.

These conditions—the passing of the Soviet and Warsaw Pact military threat to Europe and the ending of the Cold War, the increasing problems and declining performance of governance, the changing international order made vivid by the Gulf War and its aftermath, and the emergence of more diffuse, certainly more nontraditional, and perhaps not less dangerous threats—lead to the requirement for careful and comprehensive examination of the national security environment we are likely to face and the responses that are in our best interests to generate. These responses will be found in the answers to four sets of questions that raise the basic issues that must be addressed. The fact that the lengthiest set of questions applies to the defense infrastructure suggests how our principally international focus on security may shift emphasis in the future.

STRATEGY

The first set of questions deals with strategy. On the one hand, strategy can be defined precisely along well-understood lines of developing a plan of action; balancing objectives, resources, and outcomes; and matching goals, priorities, and actual policies. On the other, strategy can be enormously vague, with no clear-cut distinctions between it, policy, grand strategy, military strategy, and operational tactics. In today's case, strategy must respond to a world in transition and to threats that are in similar conditions of flux.

As noted in the Introduction, the first strategic question to be answered is how to respond to a changing, and diminishing Soviet military threat. What is the future application of deterrence as we have known it to this evolving U.S.-Soviet relationship? Can this transition be expedited wisely, can the USSR be persuaded to adopt a military posture that, from our perspective, offers minimal or acceptable threat and risk, or are our interests best served by letting events run their own course? To what degree, if any, might genuine arms reductions (as opposed to simply limiting flexibility in deploying forces) be useful as strategic instruments to the advantage of the United States or to influence the USSR to assume a more benign military posture? How should new threats be incorporated into national security planning and our strategic response, and should any limits be drawn as to what does or does not constitute a genuine national security threat? On a strategic basis, does the United States possess such a lead in its technology to permit a change in pace or urgency in exploiting these advantages?

DOMESTIC ENVIRONMENT

The second set of questions pertains to the domestic environment, and governance must be on the top of this list of concerns. The nature of the American political system and its constitutional basis of checks and balances operates most effectively when at least one of three conditions is in place. The first condition is the existence of active and widespread public consensus to support or demand vigorous and effective responses to problems by government. Absent that degree of consensus, the second condition that is needed is an extraordinary threat, trauma, or danger to coalesce massive public support around a unified response. Lacking the first two conditions, the third condition is sufficiently abundant resources to spend our way clear of danger regardless of the degree of public consensus. Unfortunately, none of these conditions exists today.

Worse, at a time when international conditions are in such dramatic flux, there is every indication that the U.S. political process is bogging down in its own mass, inertia, and inability to take effective action in the face of these and other domestic problems. The performance of government in dealing with pressing economic issues such as the debt and deficit and with complex social problems such as the battle against drugs and the plight of the underclasses must also be measured in terms of the deficient educational standards and poor learning achievements of the nation, the decaying state of physical infrastructures like the nation's health-care and transportation systems, and public perceptions over how government is addressing these problems. The signs are not promising.

Thus, the key question is whether government can and will rise to the occasion of providing for the common defense in economical, practical, and effective terms. The second question pertains to ongoing changes within that process of governance and their consequences for national defense at this time of change and challenge. The third question pertains to national support and interest for defense and what defense capability is perceived as "about right" by the public absent a single threat of the magnitude of the former "evil empire."

INFRASTRUCTURE

The third and longest set of questions addresses the infrastructure that supports defense. For our purposes, *defense infrastructure* encompasses the defense industrial base; the decision-making process for buying and obtaining the goods and services for defense; the personnel base for manning the forces; the basing and support structure for stationing, maintaining, and training our forces; and the intelligence base for producing threat alertments.

In the past, we could safely assume that the infrastructure was an inexhaustible resource. Abundant industry provided the sinews for defense, and a vibrant technological base made our weapons among the best in the world. The acquisition process turned out high-quality systems at politically acceptable costs. Either through draft or voluntary service, sufficient numbers of personnel of the necessary quality manned the forces, and the system of bases and support facilities ashore more or less fit our needs. In addition, the intelligence community generally provided appropriate and timely information on our major adversary even if political factors often mitigated taking prompt action on every valid alertment.

Just as our perceptions of the international environment should fit the changing circumstances and just as strategy must evolve to meet the challenges of a broad array of non-Soviet threats, past assumptions about national defense infrastructure must adapt to equally powerful, although often far less obvious, forces of change. The defense infrastructure is being buffeted by powerful fiscal, industrial, socio-political, and technical forces of change. The once seemingly inexhaustible defense infrastructure can no longer be taken for granted in its automatic and widespread contribution to security policy. Indeed, this single area may pose the greatest and most difficult problem facing the nation's defense posture.

In addition to changing threat perceptions, huge public debt and deficits have imposed enormous pressures to curb federal spending. The FY 1991 deficit is estimated at $330 billion, and, for the first time in history, federal interest payments on national debt will exceed what is spent on defense. Because defense accounts for about 80 percent of the federal government's discretionary spending, these pressures for cuts are likely only to be accelerated. This means that the defense infrastructure, which was based on supporting a $300-billion-a-year military expenditure and which required annual real growth simply to maintain itself, will contract. The questions are by how much and how fast.

In addition to the impact of the (greatly) shrinking defense budgets that will follow the Gulf War, the U.S. industrial base must respond to increased competition from abroad. The reasons for this are clear. Immediately after World War II, American industry was untouched, undamaged, and vibrant and thus enjoyed a monoply over the rest of the world. Ironically, through U.S. largesse, the bulk of the world's economies that were destroyed or eliminated by the war were put back into action. That monopoly advantage has long since disappeared. Today, in many areas of trade and production, foreign countries have caught up with or surpassed the United States in specific economic capacities.

The dramatic expansion in the numbers of goods and services in which the United States is no longer dominant or even competitive has accelerated the decline in the defense industrial base and exacerbated the effects of cuts in the procurement side of defense budgets. America's growing dependency on foreign-produced components for its weapons and defense support systems is, in itself, illustrative of how global industrialization and competition affect our industrial base and, potentially, our national security.

Two American political characteristics, with roots that are deep, have resulted in inhibiting the ability to develop, produce, and field weapons of war on a timely, efficient, and affordable basis. First, protection and insulation from the harmful side effects of unchecked capitalism and an entirely unrestricted industry have led to a vast array of socio-economic regulations to safeguard individuals, small businesses, and other key sectors of national life. These regulations, which affect virtually all aspects of economic intercourse, from protection of workers' health and retirement funds to safeguarding the environment, have created enormous overhead expenses for all enterprises, caused greater governmental intrusion into their activities, and thereby imposed greater costs on the overall conduct of business. We accepted these costs for balancing regulation and free enterprise and are perhaps oblivious to the current magnitude of what we are paying to maintain them.

Second, the growing distrust and lack of confidence within the executive branch, Congress, and the American public have produced a monolith of regulatory and oversight mechanisms that add enormous costs in time and money to the defense acquisition and decision-making process. As a result, it has become more difficult for Congress and the executive branch to develop coherent, rational, coordinated, and efficient acquisition policies that are economical and efficient. This cumbersome and incoherent process increases the costs and time it takes to contract for goods and services by the government and, ironically, exacerbates the effects of political distrust. By some estimates, this cost of oversight and regulation may account for a quarter of our total defense procurement bill.

Finally, and simply put, the costs of improving and fielding greater military capability and system performance increase dramatically, if not exponentially, as we continue to challenge the new limits offered by technology. In FY 1991 dollars, the British Spitfire that won the Battle of Britain cost less than $500,000. Today's equivalent fighter, the F-15, costs about $50 million. A Spitfire could fly at 400 knots and had a maximum effective weapons range of about 500 yards due to the limits of its .30-caliber machine gun and 20-mm armaments. An F-15 can fly at three times the speed of sound, and its missiles can reach out 50 to 100 times as far as the Spitfire's guns. This pursuit of technology and capability, inevitably, is going to lead to more and more "techflation" and costs that grow exponentially, not arithmetically.

The confluence of new fiscal realities, overhead and bureaucratic bloat, global industrialization, and techflation cuts across the entire defense infrastructure. The key questions must be where these trends are headed, what their consequences are likely to be, and what can and should be done in response.

OPERATIONS

The final set of questions must focus on the operational imperatives of this new, emerging environment. Not only must tactical criteria be expanded beyond assumptions pertaining to war against the USSR, the concepts for joint and combined operations must be stretched in all dimensions.

As the national security environment broadens to include a wide variety of traditional and nontraditional threats, questions about how all these changes will affect doctrine and operations must be addressed. Determining where to put future emphasis will be far from trivial. This greatly changed environment particularly applies to joint operations with strange bedfellows, conceivably including former adversaries. In this regard, Syria and the USSR are now two of our "strangest bedfellows."

THE CHALLENGE

At first cut, this is a very broad introduction to a study on maritime power and the future roles of the Navy and Marine Corps as they pertain to defending the country and its national security in the next century. It is crucial, however, to move from the general to the specific in a comprehensive way. In the past, when security was principally justified by and argued for on grounds of containing and deterring the Soviet threat, a plausible strategic framework for national strategy and the military component of that strategy could be fashioned. Maritime, land, and air forces could be assigned crucial and understandable roles against this strategic need and structure. Moreover, government, certainly until the Vietnam War began in earnest, was more trusted by the public and less complicated and convoluted regarding defense. That situation did not always lead to the best decisions, however; any system is fallible.

Debate always flourished over the proportion of budgets and the priority of roles and missions assigned to these forces and their parent services, but not over the broader framework of containing the adversary. At the tactical and technical level, intense controversy over the size and shape as well as the readiness and sustainment levels of the forces was very real. Hotly contested questions over large versus small carriers, nuclear versus diesel submarines, single- versus multipurpose surface warships, and total numbers of forces invariably set the terms for part of this debate. At the policy level, several long-standing strategic questions have polarized this debate, namely, how far forward should a forward defense be and what should dictate the *raison d'être* of the Navy? Should the Navy have the ability to operate and strike deeply into Soviet home waters or merely the ability to maintain sufficient forces to control the seas and the access to our allies?

The one underlying assumption in our framework never at stake or at issue all these years, however, was the identity of the enemy. Successive doctrines of *massive retaliation, flexible response*, and *maritime superiority* always held the adversary to be the USSR and assumed that all other threats were subordinate and could be dealt with using the same forces and doctrine. Even as we moved from a 2-1/2-war to a 1-1/2-war strategy in the early 1970s and dropped China as an enemy, the force structure and war plans remained remarkably consistent with countering a Soviet threat.

In the naval jargon, then and now, conducting operations in the Third World, such as punitive raids against Libya or Iran, took on this Soviet-based planning and were often estimated in percentages against the yardstick of potential strikes on key Soviet targets. American forces and services were conditioned to respond against the requirements levied to counter the Soviet threat, even though, in actual practice and in every case, those forces were used elsewhere and against other adversaries. Most of these uses, however, were either against client states of the Soviet Union or states that had acquired Soviet weaponry, such as the war in the Gulf against Iraq.

Thus, it was not surprising that, when U.S. naval presence was increased in the Persian Gulf and Indian Ocean in 1980 following the capture of the American Embassy in Tehran, the United States found that its forces had not been designed to counter many of Iran's weapons, which were acquired from French, British, and even U.S. suppliers. Similarly, during the Falklands War of 1982, the Royal Navy found itself hard-pressed to cope with Argentina's weaponry, which was mainly French Exocet missiles and U.S. A-4 Skyhawks, because the British systems, like those of the United States, had been designed for the Soviet threat. The days of designing a weapon for a single threat are gone, however.

Certainly, before August 1990, it was argued and generally accepted that the most applicable military forces for the United States will be maritime. The combination of flexibility, deployability, political acceptability (i.e., maritime forces can remain in international waters near crisis areas indefinitely), and the guarantee of long-standing sustainability of these forces provides precisely what the nation needs. Furthermore, the stabilizing effects of these forces are also strong arguments for their continuing utility. As the war in the Gulf has shown, however, ground and air forces cannot and should not be dismissed. Indeed, a clear shift in public atitudes towards land-based forces reflects the overwhelming defeat of Iraq's army.

Accepting the same premises as those who view maritime forces as the preferred military instruments in this new world, advocates of ground and air forces reach entirely different conclusions. Given a diminution in or indeed the elimination of the Soviet threat, likely threats elsewhere will still maintain highly capable ground and air forces that the United States must be able to defeat. Because only armies can occupy and capture territory and no doubt need airpower to support ground offensives, the Army designed to fight in Europe can be redeployed and tailored for other regions. The Persian Gulf has become the textbook case, in this view, for justifying ground and air forces for the future, although these forces admittedly will be fewer in number. Similarly, the Panama intervention, in which the United States already had access and basing in place and could bring to bear land and air forces far more quickly than naval forces, represents a second model for justifying the future force design and employment best suited to America's needs and interests.

Thus, because crisis areas outside the Soviet Union are likely to be relatively few in number and require fewer overall numbers of U.S. forces, a strong air-land team supported by maritime forces can fill the bill while contributing to the critical role of maintaining stability in Europe as the dust and debris caused by the explosive changes there settle.

Although maritime advocates will mount powerful counterattacks to this line of argument, the defense budget will be trapped in the pincers of a perceived decline in Soviet threat and a descending economic axe in the form of even greater deficits. As the 1990s progress, even if the economy experiences unanticipated growth, defense expenditures (outlays) for DOD of $225 to $250 billion or less per year rather than the current $275 billion (out of a total of $295 billion for all of national defense) could be a likely ceiling and, in any case, would become the dominant factor in planning, irrespective of the threat. Based on the arguments that follow, towards the end of the century or possibly sooner, annual defense spending in the range of 3 or 4 percent of gross national product (GNP) or about $150 to $200 billion (FY 1991 dollars) is not an unreasonable forecast of the fiscal limits of political reality, at least as seen in 1991.

In this, the most likely case, the overriding reality must be economic. No matter how logical or powerful arguments may be to maintain future levels of military capability to deal with a highly uncertain world, absent a unifying threat and even with the great success in the Gulf, defense spending must decline. The crucial questions are by how much and at what rate.

The analytical tasks, therefore, must be several-fold. First, the meaning and dimensions of national security must be clinically and closely examined to reflect the more likely demands, challenges, and realities of this new world so our basic framework for security can be reinforced or indeed recast and so nontraditional and nonmilitary threats that public attitudes now demand be incorporated into this new framework can be taken into account. This analysis should bound the future level of resources likely to be applied to defense under the most probable range of future planning scenarios. Second, within this broad security framework, the role of maritime forces must be clearly identified and their utility carefully rationalized. Doing one without the other simply will not work except by the best of fortune. Third, alternative maritime force postures must be derived and compared to identify what specific forms of maritime capability the nation should acquire.

With this national security framework, or one like it, excursions on Soviet and other threats can be conducted. For the Soviet case, this excursion can range from a still formidable Soviet adversary to the virtual absence of Soviet threat. (This latter boundary is exactly how the United States began to regard China with the accession of the Nixon administration in 1969.) Then, careful consideration of existing and emerging threats beyond that posed by the USSR must be made.

Finally, because the uncertainties appear to be so vast, positing certain scenarios or *wild cards* in which we may have guessed wrong about the future will provide a counterbalance to these other cases and form a kind of insurance policy. The economic distinction between this kind of a national insurance policy and that for an individual is that the individual's health is not normally affected by the size of the policy. That is not true for a nation that must pay the economic bill to safeguard its security. In answering the four sets of basic questions that will help define the Navy's (and Marine Corps'[1]) future direction, three specific queries apply to each category and warrant special attention:

- To what degree and how should the Navy be postured against the overall threat likely to be posed by the Soviet Union? What are alternative means of achieving these objectives, and what force structure and employment options flow from them?

- To what degree must the Navy be prepared to deal with other threats? How can this case best be made, both inside and outside the Navy, and what alternative means, including force structure options, can achieve these objectives?

- What are the essential needs, requirements, and objectives that flow from this examination that establish the case for the Navy of the future?

Answers to these questions, in turn, will set the framework for responding to and shaping how we will deal with strategy, domestic environment, infrastructure, and operations in this post-Cold War world. More important perhaps than the particular answers that follow in this book is the challenge for us to look into the next century and do our best to define and cope with the requirements of harm's way in that future.

---

1. Except where noted, Navy refers to both the Navy and the Marine Corps.

2

A Brave New World?

Looking back over the four-and-a-half decades since the Second World War ended, it is not difficult to identify how the international political system has changed, what the fundamental forces catalyzing and compelling this change have been, and what these transformations have meant for the traditional national security framework. As the metaphorical and symbolic destruction of the Berlin Wall in November 1989 suggests, analyzing the past to predict the future is no easy matter. Indeed, movie mogul Sam Goldwyn was right when he observed that prediction, especially about the future, was tough business.

To assess the scope of these global changes and their consequences for maritime power, the basic and remarkably consistent assumptions that have both guided U.S. national security since the end of the war and fashioned the security framework that has lasted so long must be examined. Determining the continuing degree of applicability of these assumptions provides useful insight in assessing the extent of global change and in defining a national security framework for the next century. This examination also will provide answers to most of the key strategic and domestic questions and will begin to suggest answers for the operational and infrastructure questions.

CHANGED ASSUMPTIONS

The nature of the threat was the first and overriding assumption. The United States assumed that the principal if not overwhelming threat to national security emanated from monolithic, godless communism, which was controlled by Moscow. Through whatever means, communism and the USSR were determined to increase their influence and, indeed, domination of large chunks of the planet. The threat was political, economic, ideological, and military in nature, and massive in scope. Virtually all other threats were seen as stemming from, subordinated to, or precipitated by Moscow. Even today, many who correctly caution patience and care in dealing with the USSR do so on the grounds that new Soviet policies under Gorbachev are only pauses in the overt, inevitable, and irreversible hostility between the two competing superpowers that must, by definition, reoccur.

Second, to counter this inexorable threat of monolithic and hostile Soviet communism, the United States embarked on a policy of containment through a series of alliances with like-minded (or almost like-minded) states, surrounding the USSR with alliances and allies to block what was believed to be inevitable Russian territorial expansion. NATO, the Southeast Asia Treaty Organization (SEATO), the Central Treaty Organization (CENTO), ANZUS,[1] and numerous bilateral security agreements were centerpieces of this policy that flourished throughout the post-war period. Rapprochement with China, beginning in the early 1970s, was a dramatic example of attempts to circumscribe Soviet power and aspirations, in this case by gaining another U.S. ally on the Eurasian continent.

Third, to offset perceived Soviet superiority in military strength and its geographic domination of the Eurasian landmass, the United States underwrote and ensured the sanctity of these alliances with primary emphasis on nuclear retaliation and nuclear deterrence. The assumption was that these frightening weapons would prevent and deter major Soviet aggression and political transgression against American interests and allies through the threat of massive destruction. Furthermore, the relatively low cost of and virtual U.S. monopoly over these weapons made them attractive components of policy.

Fourth, the United States relied on its technological and economic dominance as the engine of economic growth for itself and its friends and acted as the central bank for international

---

1. ANZUS stands for Australia, New Zealand, and the United States, who were the signatories to the Tripartite Security Treaty of 1951.

trade, business, and finance, presuming this superiority would always continue. The United States further believed that it could spend or invent its way out of danger using these extraordinary resources and their seemingly infinite availability as collateral for these endeavors.

Fifth, the United States assumed that its political process would operate on a genuine bipartisan basis when matters of real national security importance or international crisis were involved. The best means of fashioning sufficient bipartisanship to bind the nation together was through crisis, outrage, or fear, and, therefore, America's ongoing preoccupation with hostile Soviet intent became an immutable political fact of life.

Finally, Americans implicitly shared the assumption that most other people either believed as we did about the role of the United States and its legitimate objectives or were in need of education up to this level. This attitude is reflected in both American culture and government. A form of cultural arrogance and insularity, perhaps a product of heritage and history, has shaped certain of America's foreign policy responses to international challenges and brought forth both successes and failures.

These assumptions and presumptions and their associated framework either have outlived their usefulness and relevance or have been shaken by changing realties. No matter how *perestroika* and *glasnost* may ultimately affect the USSR and its behavior at home, abroad, and with its allies, threats to American security have broadened considerably, have become more complex and diffuse, and have long since encompassed more than Soviet ill will and military power. Indeed, some observers, such as George Kennan, have declared that the USSR is no longer a military threat, a view that is acquiring greater credibility.

As former national security advisor and current Chairman of the Joint Chiefs of Staff (JCS), General Colin L. Powell, USA, has put it, the Russian bear now wears a "Smokey the Bear" hat and, despite his claws, is seen as more interested in putting out political forest fires than starting them. In fact, not only is the threat-based, central linchpin of our post-war assumptions and security framework changing, but the term *threat* may be unsuitable for the future challenge facing us.

Drugs; diseases like AIDS; economic instability through debt, disarray, or disruption; the ideological thrusts of fundamental Islam; and the proliferation of modern weapons (including truly frightening and dangerous chemical and biological agents) have become a more direct and growing challenge to U.S. security than catastrophic scenarios of nuclear war with the USSR. Terrorism and environmental crises, whether devastation of Brazil's rain forests or the huge oil spill in Alaskan waters, evoke new types and dimensions of threats actually challenging our security and menacing our sense of national well-being.

Largely as a result of changing threat perceptions, the extensive diffusion of economic and political power, and nearly universal access to advanced technology, the future of alliances constructed to contain a once-agreed-upon military threat is by no means certain. In Europe, NATO was organized to contain Soviet political and military threats. Maintaining a strong military alliance when the perception of military threat is low and when economic disharmonies among major alliance partners are viewed as potentially more divisive than Soviet tank armies stationed in Eastern Europe will be exceedingly difficult.

The ending of the Cold War will increase this tension. The near revolt in 1989 by the Federal Republic of Germany concerning short-range nuclear weapons modernization and the reality of a reunified Germany underscore how much the sense of threat has changed. Indeed, a unified, powerful Germany must raise concerns based on old, disastrous experiences created by German bellicosity over the past century. Perhaps SEATO and CENTO, moribund in the last decade, are precursors to events of today and tomorrow regarding the longevity of Western military alliances.

The importance and utility of nuclear weapons are being broadly questioned. America's nuclear monopoly has long since disappeared, and it has dawned on both superpowers that possession of more than 12,000 strategic warheads by each side exceeds credulity. America's decision to launch the Strategic Defense Initiative (SDI) in March 1983 was based on President Reagan's goal of making nuclear weapons "impotent and obsolete." The summit meeting in Reykjavik in 1986 between Reagan and Gorbachev led to a flickering moment when both leaders flirted with eliminating all nuclear weapons. That moment passed. The emphasis on and importance of nuclear weapons, however, are far less today than at any time since the Cold War began in earnest.

Thus, for the first time since the Soviet Union acquired nuclear weapons in 1949, genuine and serious arms reductions and not merely arms control are a given. The elimination of an entire class of intermediate-range nuclear missiles, and the move towards a nominal 30-percent reduction in strategic weapons, a central part of the Strategic Arms Reductions Talks (START), are further evidence of this trend towards diminished reliance on these systems. As a result, the nuclear glue that bound the alliance together is decomposing.

The dominance of the United States' economy and technology once was the controlling factor in global trade and business. Those times no longer exist. Although the United States is still extraordinarily powerful, developments such as petrodollars; persistent and growing American debt, deficits, and trade imbalances; greater foreign ownership of U.S. property; and the diffusion of technology have fundamentally diluted the power and influence of the United States as *the* dominant economic power. Japan, West Germany, and the Asian "tigers" have eclipsed a significant part of the American economic sun.

Finally, the constitutional division of checks and balances and the divided authority between the branches of American government have purposely imposed fundamental limitations on making sweeping policy alterations, even given the need. The process has now mutated to the point where the degree of consensus required to enact bold policy action makes practical implementation virtually impossible. Meaningful bipartisanship is likely to be a myth. The dilemma is that, to gain political consensus, policy must be uncontroversial and without sharp edges. Yet, that policy would be so diluted as to be useless. Virtually all issues have become politicized and the political parties usually polarized. Given no single party in control of both branches of elected government, the result is gridlock and perhaps worse.

Rhetoric aside, vacuous policy actions on drugs, the deficit, the USSR, trade, education, and other issues reflect this dilemma and this political reality. In addition, a resurgence of political Calvinism has immersed the nation's capital in the 20th century's version of the Salem witch trials, burning at the public stake the careers of Senators Gary Hart and John Tower, former National Security Advisers John Poindexter and Robert McFarlane, and former House Speaker Jim Wright, and gently roasting the so-called "Keating Five" senators.

The past five decades provide ample evidence of basic causes of these changes and shed some light on forecasting how the next decade may evolve. Some of these causes and forces for change may have run their course; others may be vibrant and powerful. Still others may be assuming new prominence.

THE OLD WORLD ORDER

In simplest terms, the post-war division between East and West yielded a certain structure and stability to the international system, although recognition of this benign condition becomes clearer only in retrospect. World War II elevated the United States to its position as a world superpower. Successfully leading the alliance to victory in concert with developing economic super-miracles preemptorily matured the United States and mandated its supraposition in world events.

The American character and its highly compassionate nature were also significant factors in producing the post-World War II order. First in Japan with General Douglas McArthur's extraordinary and benign occupation and then in Europe in 1947 with the Marshall Plan, American foresight and largesse helped rebuild much of a war-ravaged planet. The humanity and compassion exhibited to former enemies was unprecedented, and, ironically, old enemies became new allies and old allies became new enemies.

Within the United States, a grateful nation wished to reward the 12 million men and women who went to war. Along with the rapid demobilization in 1945, this reward changed the nature and structure of American society and, ultimately, its value system. The GI Bill of Rights and federal mortgages for veterans were the opportunities that offered a free college education and the opportunity of owning one's home. In time, the combination provided the means of nearly unfettered vertical mobility for a large portion of what traditionally made up the U.S. lower and middle classes. The economic colossus spawned by the war provided the engine of growth for producing and distributing vast amounts of individual wealth through success in business, and the war's virtual destruction of all foreign production and, therefore, competition in the world markets gave the United States extraordinary opportunity and prosperity.

The blossoms of success, however, spread seeds that one day would sprout rivals for this wealth. Clearly, the most pronounced factor in reshaping the globe has been the diffusion of all forms of power, and much of that was knowingly and willingly accomplished by the United States.

Decolonization of the British and French empires was the most obvious example of the diffusion of political power. Since the end of the war, the number of sovereign states in the world has quadrupled. Most of these new states were former colonies. Sovereignty has bred legitimacy that has, in turn, protected these states from many forms of foreign domination. Ultimately, sovereignty, regardless of the size of the country, has led to certain amounts of authority by virtue of this protective legitimacy, and relatively insignificant countries have had no trouble ganging up on the super and major powers. The case of Lithuania and the reluctance of the USSR to resort to bloodshed is a current example of this phenomenon.

The spread of economic power and wealth is self-evident, whether to industrial giants like Germany and Japan or to those countries fortunate to sit astride precious resources such as oil in the Persian Gulf. The economy is not only global; it is interactive and interconnected to the degree where weakness or fragility at one pressure point could shock the entire world corpus into a financial or trade equivalent of cardiac arrest.

The spread of access to technology and the creation of new centers of technology outside the United States is another example of this changed environment. The United States is now entirely dependent on foreign sources for semiconductors, which are vital to the computer industry. This technology dependency is equivalent to resource dependencies of 50 years ago when the United States could obtain, for example, tin and rubber only from foreign sources. These dependencies have spread and old worries such as oil shortages are likely to return during this decade.

Militarily, the diffusion of weapons has been remarkable. Certainly many states as early as the 1950s possessed modern aircraft and submarines. Today, however, not only are weapons as modern and sophisticated as those possessed by the superpowers acquired with little difficulty, they are also supplemented by weapons of mass destruction, particularly chemical and biological weapons and, to a lesser degree, nuclear weapons. Ballistic missiles, too, are spreading. Although the extent of this threat is sometimes exaggerated, the prospect of these weapons actually being used in some form has become a reality. The appendix lists how and where these advanced weapons are proliferating.

Paralleling and reinforcing these forces for change is the power of near-instantaneous communications and the omnipotent presence of television. Television and communications, later joined by the computer and word processor, have generated instant access to the world at large. Although television may be the new opiate of the masses, it has also been a prime factor in reinforcing change simply on a cumulative and repetitive basis of exposing countless viewers to new and changing conditions. The June 4th massacre in Tiananmen Square was immediately broadcast to a largely shocked and outraged world, and the live broadcast of the Berlin Wall being effectively demolished became the most vivid symbol of the passing of the Cold War.

In the West, these changes have been largely positive and have cut across both domestic and international interests. They have been cumulative as well. It is in the East where the net effect of these forces and factors has exploded with breathtaking speed.

A NEW WORLD ORDER? THE USSR

Winston Churchill probably did a disservice when he labeled Russia as an intertwined riddle and enigma. In many ways, even with its emphasis on secrecy and general paranoia, understanding the motivations and actions of the Soviet leadership is occasionally less difficult than, say, carrying out a similar analysis of Western democracies. In the case of Mikhail Gorbachev, his two books—*A Time for Peace* and *Perestroika*—unequivocally reveal his extraordinary commitment to reform of the USSR. His analysis of socialism's failure is penetrating in the extreme. It is no ideological harangue and is probably unique in modern history in that a head of government would so strikingly criticize a system over which he presides.

The thread of reform has woven its way throughout Russian history. Peter the Great is generally regarded as the first modern Russian reformer. This thread was apparent in Nikita Khrushchev, who parenthetically attempted many reforms, including the "virgin lands" program to cultivate Russian wastelands. From 1959 onwards, he waged an uneven campaign to reduce Soviet defense expenditure and indeed oversaw substantial numerical decreases in military forces. Alas, neither *perestroika* nor *glasnost* was in Khrushchev's political lexicon, and, when he was driven from office in 1964, his controversial attempts at reform either were reversed or disappeared on their own. Most interestingly, it was Khrushchev who argued that the military rivalry with the West could and should be downgraded in its priority.

Gorbachev has not only implemented similar types of reform, he has brought along both an intellectual and philosophical framework and a political plan of action. Although how far and to what degree these reforms will go are unanswerable questions, some incontrovertible conclusions must be taken into account.

First, *perestroika* and *glasnost* are both separate, political facts of life. *Perestroika*, or restructuring, may or may not be successful in rejuvenating a petrified economy. *Glasnost*, or openness, is irreversible absent repressions of such magnitude as to make them probably unthinkable. The political effect *glasnost* has had can be seen in events in Eastern Europe and in the remarkable events taking place inside the USSR. The Soviet decision not to use military force to prevent political secession movements from taking root in parts of the empire (Eastern Europe and perhaps the Baltic states) as opposed to within the USSR (intervention to prevent civil war between Armenians and Azerbaijanis) means that this new form of politics is real and in place.

Second, the Soviet political leadership has concluded that it is not in the best interests of the state and party to continue the military rivalry with the West at current levels. In other words, militarization is viewed politically as no longer a wise or effective policy. Even the decisive victory of U.S. and Western arms against a Soviet client in the Gulf War will not reverse this strategic decision. This political judgment probably took place at the same time the Soviet military was concluding that the technological revolution in military equipment was now greatly favoring the West through its exploitation of "smart munitions" and SDI. Ironically, for different reasons, both the Soviet political and military leadership arrived at the same conclusion, namely, that continuation of previous defense policies under these situations was prescription for failure.

This interpretation is at odds with the conventional view prevalent in the West. In the conventional view, the excessive economic demands of Soviet defense spending were strangling the failing economy and had to be reversed. Thus, economic and not strategic reality led the Soviets to act decisively to change their military posture. The flaw in this analysis is the reversal of cause and effect. The true cause of the collective Soviet decision to alter policy was based on the strategic conclusion that the level of military competition with the West was unnecessary and wasteful. The effect was economic and the Soviet Union could shift its economic priorities safely and securely. To put the matter boldly: the Soviet Union has taken the threat away from the West because it is in the USSR's best interest to do so.

Third, no matter whether Gorbachev remains in power, the policy direction is unlikely to change unless a massive trauma such as civil war or economic collapse devastates the Soviet Union. The debate is not over ends. It is about means, tactics, and pace. Although a successor leadership probably would lack the charisma and the intellectual commitment to continue the breadth of reform undertaken by Gorbachev, there is no going back, even though there may be slowing down or stopping. The resurgence of the conservatives is illustrative because it is they and not the reformers who appear to have a better idea of how to make the system work.

The USSR, therefore, may be challenging the West to embark on a less military-oriented competition, because, in the USSR's view, this strategy will be in its best interest. This interesting quandry posed by Moscow is the one likely to cause the greatest debate and dissension in fashioning an appropriate American and Western response. The next chapter examines some of the reasons for the scale and harshness of this debate, its likely divisive outcome in the West, and the ideological as well as the actual difficulties in dealing with what may be a radically different type of Soviet threat and with the emergence of more non-Soviet challenges and threats.

A NEW WORLD ORDER? OTHER THREATS

No matter how the behavior of the USSR evolves, a panoply of challenges outside that context abounds. In some cases, the insularity of the Cold War simply permitted ignorance and avoidance of these challenges to determine our attitudes. In other cases, the well-being and, therefore, the national security of the United States were intimately interconnected, and ignorance or avoidance of these realities would be fatal or damaging. Consider the categories of new or emerging traditional types of challenges and new or emerging nontraditional concerns.

A world without a Soviet military threat is not a world in which the United States would be without military forces. Given the opportunity, too many potential adversaries and would-be evildoers would like to damage or challenge American interests. Saddam Hussein's defeat could sow the seeds for others like him rather than eliminate this type of idiosyncratic

threat. Because nuclear weapons cannot be undone, it is inconceivable that the United States would eliminate this entire
category from its inventory. The worry of nuclear proliferation,
the threat of chemical and biological weapons, and the creation
of a strategic vacuum that could be unhappily filled by other
powers provide absolute reasons for maintaining some level of
nuclear capability. Future levels for U.S. nuclear weapons in
this new world are proposed in later chapters.

Maintaining powerful, ready, and flexible conventional
forces, including special operations forces, is also unarguable
by serious people. No matter what arguments the Bush administration made about its policy to force Saddam Hussein
from Kuwait on legal and moral grounds before force was used,
maintaining access to resources, especially oil, is an independent requirement regardless of Soviet intent or action. Although legal denial of U.S. access to those resources by local
states is unlikely to trigger the use of U.S. force to regain that
access (here, the Arab oil embargo of 1973-1974 is relevant),
assaults on those states by external aggression or through
internal revolution could easily lead to a U.S. response.

The need for future military retaliation or for intervention
to protect or defend American interests cannot and should not
be assumed away. The United States would be derelict if it
were militarily unprepared for these situations. Indeed, the
peaceful southern border across the Rio Grande could be
destroyed by upheaval in Mexico. Such upheaval could require
defense of our territories—the traditional mission of the Army.
The Falklands conflict, the Grenada intervention, the stationing of U.S. Marines in Lebanon, the tiny but successful show of
U.S. military force in the attempted coup against the Aquino
government in the Philippines, and the Christmas 1989
Panama incursion could be the textbook cases for future uses of
force.

So, too, the use of military force to deter or intimidate a
Qaddafi-like leader or a terrorist group may become more
important. The problem, of course, is measuring the effect of
this type of use, because understanding why an event did not
occur can be highly speculative. Did the presence of force
actually prevent hostile action from occurring, or did that

presence merely precipitate an untoward act later or else-where? Answering these questions, in large part, will be inex-act and almost certainly controversial.

Military intervention for humanitarian reasons, such as preventing genocide, eliminating civil strife, and perhaps reducing human misery, also could emerge as an important future mission. The genocide in Cambodia and Ethiopia, for example, might finally gain attention and action.

The battle against drugs and the war against terrorism also require the military. The dilemma in winning the drug war is that it is not resolvable by military means alone. The effectiveness of military force in surveillance, blockade, prevention, retaliation, and preemption in the drug war is open to question—a reality not widely appreciated by the public at large. The dilemma stems from the nature of military forces.

Military forces, if they are to be effective, must be designed and prepared to fight other military forces. When they are asked to perform nonmilitary tasks, they are not automatically applicable or inherently destined to succeed. In Vietnam, for example, U.S. military forces won every battle and killed hundreds of thousands of the enemy, but the United States lost the war. The reason was not military failure but a misuse of the military and the fatal error of ignoring the broader political and strategic realities that determined the outcome.

Similarly, the stationing of military forces by the United Kingdom in Northern Ireland may provide some measure of protection for the populace, but offers no solution in defeating the Irish Republican Army or in eliminating the hatred between Protestants and Catholics.

Drugs and the demand for them stem from social and physiological needs. Supply is a function of criminality and economic distribution. The target for the military cannot be the military forces of either the supply or demand sides because there are none. Moreover, given how the drug trade evaporates into the broader intercourse of everyday life, detection and surveillance of wrongdoing become exceedingly difficult. For the same reason, the military cannot stop crime—and note that despite its militarized posture and powerful internal police, crime is an exploding problem in the

USSR. Applying the military to the drug war will provide only incomplete results at best. This difficulty does not mean the military should not be used. It does mean, however, that careful examination of what results could be achieved and what the costs may be is essential. The same line of argument applies to fighting terrorism; the limits of military power must be appreciated.

Another area in which military force is seen to have application is so-called low-intensity conflict (LIC). This unhappy and misleading term suggests that *low intensity* means less violence and less intense degrees of traditional conflict between traditional armies. In fact, low intensity relates to uses of force other than that of large armies squaring off against other armies.

As we and the French learned in Vietnam, the British learned in Northern Ireland, and the Soviets learned in Afghanistan, LICs and insurgencies are difficult to fight and often more difficult to win. The notion that a private soldier has all the skills of a Lawrence of Arabia and can right the wrongs that generally are the root cause of these conflicts is bizarre. Yet, the current thrust is that military forces should be able to perform this role.

There are, no doubt, other roles U.S. military forces could fill. If the political pressure to address the other "deficits" becomes strong enough, the military could conceivably be required to help revitalize parts of the national infrastructure or serve as a training or retraining facility to improve broad-based skills in selected technical areas. This use could be seen as a militarized version of the Civilian Conservation Corps of the 1930s, drilling, training, and preparing itself for military duties part of the time and carrying out other duties the remainder.

The fact that this approach is wasteful and certainly does not maximize military skills would be outweighed by the political reality that this may be the only acceptable means of maintaining a relatively large military force in peacetime.

Whatever direction the United States takes, a brave new world is emerging. Although the nation will need strong and ready military forces of some size for this world, there are

great doubts as to how these forces are to be justified so sufficient political and public support can be generated and
maintained. The dissipation in the perception of Soviet threat
is not sufficient grounds for determining a strategy. Much more
is required.

Concurrently, although a propensity towards violence remains part of the human condition, for the United States and
its allies and for the USSR as well, there appears to be a pronounced and probably irreversible shift towards defining security in political-economic terms instead of strategic-military
terms. The stalemate between East and West, with the threat
of nuclear holocaust playing the role of ultimate deterrent, may
finally have provided the opportunity for significantly diminishing the role and numbers of military forces maintained by
the competing alliances.

If another war comes to the West or East, it probably will
be economic and not military in scope. Of course, a trade war,
between Japan and the United States, for example, could conceivably lead to an actual clash of arms at some future date.
The extraordinary interdependencies between these and other
major trading partners, however, suggest that it can be in
neither's interest for a trade war to get out of hand. Thus, the
military contingencies stemming from economic conflicts
among industrial states are likely to remain remote unless we
are very careless or stupid.

As threats diffuse and take on vastly different form, as the
old, familiar order and framework disintegrate, and as ensuring national security becomes more complex and certainly more
difficult in the abstract, the challenges for the leadership of the
United States have never been as intricate, subtle, and uncertain as they are today.

No matter how benign the USSR may become, the United
States will be required to exercise force to protect its interests
elsewhere. Democracies, however, are rarely keen to keep large
military forces around if the perception of where and when
these forces may be used is unclear. As domestic priorities
build for using increasingly scarce resources to meet non-
defense needs, the political pressures to keep these threat
perceptions blurred will increase.

THE CASE FOR MARITIME POWER

The national security establishment, therefore, must carry out three principal tasks and, in making the case for the future of maritime power, must understand the following:

- First, determine what the enormous changes in Eastern Europe and in the Soviet Union mean for U.S. military strategy and accompanying force structure. This analysis should define a "steady state" and, from our perspective, a nonthreatening level of where we would like to see Soviet force posture and military doctrine stabilize, as well as a plan for getting there.

- Second, identify the security and defense needs that emerge from this highly uncertain new world outside the Soviet threat and use that information as the foundation for determining the requisite military capabilities we must maintain.

- Third, strive for a complete understanding of the domestic mood and American reactions to these unprecedented events to accompany the analysis and the intended plan of action.

The ultimate questions that must be answered do not deal with whether we will maintain capable military forces, for surely we will. Instead, we must learn how to make the best transition from the era we have known so well to this new, less certain world. This transition must include a new strategy for dealing with the USSR as mutual hostilities lessen and a strategy for dealing with legitimate needs elsewhere now that these conditions may no longer be successfully rationalized as lesser cases of conflict against the Soviets. This strategy must be put in the maritime context and assessed against a broad range of possible force structures, different budget levels, and an understanding of what that capability could and could not be reasonably expected to achieve.

3

To Preserve and Defend— Demolishing the Domestic Gordian Knot

Fast forward: The world order had drastically changed. Old, dangerous threats had passed. New ones were taking form. Europe was in political and economic turmoil due in part to the creation of a new Germany. The United States, after an extraordinary defense buildup, had begun an extraordinary builddown. Defense industries that were no longer needed for producing the weapons of war sought new markets and opportunities.

The newly elected President came to office with little experience in security and defense policy despite the wealth of office seekers who had more than their share of expertise. The United States turned inward to rejuvenate itself, and Congress, labeled by the President as "do-nothings," refused to address many of the larger fundamental changes in the world.

The Secretary of Defense, responding to a defense budget that was slashed to less than 4 percent of GNP, presented to Congress a radical new strategy and force structure that produced a storm of controversy. Central to the plan was reliance on a new "super bomber," advertised as absolutely impervious to defenses, and new land-based missiles with radical technology.

The Navy, electing to bet its future on buying the next-generation aircraft carrier and allowing its surface and submarine fleets to be drastically reduced in compensation, had its plans for new carriers abruptly cancelled. As a result, it went into revolt. The Army and Marine Corps were at each other's throats over expeditionary missions, and Congress was up in arms over the worst procurement scandals since the war.

Within a year or two, a new war would erupt to end this period of extreme peacetime turmoil and austere budgets. Before it did, however, a desperately depressed Secretary of

Defense committed suicide and a second was summarily dis-
charged. Interestingly, all this actually took place in 1948 and
1949.

A TRANSFORMED AMERICA

At the same time that extraordinary international changes
have been at work reshaping the world as we know it, less
visible but not less powerful or less pervasive forces have been
fundamentally transforming the political character and social
structure of the United States. These transformations are
essential in addressing the questions relating to the domestic
environment and to the defense infrastructure.

These changes in domestic politics, public attitudes, and
the process of governance reflect the broader events of what
has happened across the entire United States. Some of these
broader changes are evident; others are diaphanous, less
formed, and operating psychologically on the American mood,
psyche, and sense of well-being. Without fully understanding
the key domestic factors—the aspirations, fears, attitudes, and
perceptions of the nation and the people meant to be
protected—underlying popular support for national security,
any resulting strategic framework would be flawed and
inherently unstable at worst and incomplete at best. With the
sense of Soviet threat dissipating and with political bipartisanship more difficult to obtain, the rigid boundary that once
separated domestic and international policies has disappeared.
This interconnection of foreign and domestic policies introduces
far more complexity and pluralism into the debate over
national security.

Understanding domestic events is more crucial than ever
for defining future security needs particularly because navies
and maritime power have generally been expressed in highly
technical terms of particular weapon, sensor, and propulsion
systems, or against a carefully analyzed military threat as the
basis for planning. The changes in domestic politics, public
attitudes, and process of governance, however, which, after all,
lead to the checks that are written by Congress and endorsed
by the public to support the Navy, are no less telling or

relevant than the threat and the operational reasons for having a navy in the first place. Too often, in the wake of international extravaganzas such as the Berlin Wall or Iraq's army being demolished, we forget or ignore that domestic changes have occurred within the United States that may be as significant, or even more significant, in shaping our future.

Politics, public attitudes, and the process of governance are intertwined and, since the days of the Founding Fathers, have undergone change no less dramatic than that in the outside world. In the Constitution, politics—which is to say the means of governing—was originally seen by the drafters as a responsibility and a function of the few. Within that governing elite, the system of checks and balances was meant to prevent the likelihood of one branch or individual dominating or dictating to the others. Tyranny of government in any form was to be prevented. The inherent contradictions in checks and balances between, for example, the delegated rights of Congress and the Executive over war-making, foreign policy, and, ultimately, national security to preclude any form of tyranny by one branch of government were manageable when government was smaller and had fewer interested and participating members.

The domestic history that would bring these contradictions into great tension began just before the Second World War with the acceleration in the scope, pace, and size of government's involvement in controlling, regulating, and protecting public well-being. FDR's New Deal was the first phase of a process that the Second World War would turn into American super-government. Immediately after the war, domestic politics would become a function of another, unexpected combination of factors.

The nation had elected to reward the 12 million uniformed Americans who served their country in defeating the Axis powers. The GI Bill guaranteed a college education, and federal mortgages assured the purchase of a home. Invisibly, class distinctions and other long-term barriers to economic and social mobility would be eroded through these upwardly mobile government programs, although it would take time for the results to play out. While these phenomena were occurring, the

American industrial colossus that became the arsenal of democracy was being redirected to peacetime commerce. The destruction of virtually all other industrial competition by the ravages of the war provided the United States with the extraordinary commercial advantage of a near monopoly of the marketplace. The combination of commerce and talent would spawn enormous numbers of Americans who would become the beneficiaries of this legacy. Wealth, and the holders of wealth, multiplied. Eventually, this new, broad class of affluent Americans would use that wealth to protect or enhance their particular business or industry interests or for political reasons, which would lead to an extraordinary proliferation of individuals, groups, and lobbies clustered around Washington, D.C., to influence the branches of government.

The Cold War and the seemingly permanent Soviet threat ensured a measure of bipartisan spirit and contained the centrifugal nature of government. Active dissent—at least in advocating any toleration of the communist adversary or changes in policy—was fraught with risk and penalty. Other forces that would cause explosive change, however, were playing heavily on domestic politics and public attitudes.

Beginning in 1954 with the landmark Brown vs. the Board of Education case in which the Supreme Court took the first step in dismantling segregation, civil rights became a powerful force with effects that went far beyond color, race, religion, and sexual equality. Dissent was becoming popularized and politically acceptable. The traditional shape and structure of American society were being challenged and transformed. The civil rights movement was among the first signs of this transformation; however, other symptoms of change related directly to national security and to the process of governing.

The Camelot months of the Kennedy administration exploited and magnified the political importance of change and gave further impetus to the national aspiration that the virtues of America were real and could be cultivated and transplanted abroad. The notion that Americans would "pay any price and bear any burden" would apply to supporting causes that were both popular and unpopular. After Kennedy's assassination, President Lyndon Johnson felt morally obligated to pick up the dual legacies of his fallen running mate that became the Great Society and the full-fledged Vietnam War. These two hugely important symbols became the sparks to the smoldering problems that would ultimately explode into societal firestorms of a generation and perhaps beyond.

The Great Society and its attendant war on poverty involved noble and inspired programs to bring America's wealth and abundance to all Americans; however, legislating remedial social solutions that would work in practice was difficult. Furthermore, the budget appetite of the bureaucratic and financial support systems that sustained these programs would become insatiable.

The Vietnam War and the Great Society were summary expressions of broader problems affecting the nation. These two symbols would collide with other factors in the late 1960s and 1970s with the most profound consequences. Vietnam was the figurative last straw in the steady accretion of power by the presidency. The failure of the war and of government in waging it also carried off the residual trust and confidence the public maintained in government. The so-called imperial presidency, contributed to and impelled by every president since FDR, finally provoked Congress to reign in the power of the White House. At times, this restraint was accomplished dramatically. The War Powers Act and the stringent controls placed on executive foreign-policy power and other legislation are well known and need not be repeated here. Watergate completed the demise of the executive branch's rise to dominance in this cycle and brought public distrust of government to the lowest point since the war's end. As power swung from 1600 Pennsylvania Avenue east to the Capitol, events in Congress were reshaping that branch of government.

The end of the seniority system, the proliferation of committees and subcommittees, and the establishment of highly competent, ambitious staffs to help Congress take on the executive branch were products of this period. As a result, the involvement of Congress in all matters pertaining to national security has intensified to the point where it has, for better or worse, some very counterproductive aspects no matter how necessary such oversight and regulation may be. At worst, what has happened could represent a breaking down of the system of governance and an inability to address the tough issues that must be solved. Yet, there is more to this predicament of governance.

As public interest groups and political action committees multiplied, as lobbies and interested parties sought to influence the many more pressure points that sprung up in Congress and in the executive branch, and as the insatiable need for election campaign financing was more than matched by the treasure troves that the economy yielded, the entire political system became enmeshed in a tangled web of influence-building networks. The image of Gulliver tied down by thousands of Lilliputians is not an inappropriate parallel. As a result, it is very difficult to impose a rational scheme of decision-making. The legislative process has reached a point where it is very difficult to undo anything, let alone introduce major programs that are new and controversial.

Perhaps worse, the public has become entirely cynical with what it sees as the nonsense coming out of Washington. "Inside the beltway" logic does not carry much weight in the American heartland. Distrust and disinterest in government have magnified the shift in the public's attitudes towards far greater if not total concern with the well-being and quality of life of self or family than that of the nation and community.

These changes in domestic politics, public attitudes, and the process of government can no longer be kept separate from the dynamic and extraordinary events that continue to occur internationally, because, now that the unifying factor of threat is dissipating, the separation between foreign and domestic policy choices has been breached. As the diffusion and erosion of centralized power have accelerated the centrifugal forces of checks and balances, American attitudes towards the Federal Government have become more cynical. On the one hand, expectations of what government should be able to achieve are high. On the other, the capacity of government to accomplish these tasks is highly suspect by the public. Given the greater demands being placed on government to resolve the social, economic, and physical infrastructure deficits, the most likely outcome will be confusion and greater public cynicism in dealing with a national security agenda that has lost the catalyzing energy of the Soviet threat.

THE UNCOMMON DEFENSE

The evolution of American national defense and public attitudes towards security captures the collision of changing domestic politics, public attitudes, and the process of governance with frightening clarity and clearly defines the extent of the difficulties this nation faces in coming to terms with national security in the 21st century. The lesson to be learned is that strategy and policy have become entirely dominated by process and budget. The last time these issues of strategy, process, budget, and organization were so clearly in conflict was 1949 and the so-called "revolt of the admirals." The flavor of that story was summarized at the beginning of this chapter. Although another mutiny or, more correctly, an act of desperation by the services in the face of extraordinary pressures is not out of the question, it is unlikely to recur for reasons that will become obvious later. Still, the 1949 episode provides interesting if not relevant insights.

In 1949, debate over defense strategy, the organization of DOD, and the size of budget cuts reached incendiary proportions. The National Security Act of 1947, amended in 1949 and 1958, "unified" the pre-World War II military departments into a single Department of Defense and created the Air Force as a third military department within DOD. Roles and missions, in this case for nuclear delivery and the tactical control of air power, pitted the Navy against the other services. President Harry Truman's decision to limit the FY 1950 defense authorization bill to $14.4 billion meant that the services' budgets would be slashed to the bone. All these factors, at a time when the new national security framework was being created, produced extraordinary upheaval and internecine war among the services and within the Pentagon.

Today, the parallels are interesting: the prospect of fundamental shifts in the security framework are real; the reorganization of DOD in 1986 is among the most sweeping undertaken; the debate over future strategy and threat, now that the

Gulf Crisis is resolved, will boil up; and the defense budget, which is 22 times larger than it was 42 years ago, is likely to enter a state of free fall. The consequences of these interactions are likely to be profound and will cut across all sections of the defense community and infrastructure. Clearly, the new organizational and operational arrangements will have decisive impact on authority and influence in the Pentagon and DOD and on who makes the tough decisions. Second, the role of Congress and how Congress will address the new security environment will be of fundamental importance, and, third, all of these changes will affect the supporting private defense industrial-technical base that, no matter what else happens, is rapidly shrinking. These consequences, in turn, will be resolved and conditioned, in large measure, by American attitudes and public mood.

THE PENTAGON

The National Security Act of 1947 as amended, along with the Unified Command Plan that assigned U.S. military forces and command structures to geographic and functional areas, created the Office of the Secretary of Defense (OSD) and the Secretaries of the Army, Navy, and Air Force. In 1949, the position of Chairman of the JCS was formalized, and, in 1958, further amendment defined the operational chain of command as well as strengthened the research and development structure of the department—one of the consequences of Sputnik.

Clearly, three sets of competing authority and offices dominated DOD: the Secretary of Defense, the individual services, and the JCS. In the mid-1950s, the Eisenhower defense approach was to set an overall direction (The New Look) and let the services operate freely under that mandate. The Kennedy-Johnson years set in place the domination of DOD by OSD and its powerful and controversial Secretary, Robert S. McNamara. The Nixon administration, the Vietnam conflict, and the personality of Secretary Melvin Laird produced the notion of *participatory management*, which appeared to shift the balance of power to the services, away from OSD's tight and highly autocratic control. In reality, Laird used this technique as a means of doling out substantial defense cuts. The services came back into their own, however, and the role of the JCS became much more important as arms control negotiations assumed higher and higher visibility.

The reasons for the renewed importance of the JCS in arms control were military and political. Despite the expediency of allowing arms control to become the surrogate for U.S.-Soviet relations in the Nixon-Ford years, military recommendations and advice were a vital ingredient in assessing the security or lack thereof that would flow from any treaty. Politically, it was impossible to win Senate approval of any treaty without the full support of the JCS.

JCS influence in arms control continued into the Carter years. After Strategic Arms Limitations Talks (SALT) I was approved and negotiations on SALT II began, however, the declining level of American defense spending became a major political issue at home. The downward trend in defense spending after Vietnam that did grave damage to the health and morale of the nation's military forces became a symbol of U.S. weakness. After the USSR invaded Afghanistan and Iranian terrorists captured the U.S. Embassy in Tehran, making a mockery of America's power, this perceived decline in will and strength contributed to the precipitous decline in popular support for President Carter. The reversal in 1979 of the decline in defense spending was a response to the public perception that America had gone far enough in reducing its military power and was dramatically and visibly reinforced by the Reagan presidency.

THE REALITY OF WASTE, FRAUD, AND ABUSE

In the first four years of the Reagan administration, annual real defense spending increased by more than 50 percent. Clearly, the Reagan team took what they saw as a public mandate to rejuvenate American military strength quickly as a reason to pump billions of additional dollars into defense. Under the new Secretary of Defense, Caspar W. Weinberger, OSD set general guidance, but the services (particularly powerful service secretaries like the Navy's John F. Lehman) took the lead in making and implementing the key budget and force structure decisions. By 1984, however, Congressmen had become politically more vulnerable to the charge that the large increases in defense spending had not produced enough significant improvements to the forces to convince their constituents that all this money had been well spent.

Readiness and the morale of the forces flourished. These qualities, however, were tarnished by an alleged lack of operational competence. The failed hostage rescue mission to Iran in 1980, the bombing deaths of 241 U.S. servicemen in Beirut, and the Grenada intervention in October 1983 became rallying points for critics wishing to bash the administration either for spending too much money on defense or for not spending it wisely.

This juncture of criticism over defense management and military competence formed an explosive political mixture that would be detonated by a wave of sensational stories over alleged cases of procurement waste, fraud, and abuse. The bizarre stories about procurement scandals captured public attention and turned popular attitudes against defense. Six-hundred-dollar toilet seats and $12,000 coffee pots created the impression that DOD and its army of private contractors were inept and corrupt.

The truth was too complicated to be understood and, therefore, to be relevant to the public debate. A U.S. Senator with a $600 toilet seat draped around his neck and a Congresswoman wearing a homemade necklace of bolts that allegedly cost DOD and the taxpayer $10,000 were vivid images on the evening news that created the belief that waste, fraud, and abuse were rampant in defense. It took a second to televise and photograph those pictures; it would take columns of print and thousands of words to explain the vast DOD procurement system that administered a budget of $300 billion and more than 20 million contracts a year. Indeed, experts on the process often found themselves befuddled by the arcane, intricate, and redundant aspects of this system. Hence, perception and image made explanation of reality impossible in most public fora.

The damage and harm done were incalculable. There was a huge erosion in popular support for defense. Congress was visibly moved to take strong action to correct and rectify many of these seeming operational and acquisition failings. In 1985, the administration yielded to great pressure and, against the protests of Secretary Weinberger, convened the President's Blue Ribbon Commission on Improving Defense Management (the Packard Commission). In 1986, Congress overwhelmingly passed the Defense Reorganization Law named for co-sponsors Senator Barry Goldwater and Representative Bill Nichols. In separate legislation, Congress also established the Special Operations Forces Command to protect and provide help for those particular capabilities that Capitol Hill saw as especially relevant to future U.S. military needs.

REFORM

The thrust of these legislative and procedural actions was to enhance the stature and the authority of the Chairman of the JCS and the commanders in chief (CINCs) in the field within the DOD decision-making process, particularly as they related to budget priorities and choices within the Policy, Planning, and Budgeting System (PPBS). The establishment of an acquisition czar—the Under Secretary of Defense for Acquisition—and linkage with the newly established Vice Chairman of the JCS through complementary responsibilities of relating operational needs and requirements to the acquisition of hardware underscored this shift of authority. Thus, the Office of the Chairman of the JCS (OCJCS) would play a stronger and more influential role within DOD both operationally and budgetarily.

In essence, the three-way division of authority in the original 1947 Act between the services, OSD, and the JCS had been greatly expanded. In addition to these traditional power centers in DOD, a greatly strengthened OCJCS and the fighting CINCs began to play important and indeed potentially dominant roles

Keeping this five-sided organization balanced among all these power centers will not be possible, and, before this century ends, it is very likely that only two centers of real power will emerge: OSD and the OCJCS. The OCJCS, with the

Chairman representing the CINCs, should become increasingly involved in making key decisions, and the Chairman's role of principal military advisor to the President and the Secretary of Defense will increase his authority even more. Such a hierarchy means that the role of the services and their secretaries is likely to be oriented towards support and program management rather than broad decision-making over strategy and force structure. The JCS are likely to emerge with more influence in their collective relationship to the Chairman rather than as uniformed heads of service.

The implications of these trends, should they continue, are obvious. The successful future national security framework and the role of maritime power within that context must obtain at least the tacit support of the Chairman and the OCJCS. To continue business as usual or to bypass DOD by resorting to end-arounds directly to Congress and the media are not, of themselves, the most likely routes to success. Indeed, these types of activities could become counterproductive.

Although major organizational changes continue to unfold inside DOD, the roles, participation, and oversight of Congress in the area of national security will have a significant if not decisive effect. Congress will continue to serve as an excellent and timely barometer of public mood and opinion. Furthermore, in the early 1990s, at a time when the domestic agenda will dominate its legislative calendar, Congress is likely to remain under Democratic control—the party that has advertised itself as the champion of these domestic issues. Thus, the Republicans will be forced to follow suit in emphasizing the domestic agenda, particularly as foreign policy becomes a debate over pace and not direction.

These realities will dictate certain consequences for DOD. First, especially over the short term but perhaps for the longer term as well, the pressure to find a replacement for the illusive "peace dividend" will become excruciating. The DOD budget will become the potential target for exacting reductions, and the urge to cut defense will be enormous after the Gulf War. Following the CFE reductions, significant arms control agreements are inevitable for strategic forces. These agreements, symbolizing the further decline of the threat, will serve as grounds for making even greater reductions in defense expenditures. The original projection by the Bush administration of keeping to a 2-percent annual decline in real defense spending has long since been abandoned. With the federal debt now legally authorized to grow another trillion dollars (to $4.1 trillion) by 1995, as early as FY 1993 or FY 1994, annual defense spending could be driven to 4 percent of GNP or less to bring the budget in some measure of balance.

The distinctions between expenditures that are outlays (i.e., money actually to be spent in the current fiscal year) and budget authority (i.e., commitments and promissory notes to future spending in the "out-years") will also complicate the effect of cuts. Congress is preoccupied with the deficit and current-year outlays. The Gramm-Rudman-Hollings Deficit Reduction Law mandated that, beyond a certain level of deficit, automatic cuts or sequestration of outlays occurs. Outlay cuts, however, because they are current-year, must be immediately translated into programs that yield this year's savings. The programs most conducive to yielding immediate savings are in personnel, readiness, and operations accounts and will have instant effect on the military's current ability to fight.

Budget authority cuts in long-term, big-ticket procurement programs such as the B-2, the SSN-21, or the Advanced Technology Fighter (ATF) have effect only in the distant future and do not relieve the immediate outlay squeeze. In FY 1991, for example, elimination of B-2, ATF, and both mobile intercontinental ballistic missiles (ICBMs) would save about $150 billion in long-term spending authority but only $2 to $3 billion in 1991 outlays. Thus, Congress faces an ongoing and unresolvable dilemma in the nature of how expenditures are programmed and disbursed.

At the same time, Congress accurately reflects the public's mood. Congress will still be adamant about obtaining the most for each defense dollar spent. That the Soviet threat is becoming more transparent and less dangerous does not remove public concerns or reduce anxieties over the need to protect and defend U.S. interests elsewhere. In a curious way, the downward spiral in defense spending could trigger even greater Congressional oversight to demand more for those dollars that are spent, particularly as Congress will be forced to address, if not solve, the problems of simultaneously cutting defense programs and defense installations within their individual constituencies. Even the huge upsurge in the reputation of the military following Desert Storm will be hard to translate into actions that will reverse these downward trends.

Clearly, base closings and "pork," that is, the maintenance of constituent interests whether national defense needs them or not, will become even hotter political coals. The base-closing commission made some progress in 1989 to eliminate unnecessary installations. Far more is needed, and that will lead to extensive negotiations with DOD and a further intensification of the whole debate of where, how, and what to cut.

The fundamental dilemma is that, although Congress is neither constitutionally equipped nor institutionally capable of specifying a national security policy by which to set spending priorities, it must still appropriate an annual budget and it must respond to constituent interests. Thus, as the defense budget shrinks, the process will be extraordinarily more difficult to keep rational, and the domination of short-term, politically expedient solutions over longer term, balanced assessments is likely to become even more pronounced. This situation underscores the critical need for a framework and even a pithy slogan to impose some discipline on where and what Congress cuts.

Although Congress may have finally become saturated with all the oversight committees and subcommittees it can tolerate, the idea of loosening the regulatory and legislative controls and rationalizing and streamlining the excessive oversight requirements on defense lacks a champion. Reform of the executive branch is a useful Congressional slogan that can be and is implemented by legal statute. Reform of Congress, however, has no counterpart, as the Executive cannot dictate to Congress on these issues, and, therefore, is less likely to be seriously undertaken absent a crisis or carefully orchestrated consensus-building plan of attack.

The trends in the respective growth of Congressional, OCJCS, and OSD staffs are indicative of the oversight morass caused by the proliferation of regulatory and review groups for defense (figure 1).

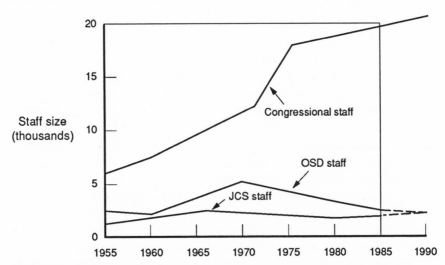

SOURCE: *Management of the Secretary of Defense,* report by the Office of Defense Study Team, October 1987.

Figure 1. Trends in defense and Congressional staffing from 1955 to 1985

All this inertia and inefficiency has slowed the process by which DOD acquires the goods and services it requires to safeguard the national defense. Few processes in life are more complicated and less understood than defense acquisition. Yet, the same acquisition procedures apply to buying both super-sonic aircraft and ice cream. Under these conditions, it may be a miracle that anything gets done.

In simple terms, the acquisition process comprises two parts: determining *what* to buy and *how* to buy it. The *what* involves a three-step process. First, the military need or opera-tional requirement must be evaluated against potential solu-tions that can include acquisition of new systems, upgrade of current systems, and changes in tactical doctrine and proce-dures that may or may not require additional capabilities. Second, these solutions must be translated into performance factors that define the technical specifications for the systems or upgrades to be acquired. Third, technical solutions must be carefully examined to determine the feasibility, availability, applicability, affordability, and capability of the technology to meet the mission needs.

The *how* refers to the strategy and specific procedures for ensuring competition and assigning the contract for a program and for accomplishing the research, development, testing, evaluation, and production. The difficulty, however, rests in determining the *what* and the *how* in a process that is subject to the extraordinary rigors, unpredictabilities, and vagaries associated with high-risk, high-technology, expensive, politically volatile programs. As a result, the process is hard-pressed to keep up with the demands that are imposed on it.

For example, rarely are alternative or different means for filling operational needs seriously explored. In part, the services have a systemic bias for platforms of advanced but similar nature to replace other, older platforms. Thus, a new tank generally emerges as the natural replacement for an older version, given the need to kill enemy tanks and provide highly mobile, protected firepower on modern battlefields. In projecting power at sea, an aircraft carrier with a displacement of about 100,000 to 150,000 tons, invariably, will become the next-generation system of choice. The argument for proceeding with the "tried and true," especially when risk in new systems can produce technical and political failure, is powerful.

In this system of extraordinary oversight, even the process of thorough testing has become politicized with a no-fault mentality. Because systems are usually so expensive, failure in testing, which, after all, must be a crucial part of the process and the only way to ensure a system will work in the most demanding combat environments, has a very low political tolerance. Ironically, then, the testing process itself becomes a volatile political problem. Rigorous testing inevitably must produce failure, which can easily generate political criticism if not active intervention as to why something so expensive is not working. Guilt by presumption follows. Especially in a budget-limited environment, the pressure to cut research programs that do not seem to work becomes intense. Hence, this vicious circle results in an understandable reluctance to embark on a great deal of costly, high-risk technical and developmental programs that, in some stages of testing, can result in spectacular failure.

So, too, the how-to-buy part of the acquisition process has significant political context. To drive the costs of acquisition down, competition and fixed-price contracting become *de rigueur* standards. The reality is that competition works best in an open and free market, and the defense business is the furthest thing from free and open. With a single buyer in the form of the government and perhaps the most regulated buying system in the world, it does not automatically follow that competition will always produce the desired results of obtaining the best for the least price. Worse, given the teaming system, contractors now find themselves teamed with one group of companies on some programs and competing against these same teammates on others. Thus, the benefits of teaming and free-flowing information exchange can never be realistically expected to take place.

The flaws of fixed-price contracting, especially in high-risk research and development programs, are obvious. As defense spending declines and pressure grows to drive the costs of buying even lower, the limits of the how-to-buy side of the acquisition house will become more exposed and fragile and probably insufficient to the task.

Cancellation of the Navy's A-12 stealth attack aircraft program in January 1991 by the Secretary of Defense illustrates the current condition and dangers inherent in the overall acquisition process. The Secretary of Defense was confronted with a program that, from all assessments, faced unacceptable costs, lengthy time delays, and unsatisfactory technical performance as a result of problems in the engineering and production of the composite materials essential for aircraft construction. The decision to cancel was generally applauded by Congress and the press, but the real cause of the failure of the program at that point rested on the flaws and vagaries of the overall system and the politics by which these weapons are purchased.

First, a fixed-price contract was mandated. Fixed-price contracting is effective and efficient when costs are known, but predictably disastrous when new technology and research and development are essential to program success. These costs are by nature, unpredictable. Furthermore, competing this contract meant that contractors were invariably going to submit low-cost bids to win and then count on reimbursement either on subsequent negotiations or contract modifications to make up the difference.

Second, to foster competition and spread the program among more than one firm, contractors were paired together against other teams. However, the winning teammates for the A-12, in this case McDonnell Douglas and General Dynamics, were competitors on the larger ATF program. Thus, the complete and unhampered flow of proprietary corporate data and technology between teammates that was necessary for success in the A-12 program was no doubt inhibited by the competition on the larger ATF program.

Third, the projected buy for the A-12 program of 620 aircraft was unrealistic. Future budgets would not support that level of procurement. Furthermore, because the average unit cost per aircraft based on this high figure would be far lower than what would result in fact, so-called sticker shock over the actual cost per aircraft was inevitable.

Last, some of the operational requirements (unrefueled range, internal bomb load, and takeoff performance) were overstated, and modifications and changes to aircraft specifications in the contract incurred cost and time increases and were exacerbated by the uncertainties of dealing with new technology. Hence, even before the A-12 contract was signed, its fate was probably predictable. Program cancellation, however, does not diminish the advantages of stealth or the need for a new strike aircraft.

The statutory establishment of an acquisition czar in DOD was viewed by the Packard Commission and Congress as an important step in the solution of the procurement problems. That positive effect has yet to be proven. Although the establishment of program acquisition executives in each of the services who report directly to service secretaries and then to the acquisition chief is an attempt to streamline the process, in essence, a side-by-side or parallel hierarchy has been put in place. This hierarchy draws on the same basic staff as the original acquisition structure and, because of this duality, whether streamlining will take place remains to be seen. In any event, double tasking of many of the same staff elements will occur. How this improves the process is not clear.

At the same time that the acquisition process inside government is becoming more unworkable, a radical transformation of the American commercial defense industrial base is taking place. A decompression, perhaps implosive, is about to occur. The size of future defense budgets will determine the extent, but it appears, in 1991, that, at a minimum, about a third or more excess industrial capacity exists than the levels of anticipated defense spending will support. Furthermore, the effects of government actions in the overall contracting and costing process have led industry to believe that there can be little or no profitability in many of the larger new programs. Figure 2, which was prepared by General Dynamics, illustrates industry's perceptions.

The history of the decline in U.S. commercial shipbuilding in the 1980s is a possible precursor of things to come for the aerospace business. U.S. shipbuilding compressed to less than 50 percent of the pre-1980 capacity. Examination of the state of commercial defense companies, whether through stock prices, debt-to-equity ratios, or profitability, indicates ill-health. One of the first victims of this austerity has been corporate research and development spending. Another victim has been innovation and independence in designing new systems.

The Navy's problem is that its procurement needs straddle both the failing shipbuilding and aerospace industries. As corporations are restructured or cut back, the notion of applying more competition will be irrelevant. Costs are liable to rise and the price of maintaining whatever commercial base survives could be quite high. For example, now that the SSN-688 program has been completed in terms of authorizing all the ships to be bought, the SSN-21 will provide the bulk of the work to keep the two remaining commercial nuclear-construction shipyards afloat. If the SSN-21 program is reduced or eliminated, even if a less-expensive SSN design is approved, these yards cannot stay in business as they are now structured. Cutting them back, however, does not proportionally cut the cost of their total overhead structure or the costs of maintaining expensive nuclear construction capabilities. As a result, both of those factors will drive the price of future SSN-21s upwards. Ironically, cutting back will greatly increase unit costs at a time when the budget is contracting.

(a) A typical program costing $4 billion in 1976

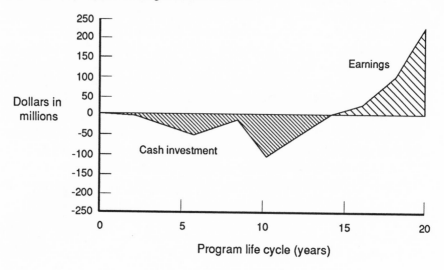

(b) A typical program costing $4 billion in 1986 through 1987

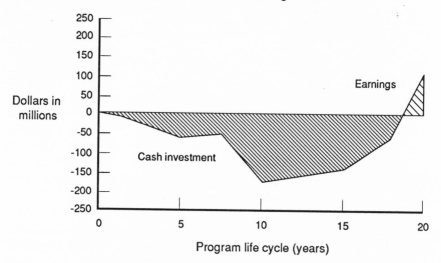

SOURCE: General Dynamics Corporation.

Figure 2. The realities of defense contracting

These same trends apply to buying aircraft, sensors, weapons, and virtually every item the Navy needs. As a result, the services will not only be dealing with a differently structured industrial base. The services will also have to deal with perhaps fundamentally different types and means of procurement. Low-run, long-term procurement in which production lines could be geared up rapidly in an emergency, combined with fewer days' worth of inventories of weapons and other operational consumables, represents one means of new thinking to respond to these industrial realities. Many more will be required.

An important conclusion can be drawn from all this. The acquisition process has been given neither sufficient tools nor enough real reform to deal with future problems and will not be able to respond adequately until additional crucial steps are taken. First, Congress must streamline and codify the laws, rules, and regulations that pertain to DOD acquisition. The rules are overlapping, contradictory, and vague. There are too many of them, and the cumulative effect has been to strangle the proper functioning of the process.

Second, legislative and executive branch oversight of these defense programs must be more realistic. On the one hand, the current oversight is overly oppressive and expensive. Both the Packard Commission and other studies have found that oversight of defense contractors may be costing the government an additional $10 to $20 billion a year. On the other hand, the public interest must be protected against fraud and wrongdoing. A system like the Securities and Exchange Commission, in which there is less direct oversight by government and far more by industry, with greater penalties for wrongdoing, could be put in place.

Third, well in advance of DOD's budget submission, Congress must provide broad policy guidelines that indicate its view about the size, structure, and general operating criteria for the forces. In addition, a budget summit should be held to reach agreement on the necessary spending levels. With these guidelines, DOD can then produce a defense program that is responsive, in advance, to the will of Congress and that avoids some of the major obstacles that keep DOD from deriving the maximum effectiveness and efficiency for the dollars spent.

Absent these necessary reforms, the future appears far more turbulent, especially as declining defense budgets mandate even tougher choices and as the defense infrastructure, in particular, continues to erode and, in too many cases, weaken.

THE DOMESTIC FLOOR FOR DEFENSE

In setting a future course and direction, however, there may be one overriding factor: the minimum level of military capability the American public will intuitively support, even without the presence of a powerful and menacing Soviet military threat. To date, no reliable or accurate polls have been conducted on this question, but the prototypical American view rests on the notion of "keeping one's powder dry." Experience and history are such that most Americans would support a certain level of military capability. Based on purely inductive and intuitive estimates, if the Soviet military threat required minimal U.S. countervailing forces, it is still likely that the public would want a substantial defense capability. Maintenance of the nuclear deterrent is also inevitable under these circumstances, especially with concerns about the proliferation of nuclear-weapon-capable states.

Based on the need for forces to respond to non-Soviet contingencies, and in keeping with superpower status and national mood, by the end of the century, total active-duty personnel levels are not likely to decline below 750,000 to 1,000,000, or about 40 to 50 percent of today's manning if public attitudes are accommodated. That decline would equate in the year 2000 to about 2.5 to 3 percent of annual GNP for defense or, in current dollars, $150 to $200 billion annually. The point is that, if a *floor* does exist below which the public will not permit U.S. defense capability to go, determining that level and making it the foundation for constructing a future transition strategy provides a solid and largely unassailable starting point.[1]

1. This floor was established by polling about 100 media reporters. Each was asked the same questions, namely, how much military the public felt was needed if and as the Soviet threat dissipated and what spending level would be required to support this level of defense.

Interestingly, the lowest point in defense spending since the Eisenhower administration is about $200 billion in current-year dollars.

For purposes of constructing a framework and strategy for the future and the first decade of the 21st century, at a minimum, it seems that this defense floor will not be less than 750,000 to 1,000,000 personnel in uniform and about $150 to $200 billion a year. With this floor established, the next step of this transition strategy is to deal with the Soviet Union in strategic-military terms. If there is debate over the concept of a floor and its level, these terms should become the focal point for discussion. It is also true that, at this floor level of defense, residual and contingent capabilities to counter the Soviet military in the days when that threat is seen as minimal will be maintained. This plan is a reversal of the traditional logic for planning forces, in which other threats were to be dealt with as lesser-included cases of conflict with the Soviet Union.

Public support can also be put to good use in overhauling the supporting infrastructure. Not only is the acquisition process in trouble, but, as noted, the defense industrial base is failing, and the supporting shore establishment is simply too large and expensive. Thus, perhaps a crucial part of the Gordian domestic knot to be slashed relates to the defense infrastructure, which must be modernized for the 21st century to make it compatible with the needs of a future defense-resource strategy.

4

The Shape of Things To Come

In the past, forecasts made in one decade about the next, whether offered in 1950 about 1960 or in 1970 about 1980, tended to conform to the natural progression of history. "Steering by the wake" and extending the present into the future were popular and reasonable forecasting methods. Although there were huge surprises along the way, both good and bad, few *step functions* radically altered the course. The tyranny of the past exerted powerful influence on the future. Events in 1989, 1990, and early 1991 have certainly changed that condition.

Now, gazing ahead ten years to the year 2000, we do not know whether this step function has run its course and whether we are, in fact, at the "end of history," at least regarding the post-war world. This uncertainty means that deductive and inductive reasoning are essential in thinking through the future with proper balances of realism and imagination and that boldness and clarity are necessary in brainstorming the wild cards (i.e., the dramatically unexpected and unpredictable events that could occur). Einstein's view of a universe that is finite but unbounded is a good starting point for speculating about future international relationships that are likely to hold the most important consequences for U.S. national security in general and for the Navy and Marine Corps specifically. The major interactions include:

- Future U.S.-USSR-European relationships, both inside and outside Europe

- Future trends and events in the Near and Middle East, the Northwest Pacific, the Indian subcontinent, and Latin America

- Unexpected wild cards, either regionally or globally, including economic, environmental, or widespread violent civil catastrophe

- Post-war events in the Gulf and Middle East resulting from the liberation of Kuwait.

From these considerations, specific answers to the major strategic and operational questions will be refined, and general responses to the domestic environment and infrastructure questions will be identified and developed in later chapters.

THE USSR AND EASTERN EUROPE AFTER THE COLD WAR

For reasons combining geopolitics, ideology, and necessity, the Soviet-oriented, post-war national security policy of the United States was anchored in Europe. The framework was designed around an Atlantic alliance that, in turn, drew its political support and consensus from the military and political danger posed by the Soviets. The highly visible and extraordinary changes taking place within the Soviet Union and its empire today challenge this traditional framework so much that the question "will NATO survive?" is no longer of only academic interest. Indeed, in the near future, there conceivably could be no military need for NATO. Put another way, if the Cold War is truly over and NATO has persevered, what is the reason for continuing a military alliance once the military threat has passed? If some European security framework is required, could not the Conference on Security Cooperation in Europe (CSCE), the European Community 1992 (EC 1992), or the Western European Union (WEU) fill that role with or without U.S. involvement?

On the other hand, prudence counsels that dispensing with an alliance that has worked so well may be more than foolhardy. In this case, there would have to be near-perfect certainty that Soviet conduct and behavior have truly altered before reducing or dissolving NATO's role or switching to an alternative structure. Therefore, if prudence is heeded, the allies should not move precipitously. Even as the threat diminishes, a new future basis for maintaining the Atlantic alliance may displace the strategic-military rationale that has held NATO together for 40 years. For example, NATO could emerge as a political-economic organization with a far less important military component, or, perhaps in concert with parts of the former Warsaw Pact, it could take on a verification role in an era of major arms reductions as well as provide an insurance policy for guaranteeing future stability in Europe by virtue of a minimal but real military presence. The advantage of continuing the NATO structure as opposed to having EC 1992, WEU, or CSCE fill that role rests in the assumption that the United States would be kept as a key partner. A hybrid structure of NATO plus a WEU or EC 1992 component, however, could provide a vital security function. Each of these conditions must be carefully examined.

In approximate terms, several interrelated factors will define the future directions and status of Europe, and the roles and levels of involvement of the two superpowers as the 21st century draws closer. Events within the Soviet Union and Eastern Europe, within NATO and the European community, within the newly unified Germany, and, of course, within the United States will be the main ingredients in this new dish, although it may be the future of Germany that determines how well or how badly this political recipe turns out.

Due to the stunning changes and departures from the past in the Soviet Union, its future may be the most difficult to predict. Yet, an outline is beginning to emerge that indicates the direction the Soviet Union would like to take.

This outline is the base case in that it probably represented Gorbachev's original thinking and intent. To be sure, the turbulence inside the USSR could derail what was started several years ago. This contingency, however, represents one of several planning possibilities for future scenarios. The former Soviet "empire" appears to be changing into some type of federation or commonwealth under what Soviet spokesman Gennadi Gerasimov calls the Soviet version of the Sinatra Doctrine—of doing business in "their own way." Events in Eastern Europe have led to more independence for the local states. Regardless of whether such a federation comes to pass, the former empire can no longer be considered in the same political terms. Indeed, a Finland-type or neutral status could result for one or more of the Eastern European states.

Within the Soviet Union, the ground rules for political dissent have been set. Internal secession and widespread disruption or civil war, as in Azerbaijan, will not be tolerated. The Baltic states, however, are another matter and may fall into the category of empire. They probably will be granted some form of limited hegemony along the lines of Finland or will become neutral like Austria provided they respect Moscow's directions for an orderly transition. Even if events in the Baltics produce further crackdown, that will probably be only a temporary condition.

Concerning overall Soviet military strength and deployment in Eastern Europe, in the scenario presumed, both levels will be reduced and probably by a significant amount. The pace and scope are likely to be determined by the problems of assimilating these forces back into Soviet society at a time when the economy is already suffering. Regardless of what happens to Soviet forces stationed in Eastern Europe, Soviet emphasis on strategic nuclear forces will continue. Even with substantial nuclear and conventional arms reductions in sight and lower numbers of forces and nuclear warheads inevitable, modernization will continue. The strategic and awesome effects of nuclear weapons will still have great significance for the future security of the Soviet Union.

Elsewhere and certainly for the shorter term, lower-profile Soviet worldwide military presence could well follow, certainly in this scenario and possibly in every scenario. Military support for Cuba and Afghanistan has been abandoned. The peaceful transition of governments in Nicaragua could be viewed by the Soviets as good reason to consider cutting their losses in the Third World. The need for foreign exchange, however, will continue to make foreign arms sales attractive, and, indeed, a flood of demobilized Soviet equipment could possibly enter the marketplace, as the recent, unsuccessful attempt to sell T-72 tanks to the French Government illustrates. With the electoral ousting of the Sandinistas in Nicaragua and the Soviet Union's ideological fight with Cuba, however, U.S. fears of Soviet Third

World involvement will be lessened as Soviet overseas presence and influence decline.

Eastern Europe, meanwhile, is undergoing a *glasnost* of its own. The Gorbachev strategic assessment appears to have been that Eastern Europe could be simultaneously made into a strategic buffer zone or *cordon sanitaire*, protecting the Soviet Union from potential abuse from the West and serving as the source for Soviet economic growth. If Gorbachev's assessment holds, the benefits of an economically rejuvenated Eastern Europe stemming from this liberation will feed into the Soviet Union sometime in the future when the Soviet economy would be able to assimilate this richer diet. The problem is that Eastern Europe may not progress so well economically.

Assuming that this rationale is correct, Gorbachev probably envisaged a two-step or two-phased course of economic development permitted by the ideological and perhaps military detachment of Eastern Europe. The first phase was economic development in Eastern Europe; the second phase is a jump-start of the Soviet economy by the rebuilt economies of Eastern Europe after *perestroika* has made the Soviet economic structure viable.

The Warsaw Pact is now defunct. The current political direction in the East appears to be a federation of Central European states still politically aligned with and supportive of Moscow but economically more pluralistic and certainly decentralized and detached from the USSR. Should this scenario unfold, the political pressure on NATO for change in kind will be irresistible and inevitable.

In such a scenario, by the year 2000, the USSR would have evolved into a much more traditional type of state with a social-democratic rather than a communist-authoritarian cast. It is extremely unlikely that the USSR would be able to achieve the economic standard of living of a Western European state; its standard of living in the year 2000 may be above only that of a Third World country. Although residual hostility with the United States is likely to preclude direct alliance or an outright and ideologically unfettered friendship, a polite but proper relationship is a possible long-term outcome, especially if genuine and significant arms reductions play out. The USSR may, in fact, take on a larger interest and role within Europe as economics come to dominate Soviet strategic calculations. Of course, myriad events and wild cards could completely discredit all this speculation, and how the USSR deals with its domestic condition will be central in what the future will bring.

For strategic planning purposes, however, certain conclusions can be drawn from this projection of trends in the USSR and its empire. All things proceeding equally, the following conclusions form the foundation for identifying the essential elements of a future Western strategy:

- The Soviet Union is moving away from its past, heavy reliance on military power as the central ingredient in ensuring national security to what George Kennan has called more moderate and traditional policies that are not dependent on such high levels of armed strength.

- Powerful, well-equipped forces, in much fewer numbers and postured for direct defense of the USSR, will be maintained into the foreseeable future. Although the steady-state levels for Soviet forces are by no means fixed and could continue to decrease, even to decrease dramatically, the decreases are limited largely by constraints in assimilating large numbers of former troops back into the civilian economy. Emphasis on strategic nuclear forces as the bedrock of deterrence will continue even at lower numerical levels, especially as conventional forces are further cut.

- The ideology of (democratic) socialism, as opposed to traditional Marxism-Leninism, even in an increasingly pluralistic Soviet empire and USSR, is not in doubt as the guiding social philosophy. The domination of the Communist Party, however, is on the decline, and the office of the executive president and the government vice the party apparatus appear to be the emerging holders of long-term authority.

- Although events could go wrong, the time it would take for the USSR to plan and launch a successful military attack on the West is becoming so great that the

traditional concept of warning time is no longer relevant. Under these circumstances, the issue for the West
would be catalyzing political agreement that a Soviet
attack were plausible or pending so a response could be
mounted. Put another way, the former Warsaw Pact
poses no military threat to the West, and a Soviet threat
would not be reconstituted in less than a year.

- All this is not simply and strictly a function of Gorbachev, although his charisma and prestige as well as
  authority were responsible for these changes. Another
  leader would not necessarily alter direction, although
  the pace and scope of change would very likely be different and probably much slower.

- Even if the current sweep of reform in Eastern Europe
  and the Soviet Union does not go smoothly, for the
  foreseeable future, the risk of hostilities and threat of
  military attack from the East is at a post-war low and
  unlikely to increase in the near term (one to two years).

It must be emphasized that these are the minimum essential points on which a future security strategy for transition
should be constructed. There will no doubt be additional
requirements that can be adjusted as the progression of events
in the Soviet Union permits. If, for reasons of crisis or desperation, the Soviet Union were to resume a threatening military
posture, the West would still be able to respond and to recover
in time.

Should some of these events go very wrong in the Soviet
Union or in the Eastern bloc and lead to crisis, however, the
consequences for the West are by no means crystal clear either.
Civil war, secession, *coup d'état*, failure of *perestroika*, or dissolution of the Soviet empire or the Soviet Union need not
automatically lead to conflict or confrontation with the West.
Introspection and isolation on the part of a politically deci-
mated USSR, along the lines of the China experience after
Tiananmen Square, are certainly possible.

Should events go right in the sense that pluralism and economic improvements take root and *perestroika* becomes a Soviet Marshall-type plan of self-help that works, it will be a

decade or more, perhaps, before the economy begins to show real improvement. As a result, the West would have ample time to anticipate, if not to react to, negative consequences of this progression of Soviet successes. Several exceptions to this generally stable flow of events, and four wild cards beyond the scenarios of civil war or political disintegration of the USSR, deserve particular scrutiny.

SOVIET WILD CARDS

The first Soviet wild card plays on the basis of renewed hostility towards the West becoming a crucial component of a political policy to restore a shattered Soviet domestic consensus or impose harsh austerity programs. Such a policy would probably be precipitated by the threat of or actual collapse of the economy. This reinstatement of Stalinist-like policies and resurgence of the Soviet military threat could occur within Eastern Europe as well, but it is more likely to occur only in the Soviet Union.

The second wild card is a collapse of the economies in the Soviet Union and in Eastern Europe. Unlike the scenario in which hostility was rekindled, in this case, there would be the need for massive Western infusion of economic assistance on both strategic and humanitarian grounds to stabilize the USSR. This could be a Marshall-type program that was based on a political and economic assessment that the West's interests were served by a surviving USSR and Eastern Europe.

The third wild card is the misuse, mishandling, or theft of Soviet nuclear weapons due to riot, revolution, or civil war. This possibility is remote but not unthinkable and has been discussed privately between the U.S. and Soviet governments.

The final and most likely wild card to play out concerns the future of Germany. The legal and political terms and conditions of unification have been completed, and now full assimilation of East Germany by what was West Germany is under way. The establishment of "one Germany" has been achieved with stability and safety. Now, the task must be to perpetuate this extraordinary achievement and ensure lasting German stability. Failure in this regard raises frightening specters ranging from a militarized Germany to an arrogant and uncaring superpower.

All this suggests a future Soviet Union and Eastern Europe likely to take one of several forms. Barring economic or political collapse, that future is not bleak for the West. Using a descending order of Soviet political and military control as the measuring stick, the first possibility is an amalgam of what exists today, with the nations of the former Warsaw Pact remaining the centerpiece of Soviet policy and strategy in Europe and with open markets, political emphasis on pluralism, and less reliance on military forces. This possibility could be called the Confederation and Union of Soviet and Central European states and would be a non-step-function transition.

The second possibility is a demilitarized Eastern Europe with relatively small local East European armies, perhaps of a constabulary nature. Soviet forces would be withdrawn to inside the USSR, although Soviet political hegemony would continue in Eastern Europe, modified by open markets and free borders with the West.

The third possibility is a neutral or Finland-type Central Europe that is still in the shadow of Soviet power and aligned economically but not militarily. In this case, Central Europe would emerge as a quasi-independent but neutral entity.

The fourth possibility is a Balkan-type Central Europe in which each of the states operates on a more or less independent but friendly and competitive basis. In this case, the USSR could well grant sovereignty to various regions and republics as set forth in the Constitution of 1936. The USSR would become a smaller country, having spun off its empire and some of the republics.

Barring the playing of a wild card, in a strategic sense, the way in which events are proceeding within the Soviet empire can be translated into Western responses. One result for the West of this revolution in the East will be the need for fundamental reappraisal by NATO of the entire Western security framework. It may be impossible for NATO to continue on as before without such a review and perhaps more impossible after. Political events, however, have moved so quickly as to make this review imperative. It should be started in the next year or so. The dilemma is in fashioning an appropriate and politically acceptable response to these dramatically changing conditions that can be accepted and approved by each of NATO's 16 nations.

At no time in this century have the opportunities and prospects for genuine peace and long-term stability in Europe been greater. Aside from the threat of a wild card, even the fear that somehow all this is camouflage for hostile Soviet intent and action is simply not plausible. Gorbachev and the Soviet Union are not even remotely similar to what Hitler and Germany were in 1935. In both the NATO and former Warsaw Pact alliances, the basic causes of the two world wars and the hostility between the blocs that followed Germany's defeat in 1945 appear to have been put to rest. The major purpose of the Atlantic alliance—to demonstrate sufficient political and military strength and resolve until such time as Soviet belligerence was overcome—appears to have been achieved. This approach has allowed the traditional and long-standing social-democratic preferences that took root in the 19th century and are inherent in the social structure in Europe to condition Soviet thinking. As a result, Marxism-Leninism is accommodating to these long-term trends and Gorbachev's Soviet Union stands the chance of becoming a more democratic type of state, even if it does not adopt all the values of a Western social democracy and even if the conservatives emerge ascendant over the reformers.

WESTERN EUROPE AFTER THE COLD WAR

For the past 45 years, the threat has also put Western Europe in fundamental strategic tension with the United States over how to contain the Soviet Union. For the better part of those years, Western Europeans, to the degree such a term applied, viewed nuclear deterrence as sufficient to prevent Soviet political and military encroachment. It was defense on the cheap from the European perspective and also meant that expenditures on conventional forces could be slighted. Except for the United Kingdom and France, NATO's European members were relieved of the extra burden of fielding nuclear forces, which created a double savings. Furthermore, for much of the Cold War, the automatic escalatory nature of *flexible response* enabled Europeans to believe the threat of strategic nuclear exchange would spare wartime damage to Europe for two reasons. First, war would never come because the threat of nuclear devastation was too great. Second, if war did break out, the United States and the USSR would become the principal nuclear battlefields as each side tried to eliminate the great striking power of the other.

The United States, of course, sought to keep the nuclear "threshold" as low as possible so that any conflict could be contained to Europe and blunted at the inner-German border. The qualitative and quantitative growth in Soviet strategic nuclear armaments in the 1960s and 1970s eroded U.S. nuclear superiority and gave obvious if not reluctant credence to the arguments for enhancing conventional military capabilities, an area in which the West was perceived to be at a disadvantage.

The glue that bound the alliance together and kept these strategic tensions from shattering NATO was flexible response. Under this doctrine, Europeans could emphasize the strategic nuclear deterrence benefits of policy and pursue defense on the cheap. The United States could argue for conventional force improvements and proceed in that direction. The elasticity of flexible response was also its brilliance because it stretched enough to permit the United States and its European partners to head occasionally in opposite strategic directions. Now, the political need for keeping the current version of flexible response and for maintaining the current levels of deterrence appears to be evaporating as the threat recedes.

Working out the next version of flexible response or its replacement is a crucial consideration in defining the basis for a future NATO framework. A formula to replace flexible response must be found that will permit the alliance to maintain strategic purpose and substance while leaving enough room and space for major differences of strategic opinion. If such a formula cannot be invented, the consequences for NATO are altogether too obvious.

As Western Europe reverberates from the enormous changes transforming the East, the approach of EC 1992 and a more economically integrated Western Europe offer attractive and realistic alternatives for a future political structure. Despite the limitations to economic integration raised by several questions—a single currency and a unified tax rate being the most obvious—movement towards a United States of Europe is far from impossible. The disappearance of the Warsaw Pact military threat and the effect of declining U.S. military presence and involvement in Europe will reinforce those pressures for Europe to become independent and unified.

Meanwhile, the political pressure for decreasing defense expenditure is irresistible and is likely to become overwhelming in Europe. The British and French are unlikely to draw down on their nuclear deterrents as this is the one guarantee of strategic independence neither would wish to forgo. As the new century approaches, however, the central strategic themes of forward defense and flexible response are surely to come into question and perhaps disrepute if democratization and pluralism persist in the East and as conventional force reductions occur through arms control or unilateral actions.

In developing a new security framework, the following considerations should shape future planning:

- The continued existence of powerful but admittedly fewer Soviet military forces and a period of transition for the new Soviet defense doctrine to take root and clearly show future Soviet intent and behavior

- Continuation of some type of NATO alliance, but with a restructured and reduced military component

- A Western Europe on the one hand compelled by geography and the advantages of integrated economies towards a United States of Europe but, on the other, retarded by basic economic and political differences among individual states that will delay this process

- Momentum towards significant arms reductions

- Acceptance that the Cold War is over, at least in Europe

- Political, cultural, and economic reasons to assist in the redevelopment of Eastern Europe that will translate into the flow of investment and creation of fiscal, trade, and monetary policies to achieve that end

• The understated concerns that a powerful, unified Germany could dominate Europe.

EUROPEAN WILD CARDS

Wild cards in Western Europe would stem from one of the following categories: domestic reactions to crises in the East, political turbulence at home leading to the election of new or more radical governments, and overreaction to future miscalculation on the part of the United States. Crises in the East would have to be massive and brutal in the extreme to resurrect the Western fear or threat of military action. Soviet incursions into Hungary in 1956 and Czechoslovakia in 1968 set a pattern that, if repeated, could easily generate powerful Western responses. A Soviet Tiananmen Square type of repression would not be tolerated by the West. In general, Western responses to Soviet actions will tend to be in kind so that "democratization" and pluralism will no doubt be favorably received. Repression, however, is a wild card that could reverse all the good that has occurred.

Political turbulence in the form of minority domestic parties coming to power and control of governments that would lead to fundamental policy reorientation is clearly a wild card. A Socialist Party victory in the Scandinavian and European low-land states or a future Labor or Green coalition government in Britain could shake or even dissolve the alliance. It is ironic that a socialist party could come to power in the United Kingdom that, in some ways, would be to the political left of Gorbachev, although events in Moscow and Prime Minister Margaret Thatcher's abdication in November 1990 make it more likely that the conservatives will win the next British general election. A unified and militarized Germany is another wild card that can and must be prevented from ever occurring. It is also fair to say that, as the Soviet military threat diminishes, the popular tendency in Europe to lessen dependence on NATO's military role must grow.

How then can and should the alliance debate its future, given these dramatic changes and huge uncertainties that lie ahead, and what should the role of the United States be in all this?

NATO can fill three crucial functions. First, it can remain as the West's best political insurance policy should events in Eastern Europe and the USSR go sour. To serve as a guarantor, NATO must maintain a certain level of active military strength, including U.S. forces in Europe, and a great deal of political cohesion. Second, the alliance can serve as a transition or bridge into the next century and the post-Cold War world by encouraging mutual arms reductions, extending confidence-building measures more deeply into what constituted both alliances, and providing part or all of the verification framework to ensure that arms reductions are carried out to the letter of the law. Third, the alliance can become the mechanism for enhancing stability in Europe by serving as a possible conduit for economic development and, conceivably, the centerpiece of a broader alliance system in Europe that could include states from the East and be complemented with a CSCE, WEU, or EC 1992 parallel structure.

To carry out these functions, NATO needs a new statement for its *raison d'être*. It needs a plan of action to carry out these three functions as well as a fallback position should wild cards or untoward events lead to greater tensions and mutual hostilities raging again in Europe.

One component of this action plan must be military in nature, both to challenge the former Warsaw Pact and USSR to draw down their forces and to maintain enough military strength to defend Western interests. In this regard, NATO should challenge the USSR to propose mutual force levels that are seen as nonthreatening to both sides and to respond to NATO proposals of what NATO perceives as a proper basis for future Soviet and Eastern European force structure and doctrine.

Given the bilateral U.S.-USSR strategic arms talks, the CFE Treaty, and the multinational CSCE, finding the most appropriate mechanism could be a chore; however, unless NATO, inspired by the United States, takes the lead in this effort, these opportunities will be lost. Chapter 9 presents a strategic framework to accomplish this task.

REGIONAL FOCAL POINTS IN THE POST-COLD WAR WORLD

The Middle East

To the degree that current regional powder kegs are likely to persist into the future, as Iraq's invasion of Kuwait showed, the crescent of crisis running from the Mahgreb in the Mediterranean to the Strait of Hormuz in the Gulf will provide ample cause for American concern and involvement no matter how these great events in Europe turn out. Although the Gulf War is over, achieving peace may take months or years. There are, however, several points to be drawn from the Gulf War.

First, the prospect of facing a well-armed, well-equipped adversary with weapons of mass destruction no longer resides in a purely hypothetical domain.

Second, the prospects for some form of long-term U.S. military presence on the ground in the Gulf as well as expanded maritime deployments cannot be disregarded. Whether Saudi Arabia becomes the next century's form of NATO to require and justify U.S. force structure, the shift of strategic axis from West Germany to the Gulf is unmistakable.

Third, given the politics and instability of the region, the problems in defining an effective and viable future security arrangement will be huge. With Iraq's defeat, massive rebuilding of Kuwait and, at some stage, Iraq must proceed. The role of Iran must be defined, and the Gulf must be provided with a mechanism that leads towards establishing peace and stability in the region. This mechanism cannot ignore the Arab-Israeli-Palestinian impasse.

The Arab-Israeli conflict will doubtlessly prove resistant to any winds of change sweeping aside historical animosities and thereby altering traditional U.S. assumptions and policies in that region. The fundamental divisions over sovereignty, territory, and religion are not likely to dissipate. Consequently, dealing with Israel and its immediate Arab neighbors will continue to pose a significant challenge and will be an important ingredient to future U.S. national security planning.

Meanwhile, Arab money continues to recirculate in the West as well as into the acquisition of U.S. holdings and property. The degree to which foreign holdings of U.S. assets would prompt specific policies towards ensuring stability in a particular region remains unclear but could become a future reason if not grounds for U.S. action. For purposes of national security, the crescent of crisis poses even greater weight for vital American interests in this post-Cold War era. Throughout the Middle East, the threat of terrorism looms large and more dangerous should it incorporate nuclear, chemical, and biological weapons. Chapter 6 focuses on the possible military consequences of these phenomena.

Southwest Asia

The Indian subcontinent and the conflict between the soon-to-be largest populated country in the world and its Islamic neighbor are also important for the United States. Both India and Pakistan are nuclear-weapon-capable states or so close to that capacity to make little difference, and both possess a growing ballistic missile capability as well. India, however, which has aspirations beyond just defending against its northern neighbor, has been steadily emerging from the enormous burden of feeding her massive population, and, with that emergence, a dynamic and entrepreneurial middle class is developing. Not only does India have increasing worldwide business interests, its "strategic" interests also are expanding.

As the world's largest democracy and soon the world's most populous state, India increasingly views itself as a global power. India's military capability has grown, and its navy has acquired nuclear submarines. Concerns about maltreatment of Indians in Africa have stirred xenophobic feelings perhaps dormant since the Mogul empire. Although it would be folly to declare India a pressing national security concern for the United States today, it would be absolute folly to disregard the possibility of future tensions and strains. This point is further reinforced by India's tenuous peace with Pakistan and the fear that another war could trigger the use of nuclear weapons by either or both neighbors.

The Northwest Pacific

The Northwest Pacific, with its crisscrossing of American, Japanese, Chinese, Soviet, and Korean interests, could become a dramatic focal point for many of the consequences stemming from other extraordinary but less visible changes taking place worldwide. In the aftermath of Tiananmen Square, China has withdrawn itself from the active international role it had been playing. The policy of economic modernization and reform without the loosening of political control is proving unworkable, and China's ambitious modernization plans probably will fail unless a little *glasnost* is applied.

China's economy is both the key to and the Achilles heel of stability in the region. The combination of China's repressive political system and its leaders' failure to raise their country's standard of living above that of a Third World country creates both internal and external pressure. Without political reform, U.S. friendship is unlikely to be as deep as it was in the past. Without economic reform, the burden for help will increasingly fall at the feet of China's wealthier neighbors—particularly Japan and Korea. Failure to help China could lead to further strains in the region, and all this political and economic interaction cannot ignore the shadow of China's military power, which includes nuclear weapons.

The two Koreas appear ripe for some sort of federation or unification, certainly by the end of the century. South Korea's economy goes from strength to strength and, with the lifting of the restrictions on entry into its stock market in 1992, will be a magnet attracting foreign investment. Combining the economy and population of the South with the resources and people of the North could produce an economic miracle. To be sure, this process will not be automatic, although the barriers to reunification will certainly have shrunk once Kim Il-Sung and his son are gone.

At the minimum, U.S. troop reduction in Korea is inevitable, and the prospect of conflict in the peninsula is surely eclipsed by the suggestion of federation. Such a federation is not necessarily going to prompt unanimous approval in Japan, China, and the Soviet Union because an economically powerful and united Korea will pose a considerable commercial and, perhaps one day, strategic challenge to the neighborhood.

By far, the future of Japan poses the most potentially complex strategic, economic, and social questions. Even before the government of Prime Minister Toshiki Kaifu was badly embarrassed by its indecision in responding to the Gulf Crisis, time was running out for Japan to defer broader policy questions over its security relationships with the United States, over the future of the mutual defense treaty, and on the constitutional limits on the Japanese Self-Defense Force (JSDF).

As the Soviet threat dissipates and the prospect of a return of all or some of the four northern islands still occupied by the USSR grows larger, the entire foundation for the security alliance with the United States must be brought under scrutiny. The territories represent much of the emotional resentment the Japanese still harbor for the Soviet Union. As this thorn is plucked from the strategic flesh, Japan may well have no other choice but to examine its past assumptions about threat.

No Japanese politician in the ruling Liberal Democratic Party (LDP) is anxious for this review to occur. Once questions are raised over the nature of the threat, continuing strategic dependence on America, and the role of the JSDF, an unraveling and deterioration of the U.S. relationship, exacerbated by the fundamental economic and trade tensions, could easily occur. So, strategically, Japan is in a condition of limbo, happy with the past and reluctant to look at the future for fear of breaking with the United States.

Economically, the strains of achieving superpower status are beginning to show across Japanese society and culture. At the heart of the Japanese miracle has been extraordinarily hard work and a sense of community that has fostered an ethic of organization above self. As Japan accumulates enormous wealth and as Japanese corporations and land garner astronomical value, there is growing social dissent over equity and the distribution of those riches. An increasing number of the Japanese middle class, the backbone of industry, are asking for their share of this wealth. This clamor could become a ground swell of demand. The showing of the Japanese Socialist Party in the elections in the summer of 1989 reflected popular unhappiness with the ruling LDP, partially due to scandal, partially due to an unpopular excise tax, and partially due to this perception of economic inequity. Although LDP's victory in the Lower House elections in February 1990 reversed this trend, the party has not dealt with the dissatisfaction raised by the equity differences. This problem can only get worse unless addressed, and the current LDP leadership may not choose to address it.

At the same time that this societal strain over fairer division of the nation's vast wealth is growing among the working classes, the elite are disposed towards reexamining Japan's economic and political role in the world, particularly as "Japan bashing" in the United States becomes widespread. A resurgence of nationalism is whispered as an unwelcome response to worsening relations with the United States.

Threats of a militarized Japan remain distant unless wild cards come into play. A trade war, U.S. insistence on Japan shouldering even more of a defense burden for itself or in supporting us in the Gulf, and a resurgence of Japanese nationalism are conceivable wild cards if the relationship with the United States were to be mishandled. That can be avoided if both countries are serious in reducing the grounds for tension and disharmony. The real wild card that could throw everything into a cocked hat is whether these societal divisions over equity erupt into crisis.

Under those remote circumstances, a future Japan could take one of several directions. Japan could abrogate the mutual defense treaty with the United States and disassociate itself from the U.S. defense umbrella, or Japan could assume a larger, more independent role by acquiring a stronger defense capability through defense industries at home or abroad. The latter would be a version of structural vice manpower rearmament and would challenge the United States directly as an arms supplier and implicitly as a potential military superpower. Indeed, a year ago, the thought of a nuclearized Japanese defense force was inconceivable. Given the changes worldwide, the probability has now risen, even infinitesimally, above absolute zero.

The problem that Japan and the Northwest Pacific hold for the United States is the reverse of NATO's dilemma. In the Pacific, no universally shared or agreed-on sense of threat rallied the key nations into alliance. The decline in the Soviet threat, therefore, is likely to have less effect on the region. On the other hand, economic rivalries have been intense and will become more so. In NATO, the Soviet threat maintained a countervailing pressure on economic and political centrifugal forces; the same was not true in the Pacific. Bilateral relations, however, were the backbone of U.S. policies in Asia. Now, those bilateral relations, from the U.S. perspective, are seen as shifting to an economic basis. For the regional states, that is where emphasis has always been, so there is likely to be even greater pressure exerted on the economic side.

To the degree military forces have actually created regional stability, American military presence may remain unchanged as the Soviet threat recedes because this threat was not perceived by all the regional powers as large. American presence may even grow. Linking this stabilizing quality of military presence to a security framework that inevitably will evolve more and more on economic lines will become one of the most crucial considerations for future security planning.

Throughout this transition, U.S. access to military bases in the Pacific will decline. In the Philippines, domestic politics, the size of U.S. aid packages, and local resentment over alleged American abuse of Philippine sovereignty will reach a point where the political costs of maintaining the bases at Clark and Subic will be too great. American withdrawal will occur well before the end of the century. This withdrawal probably will not lead to complete loss of access to these bases, but will lead to access at a much lower level.

To lesser degrees, the popularity of U.S. military presence in Australia will decline and the controversy with New Zealand over nuclear weapons policy may never be healed, but it may no longer matter. In any case, the long-predicted withering away of U.S. access to overseas bases is occurring and can no longer be considered as idle speculation.

Although the situation in Southeast Asia remains chaotic, the major security interests of the United States will rest between waging a drug war to close down the "golden triangle" of supply and stop the flow of illegal drugs into America and perhaps scoring a major coup by improving relations with Vietnam. These interests will have relatively little effect, however, on future U.S. force planning.

Latin America

The final region that will affect U.S. national security is Latin America. The dangers there are threefold: drugs, dictators, and destabilizing social, political, and economic forces. The implications of drugs for national security will be expanded upon in later chapters. Suffice to say that the U.S. military will play a larger role, but one with little chance of major success. To defeat drugs, demand and supply must be addressed. To date, the only law drug dealers have not violated is that of supply and demand. Military forces may have value in stemming the supply side, although that is doubtful because the supply far exceeds the demand. On the demand side, military forces simply are not relevant.

Meanwhile, most of the annoying left-wing dictators in Central America are gone. Even though Castro has proved long-lived and may remain in power, in realistic terms, he is a minimal national security concern.

The last and most dangerous d—destabilization—could spill over. Revolution or chaos in Mexico is the most obvious scenario. Aside from protection of the border, however, the implications for national security seem to fall outside the realms of U.S. military forces and into the thrall of other policy instruments.

THE UNPREDICTABLE WILD CARD

From this perspective, the 21st century, does not appear particularly ominous, provided no step function or wild card causes the world to explode in our faces; however, a number of crises could occur. The Gulf War could have had a tragic twist had Iraq fought competently and used chemical weapons; an Arab-Israeli or Indo-Pakistani war could escalate to weapons of mass destruction; a militarized, aggressive Germany could threaten Europe; a hostile, aggressive, or volatile USSR and Eastern Europe could emerge; a rearmed Japan could cast its shadow on the Pacific; or some terrorist-induced calamity could change the course of events. By and large, because the likelihood of each crisis is low and because each is preventable by virtually all concerned, we are not faced with impossible tasks in creating future policy. Clearly, U.S. national security policy for the future must include what we do not want to see happen. That approach is manageable vis-à-vis the more obvious and improbable wild cards.

The surprises, however, rest in what is really unpredictable. Suppose, for example, environmentalists are right and the next generation of the Four Horsemen of the Apocalypse includes the greenhouse effect, depletion of the ozone layer, deforestation, and overpopulation. National security policy could abruptly shift focus. As ludicrous as it sounds, if the environment becomes perceived as a resource no less vital than oil, and if we were prepared to repel a Soviet attack against the oil fields of the Gulf, would we contemplate similar action to save rain forests in Brazil if their extinction were to produce an environmental catastrophe that could destroy much of the agricultural capacity of the United States? The case of Iraqi environmental terrorism in loosing the huge spill and igniting nearly 1,000 Kuwaiti oil wells will not be lost on the world at large.

In the mid-1980s, when the spread of AIDS had no obvious limits, the National Institutes of Health reckoned that, if the disease spread similarly to the influenza epidemic of 1919, virtually the entire federal budget would be required for medical treatment. Now that national security is no longer seen exclusively in terms of a Soviet threat, new types of threats are likely to be in competition for resources. One of the future tasks must be to define national security in a politically realistic manner so that appropriate needs are included and inappropriate tasks can be assigned to other responsible areas.

The most likely wild card that will directly challenge national security is weapons of mass destruction and transnational or terrorist groups. The consequences of terrorist actions with these weapons are so great that they must be given careful consideration. Indeed, superpower cooperation in this area in exchanging information and intelligence and even in taking mutual action is crucial.

In summary, the security challenges and environment of the next century will be more complicated, diffuse, interconnected, and, in some areas, more dangerous. The two principal regions for U.S. planning—Europe and the Middle East—have undergone radical change. As the U.S.-Soviet strategic competition dissipates, economic and political issues are more and more likely to dominate security concerns. In this regard, the United States will have to learn to deal from a position of lesser strength as other industrial powers either close the gap or pull ahead of the United States economically and technologically. Although diminution of the Soviet military threat will likewise lead to diminishing our own military forces, the future role of military force will be crucial for ensuring stability and, no doubt, for actual use, although U.S. force is likely to be used only in relatively discrete, small doses.

Instead of containing or preventing communist-inspired aggression, the theme for future U.S. security policy could shift to ensuring the safe transition to this new world and providing important stabilizing qualities so that untoward events and crises do not take place. If this can be done, the next phase of U.S. national security policy in this new world can be at least as successful as the policies of the past 45 years have been.

5

The Soviet Threat:
Diminishing and ... ?

The changes in the Soviet Union imposed by Executive President Mikhail Gorbachev through *glasnost, perestroika,* and his own dynamic and extraordinary persona have been so striking that traditional analysis of Soviet conduct and prior assumptions about Soviet behavior must be carefully reexamined. This examination does not mean that wholesale invalidation of a generation of policies and assessments concerning the Soviet Union should result. Certainly, no matter how different the future is from the past and present, there will be some continuity. Thus, trends and threads in the evolution of Soviet strategic thinking will be extremely useful in determining where the Soviet Union may be headed and what, if anything, the West must do in response.

Regarding the defense of the homeland, which has been and will remain the highest of Soviet priorities, thorough examination is revealing because many of Gorbachev's policies of today sprang from yesterday's initiatives and, in some cases, even from some of Nikita Khrushchev's "harebrained schemes." The starting point for review can be placed at the death of Stalin in 1953, because the iron lock of that despotism was loosened and the rise of Khrushchev brought early although powerful signs of policies that would eventually mature into *glasnost, perestroika,* and the phenomenal events reshaping the USSR today.

Soviet and Russian paranoia over direct military threats to the homeland cannot be overstated on strictly emotional grounds. The pitfall in the United States, however, is subliminally permitting Soviet emotional and patriotic responses to what constitutes genuine defense of the homeland to obscure Soviet hard-headed, pragmatic strategic judgment. Of course, the Soviet Union abhorred and mourned over the devastation of invasion as did the Russian and Tsarist empires of earlier centuries; of course, the Soviet Union paid the extraordinary price of enduring some 20 million killed in the Great Patriotic War; and, of course, the Soviet Union, from its perspective, had ample reason to fear the United States and the threat that another war could break out as the Cold War waxed and waned in intensity.

SOME USEFUL HISTORY

The paranoia of Stalin and Stalinism was kerosene for whatever sparks East-West tensions struck. The successful Western policy of containment, the series of alliances surrounding the Soviet Union, and American monopolies in nuclear, then thermonuclear, and, finally, strategic delivery vehicles were perceived by Stalin as clear and present dangers. The ruthlessness of Stalin and the physical elimination of those with opposite views (including, at various times, supporters who carelessly took the wrong side of an issue) made certain that debate over the external dangers was limited to prescribed boundaries.

From 1955 onwards, after removing the two other members of the post-Stalin ruling *troika*, Nikita Khrushchev began a strategic reassessment of the state of the Soviet Union and the external threats to Soviet security. Several critical events helped him. Perhaps most significant was the Soviet invasion of Hungary in 1956. This dangerous crisis was filled with strategic uncertainty because the Soviets did not know how the West would respond and whether Soviet nuclear inferiority would be readily used as political blackmail by the United States to force a showdown and Soviet backdown over Hungary. For a number of reasons, the United States and the West did not and could not take strong counteraction. The lesson for Khrushchev was that the sanctity of the Soviet empire in Eastern Europe was inviolate as far as the United States was concerned, regardless of military balances and despite U.S. rhetoric about rollback. This conclusion meant that there could be broad Soviet policy scope no matter the degree of strategic imbalance. This crisis led Khrushchev to develop several broader strategic conclusions regarding the defense of his country.

First, in his view, even a relatively few nuclear weapons deterred conflict with the West and gave the Soviet Union a protective umbrella under which there was a great deal of maneuvering room for pursuing even dramatic foreign policy initiatives safely and securely. This view, in part, led to the initiative for the neutralization of Austria and the withdrawal of all occupying forces in 1959. Khrushchev further reckoned that perhaps a kind of minimum nuclear deterrence could be put in place that did not require large numbers of weapons of mass destruction. In the interim and until that condition was reached, however, Soviet defense interests were best served by emphasizing strategic nuclear systems, as they were the principal shield for preventing war.

Second, under this condition of nuclear stalemate, there was less need for conventional forces, as conflict in Europe would be deterred by the threat of nuclear war. If, by some fluke, war came, the threat to use nuclear weapons would either limit the conflict or escalate it. In the latter case, conventional forces would be eviscerated in a nuclear holocaust. Hence, their importance to Khrushchev was substantially reduced.

Third, exploitation of the revolution in military technology that would allow ballistic and cruise missiles to be mated with nuclear warheads and other advanced weapons systems to be procured, ultimately would prove less costly to the Soviets because, at a future date, minimum deterrence would permit fewer numbers of these advanced systems to replace much larger numbers of less advanced, but individually cheaper, weapons.

Fourth, arms-control initiatives could be pursued once the Soviet Union attained a certain level of technical competence in the manufacture and control of nuclear systems.

These views were translated directly into Soviet defense policy (although not without great debate and not without some recantation after Khrushchev's misjudgments concerning Soviet policy in the so-called southern hemisphere backfired and led to the Cuban Missile Crisis). Furthermore, the defense buildup of the Kennedy administration to close a missile gap that did not exist gave his critics sufficient ammunition to blunt these thrusts. By 1964, Khrushchev's authoritarian style, as well as his failure in stimulating the economy, led to his downfall in a *coup d'état* that put Leonid Brezhnev in power.

In January 1960, however, and surely not without some appreciation of the Eisenhower administration's strategic policy, Khrushchev publicly unveiled his strategic *new look*. The Soviet Union unilaterally reduced one million reserves from its force structure and embarked on policies to put principal emphasis on strategic nuclear forces. Strategic emphasis not only corresponded to what were identified in ideological terms as the correct objective factors, it also permitted and encouraged technical modernization and, ultimately, would permit reduction of the more costly conventional forces, freeing up resources for a chronically ill economy. The defense budget was substantially reduced.

The history of that debate from 1959 and the 21st Party Congress until 1961 and the extraordinary 22nd Party Congress is well documented. The upshot for the Soviet Navy was that the naval missions were defined almost entirely in terms of defending the homeland from Western sea-based nuclear strikes. Defense could be achieved through some mix of capabilities for nuclear deterrence, of which the Soviets had little, and destruction of the West's sea-based platforms, of which the Soviets had less. Emphasis was placed on the latter, that is, attempting to limit damage by destroying U.S. sea-based nuclear systems, at least until a substantial Soviet strategic nuclear deterrent capability could be acquired. Although destroying the U.S. Navy's aircraft carriers would be difficult because of American military superiority at sea, the destructive power of nuclear weapons was a great equalizer if properly employed. The problem resided in the difficult issue of antisubmarine warfare, to which neither the Soviets nor anyone else had immediate solutions.

Ironically, the Soviet surface fleet, which Khrushchev regarded as "floating coffins" at the time, was saved on the grounds that surface ships were needed as part of the multidimensional effort to destroy enemy submarines and, later, to protect one's own. Like many weapons systems that are operationally versatile, the cloth was cut to fit this new jacket and surface ships were rationalized as important parts of this new strategic mission to attack and to defend ballistic submarines. Protection of the seaward flanks was more of an exclusionary mission designed to prevent the allies from making lodgments that could threaten Soviet bases in Murmansk and the Baltic.

Interestingly enough, during this period and for at least another decade, the U.S. Navy completely discounted how the Soviet Navy was actually evolving and ignored the strategic nuclear bias mandated by Khrushchev. The U.S. Navy, despite the aircraft carrier's role as a nuclear delivery system against the Soviet Union, argued the next war at sea would resemble the last. Soviet submarines were assessed as a much larger equivalent of Hitler's U-boat fleet and the war at sea would be fought over defending the sea lanes and the resupply and reinforcement sea bridge to Europe.

This strategic underpinning to the Soviet Navy has remained a central component ever since. Although debate has shifted as to (1) where the balance between strategic deterrence and defense should rest, (2) the degree to which nuclear and conventional capabilities were required, and (3) the optimum force structures and platforms needed to carry out these tasks, the Soviet Navy has remained principally configured to defend against, and therefore deter, attack from the sea, particularly nuclear attack.

Several broader points can be extracted from this brief history of the 1960s. First, there was a direct correlation between the views and policies of the main political leadership and how they affected, in this case, the navy. That correlation was imperfect across every area but direct in terms of the main thrust for designing and employing the navy.

Second, the United States lagged behind in producing an accurate assessment of Soviet strategy and intent by a decade or more. Although that assessment might not have altered the shipbuilding plans for the U.S. Navy one iota, that gap could have produced significant erroneous and wasteful decisions for the United States.

Third, and most important, Khrushchev had an apparent although far from precise understanding that military competition was insufficient reason for pushing an inevitable arms race to higher and higher levels of military forces and defense spending. At some point, enough was enough. However incompletely conceived, a sense of limits on defense and an instinctive urge for redefining the military competition at "reasonable" levels were present in Khrushchev. Some of these lessons were not wasted on Gorbachev.

The Brezhnev leadership was very much status quo, unwilling to take political risks to advance Soviet society and willing, as it now has become obvious, to serve as caretakers. Even so, debate, in this case over defense, was fierce. The military build-up under President Kennedy, the Vietnam War, and the Soviet invasion of Czechoslovakia in 1968 to stamp out the Prague Spring independence movements all were grounds for the Soviets to moderate the Khrushchev approach of favoring strategic nuclear systems and downgrading conventional forces.

For nearly 20 years, from Khrushchev to Gorbachev, Soviet military doctrine and the naval applications proceeded along fairly clear lines. To the central core of dealing with strategic nuclear war was added increasing theater nuclear and conventional warfighting responsibility and capability. In part as a response to the NATO and U.S. strategies of flexible response, wherein the West was doctrinally prepared to counter Soviet military incursion at every level of nuclear or conventional conflict, and in part because the Soviets understood that Khrushchev's reliance on the strategic choices of either nuclear war or nothing at all left few good options, the Soviets expanded their theater and regional military capabilities. At the strategic nuclear level, the Soviets continued to improve their forces numerically and qualitatively, eventually acquiring solid-fuel, highly accurate, multiple-warhead ballistic missiles. Although calculation of the strategic balance between the United States and the USSR was driven as much by political expediency as anything else, by the time of Gorbachev's accession to power in 1985, the Soviets had achieved at least strategic nuclear equality with the United States. Indeed, many in the United States claimed the Soviets were just plain superior.

During the Brezhnev years, the military component in the overall policy of the Soviet Union increased. The reasons why the Brezhnev leadership permitted, tolerated, or encouraged this emphasis on military force are clear. First, the leadership feared that Khrushchev's discounting of the importance of overall numbers and capability in the nuclear age would lead to significant American advantages through exploitation of U.S. technological and technical superiority. Some balance or perhaps imbalance in the Soviet favor was important. Second, there is evidence and some logic that enhancing Soviet military capability was thought by certain members of the Central Committee to be one way of improving the industrial-technical base of the USSR. Finally, some in the Kremlin believed greater military force was necessary both to legitimize Soviet superpower status and to provide more authority in conducting foreign policy. These conclusions were a logical response to the realpolitik and balance-of-power politics practiced by President Nixon and his National Security Advisor, Henry Kissinger.

Throughout this period, the Soviet Navy's missions can be characterized as defending the state from seaborne attack and protecting "state interests." In the former, strategic deterrence assumed more importance as more and truly capable Soviet ballistic missile submarines (SSBNs) became operational. The mission of protecting these forces in highly defended bastions near Soviet homewaters therefore increased in its priority.

Strategic defense was more difficult. Defending against the aircraft carriers could be accomplished either by saturation attacks with large numbers of cruise missiles, submarines, and extensive jamming, or by nuclear evisceration. Hunting the enemy's SSBNs, however, was another issue. As U.S. sea-based ballistic missiles acquired intercontinental range (from 1,200 miles for the Polaris A-2 to 6,000 miles for the Trident D-5) and as U.S. submarines became acoustically more invisible, strategic ASW became a very low payoff mission. To date, neither the Soviets nor anyone else has resolved this problem of ASW detection.

Protecting state interests was akin to what had once been called gunboat or peacetime naval diplomacy. To carry out its now worldwide wartime missions, the Soviet Navy had to sail most of the seven seas. The presence of these units provided instruments to the political leadership should they care to exercise them for peacetime or crisis diplomacy. Hence, the strategic need for distant deployments could yield political benefits, or so the conventional Soviet naval wisdom argued.

Meanwhile, from the late 1960s onward, strategic arms control increasingly occupied center stage for U.S.-Soviet relations. The Soviet Union gained two particular advantages from these extensive and ongoing negotiations: (1) it came to realize it could ultimately understand U.S. strategic views, and (2) it was able to unscramble the chaotic nature of the decision-making process in Washington, which for the longest time was genuinely believed by the Soviets to be a part of a purposeful American disinformation plot. The confidence the Soviet Union gained in more thoroughly understanding and appreciating how the United States regarded key strategic issues was a silent but powerful contributor to some of the reforms Gorbachev would make.

Within the Politburo, there was powerful dissent over the status-quo style of leadership. As the average age of the Politburo increased and Brezhnev became enfeebled, the more lethargic an already ponderous leadership grew. The main dissenter, Yuri Andropov, we now know from Gorbachev, was anxious to set in place some new thinking. Death, however, was to cut off Andropov. Ultimately, it would fall to Gorbachev to assume the mantle of originator and protector of new thinking.

NEW THINKING

As has been argued earlier in this book, by the time Gorbachev assumed power in 1985, he and a growing number of Politburo colleagues had come to the conclusion that the excessive militarization of the U.S.-Soviet rivalry was counterproductive and wasteful. Khrushchev had reached this conclusion on intuitive and visceral grounds. Gorbachev was more analytical and reasoned that even unilateral force reductions could be accomplished with no political risk to the USSR. From a strategic perspective, the superpowers had no reason to embark on World War III. Furthermore, so many nuclear weapons were in place that neither side could exploit them politically. Therefore, it was pointless to continue the military rivalry at such high levels. Clearly, the Soviet economy could benefit from slackening the grip defense held on the budget.

In 1991, the military proof of Soviet intent is still in the adolescent stage and, metaphorically, may not be fully mature until 1992 or 1993. By then, the doctrine of *reasonable sufficiency* and the cuts Gorbachev has made in the defense budget will have highly visible effects. Yet, the collapse of the Warsaw Pact as a fighting force, particularly with the coming withdrawal of all Soviet forces from what was East Germany, from Hungary, and from Czechoslavakia and the promise to withdraw all forces from Eastern European states by 1994 provide evidence that what Gorbachev says he will do will occur. Soviet military deployments and force structure in Asia are being similarly cut back.

Still, national defense demands that the United States must double- and triple-check its assessments about Soviet intent and action before responding or taking major new initiatives. What the Soviets cut today could be replaced tomorrow. Therefore, answers to the following questions are crucial:

- First, what is Gorbachev's view about the future political status and composition of the Soviet Union and the Soviet empire?

- Second, doctrinally and practically, what does this reduction of forces mean for the future direction of Soviet military capability as well as future prospects for arms reductions?

- Third, how is this likely to change the navy?

The first question was answered earlier. To the degree that a future design can be predicted for the East, Gorbachev has elected to move towards a commonwealth or confederation of Eastern European states with the USSR. Inside the USSR, a miniconfederation is likely, with Moscow and the Russian Soviet Federated Socialist Republic at the core of perhaps ten republics. The remaining republics, and this may take to the beginning of the new century, will have limited autonomy and independence but will still be politically beholden to Moscow. Should this structure unfold, Western fears over Soviet territorial aspirations must be mitigated.

The future direction of Soviet military doctrine and structure appears headed towards a smaller, qualitatively improved force in which reasonable sufficiency and a *defensive offensive* will become the stylized, abbreviated expressions of intent. From the Soviet perspective, the military threat that literally rings the USSR is declining and, indeed, can be dealt with by defensive forces largely confined to the USSR instead of forces stationed outside the Soviet Union that are designed to launch huge offensives into Western Europe. The future United States and NATO threats, therefore, can be countered with fewer forces and indeed with little or no Soviet military presence in Eastern Europe. A unified Germany will still require residual Soviet military capability, especially by the end of this century.

The military threat from China is limited and can be dealt with by a combination of nuclear forces and, perhaps, a thinned-out or even trip-wire conventional defense along the huge border. It is from Iran and Turkey, where the crescent of crisis abuts the soft underbelly of the USSR, that threats are likely to emerge.

The nature of these military threats is that of an incursion or encounter rather than a full-scale invasion. The ideological and political threats of religion and culture are likely to pose the greatest challenges to the USSR, but, in the Transcaucus regions, the Soviets will still be sensitive to potential military threats from the southern borders.

Southern Asia and Indochina do not pose a particular concern to the USSR, and India and China provide a counterbalance to each other. In fact, envisioning a situation in which India could constitute a future military threat to the USSR is difficult. Should the two Koreas reunite, demilitarization of the peninsula should follow. The rise of Korea as a greater economic power could well be to the benefit of the Soviets for the next several decades because Korea would probably find investment in the USSR a small price to pay for unification.

If there is a wild card for the USSR, it may be Japan. Barring the extraordinary unlikelihood of a rearmed Japan, tensions between the USSR and Japan will be political, economic, cultural, and racial. More than likely, Japan would be regarded militarily as a lesser-included case of a China contingency. Should Gorbachev have returned some or all of the northern territories to Japan in 1991 or soon thereafter, Soviet-Japanese relations could improve dramatically. Indeed, from a strictly strategic calculation, it may be surprising if the USSR does not return these territories. The immediate issue for the first half of the 1990s is the degree to which Japan's decision to support economic development of the USSR reinforces or erodes that good will.

The general plan Gorbachev has set and will most likely follow, at least as basic defense principles, is to rely on fewer, more capable strategic nuclear systems (both offensive and defensive), cut back substantially on conventional forces, and move to a defensive doctrine for the immediate protection of Soviet territory. By the year 2000, the total number of active-duty personnel in the Soviet military is likely to be less than two million, perhaps much less. This level would be not less than and probably far more than a 50-percent reduction from current levels. The number of reserve forces, border guards, and the like will also decline. The largest impediment to these reductions is likely to be the ability of the civilian economy and social structure to assimilate such large numbers of people.

Obviously, depending on the follow-on negotiations to START and excluding crisis or unprecedented nuclear proliferation, the Soviets are likely to move to well under the nominal 8,000 warheads permitted by treaty. In the end, they will probably have 4,000 or less. The bulk of these warheads will be land based either in silos with multiple independent reentry vehicle (MIRV) or mobile multiple- and single-warhead missiles. The ratio depends on START agreements. The Soviets will also maintain probably between 20 and 30 SSBNs, mostly *Typhoons* and *Delta IVs*.

Conventional forces will be modernized and set at lower numerical levels. The doctrine of the defensive offensive, that is, absorbing the first blow of an enemy's attack and then repelling the attacker, should dominate planning and force design, although more emphasis on the defensive aspects is likely. Similarly, some (non-naval) force-projection capability to 500 or 1,000 miles outside of Soviet borders will be required.

How does this translate to the Soviet Navy? If the foregoing is the base case, the consequences for the navy will probably take on fairly predictable forms. Other possibilities for the future Soviet Navy cannot be excluded, however. These other possibilities are discussed after the base case.

Assuming Gorbachev's view prevails, the major missions of the Soviet Navy would converge around deterring nuclear attack and, from the days of Sergei Gorshkov, protecting state interests. A residual mission would be to defend the country against other forms of seaborne attack, presumably of a conventional nature, but this mission would be mostly contingency based. The bastion and SSBN-protection missions would loom large. The strategic-ASW and counter-SSBN missions would have declining importance as the threat receded and would provide a less persuasive case for rationalizing force structure.[1]

The tactical means to carry out these missions would continue to reside in more or less balanced forces consisting of attack submarines (SSNs) and land-based Soviet naval aviation. To the degree surface forces are required, the larger destroyers and cruisers with multipurpose capabilities will be among the surviving forces. Future forces will be multipurpose in any event.

Assuming the Soviets maintain 20 to 30 SSBNs, probably 60 to 80 SSNs would be kept for their protection and perhaps an additional 20 SSNs would be kept for other purposes. In other words, the Soviets will probably have a force of 100 to 120 SSNs at or before the end of this century. What this means for reserve forces and "mothballed" ships is open to debate; the recommendations in chapter 11 cover some of these more interesting points.

---

1. This view is confirmed by informal remarks made by General Mikhail Moiseyev, Soviet Chief of the Defense Staff.

Future Soviet naval developments could take several other excursions. With successful, successive START agreements, the Soviet Navy could abandon its strategic role and concentrate more on traditional missions akin to the U.S. Navy. Because the prospects of war in Europe are likely to grow even dimmer, an anti-sea-lanes-of-communication (anti-SLOC) campaign for a conflict unlikely to happen and for which no belligerent would be equipped seems illogical. Perhaps a sea-control or local power-projection force in distant regions could become a focal point for naval use.

Alternatively, the Soviets conceivably could increase the proportion of their nuclear-deterrent force at sea. This increase might produce a navy that would be smaller in size than the base case and with greater emphasis on strategic missions. Given Soviet historic preferences for an investment in land-based systems, a move towards a sea-based deterrent as the backbone of Soviet strategic might is just not very compelling.

Finally, although the Soviet Union will almost certainly reduce its navy in size, the Soviets could choose to embark on a more extensive modernization and research and development program so that the Soviet Navy, pound for pound, would be the best in the world. This modernization could occur no matter whether the navy was biased in favor of strategic missions or conventional ones.

It is easy to be lulled into the sense that all this could be benign simply because the USSR is following less militarized and belligerent policies. These policies could change. Whatever form the future Soviet Navy takes, it will no doubt be a very capable force. Still, the Gorbachev reforms generate a few interesting opportunities for the United States.

OPPORTUNITIES?

First, assuming Gorbachev continues towards reasonable sufficiency and a more defensive orientation, what types of naval postures would we find less threatening that would still protect legitimate Soviet interests?

Second, is there a way for us, either through discussions and negotiations or confidence-building measures, to induce the Soviet Union to adopt this posture or to give us good reason why it will not?

Third, how can we plan a force for this transition period that will enable us to stay the course safely regardless of whether the Soviet Navy is transformed to a nonthreatening entity?

To the degree the Soviet Navy can be encouraged to assume a less-threatening posture, strategic and force-structure prerequisites can be identified. In terms of strategy, to be sure, direct U.S. attack of a non-nuclear nature against the Soviet homeland would be opposed by whatever Soviet forces remained. Soviet shifts towards a nuclear deterrent posture in the bastions does not seem especially worrisome, however. The counter-SSBN and anticarrier missions should concern us most.

The strategic nuclear shift is directly transferable to force structure. The Soviet Navy must simply reduce its SSNs and advanced diesel submarines. In fact, rough equality in numbers of SSNs on both sides, provided it produces substantial Soviet naval cuts, is clearly in our best interests.

Soviet projection forces have always concerned the United States, but, in this category, too, the Soviets have legitimate reasons for maintaining these forces. The question is at what level? By arbitrarily setting a level of, say, the equivalent of two Marine Expeditionary Brigades (MEBs) for the Soviet Union and ensuring that we would maintain the ability to counter these forces should we have to, there can be grounds for mutual agreement.

In sum, a Soviet Navy that moves towards nuclear deterrence and protection of its at-sea SSBNs and that reduces its SSNs and agrees to limits on its projection forces is something the United States should pursue. (See chapter 11 for policy actions and recommendations.) A need remains, however, to ensure close scrutiny over Soviet transition to a future naval posture.

In addition to the confidence-building measures and whatever treaty verification mechanisms are established, the following four areas require scrutiny:

- High-level, navy-to-navy exchanges should be conducted to set forth the strategy, positions, and future directions of both sides. Indeed, the CNO might be well-advised to correspond directly with the Soviet Navy's commander in chief to obtain this information. The response would be revealing. Failure to respond meaningfully would send a message; dissembling would be a second, obvious sign; and any candor and truthfulness shown would be useful for further collaboration.

- Close scrutiny of the debate inside the Soviet Union on doctrine and on uses of the navy must continue. This analysis is crucial, especially as *glasnost* opens debate and access to debate.

- Observation of Soviet naval training, exercises, and operational deployments can provide actual evidence of intent.

- Soviet building and modernization plans must be carefully assessed.

The conclusion for the United States regarding the Soviet threat must be this: there is more than indication of fundamental change and Soviet movement towards a defensive posture charged with the immediate defense of the territory and borders of the USSR. The challenge is to induce the Soviet Union to continue this transition along lines we believe are most benign. At the same time, the United States must design its strategy to set the pace of this transition. If all goes well, at some future date, the United States will be better off, more secure, and, on relative terms, in a stronger position. If all does not go well, the United States can abruptly halt this transition and remain strong and well postured for whatever is required. This view forms the heart of the conclusions and prescriptions that follow.

6

Big, Bad Weapons ... But

Few military phenomena have attracted as much attention as the spread of advanced weapons systems,[1] and that was before the Gulf War. These weapons have spread literally to every part of the globe. If the specter of U.S. military units being eviscerated by a nuclear weapon or gassed through chemical attack by a rogue state was ever pure fantasy, one conclusion from the Gulf War is that these contingencies must be seriously addressed in planning, training, and in acquiring weapons systems. Even more fundamentally, operations in these non-Soviet contingencies will require root-and-branch changes in many of the basic assumptions that held when the USSR was the principal military threat for force design and use. Put another way, open-ocean, deep-water ASW and long-range AAW simply may not be relevant in many operational conditions outside the Soviet threat. Furthermore, dealing with potential new allies as diverse as Syria and the USSR could form the basis for a new, combined-operations doctrine.

Conventional wisdom has held that the spread of advanced weapons systems automatically changes the balance-of-power equations for both local and external states and poses much greater risks for those who would consider involvement or

---

1. The terms *advanced weapons* and *weapons of mass destruction* require careful definition and distinction. The term *advanced weapons* must include all types of modern combat systems, from ballistic missiles to advanced aircraft, submarines, and cruise missiles and from advanced sensors and command, control, communication, and intelligence (C^3I) to chemical, biological, and nuclear agents. The term *weapons of mass destruction* should be limited to chemical, nuclear, and biological agents. Thus, a ballistic missile is an advanced weapon that may or may not be a weapon of mass destruction, depending on what is carried in its warhead.

intervention in a particular region. The questions of whether that conventional wisdom is correct and how threat perceptions are likely to change in the future when even more highly capable military systems will be available in both quality and quantity must be examined, especially in designing those forces that are likely to play leading roles in any expeditionary assignments. These two sets of challenges posed by non-Soviet contingencies must occupy more of our collective efforts.

* * *

Fast forward: Consider this scenario. It is the year 2000 and the shaky truce between Iraq, Kuwait, and Saudi Arabia has finally failed. U.S. and UN forces, in line with the treaty setting the truce, are ordered to redeploy and marry up with prepositioned equipment that has been maintained in Saudi Arabia and Kuwait since the Iraqi invasion was repelled in 1991. The U.S. operational commander has been ordered to deploy one U.S. airborne brigade and two tactical fighter wings to prepositioned sites in Kuwait.

Just before their deployment, unlike the 1991 war, biological and chemical agents contaminate the sites, making them unusable by the United States or, for that matter, by any forces. No direct evidence points to Iraq as the perpetrator, and a fundamentalist terrorist group has taken credit for the attack. Cleanup and decontamination will take weeks. The commander's alternative is to use a Marine Expeditionary Unit supported by elements of an amphibious brigade, but the shallow water and constricted shipping routes of the Gulf and the need to bring those forces close to the shore raise very real operational risks.

First, Iraq has developed a strong in-shore navy, and the presence of highly agile diesel submarines armed with under-the-keel torpedoes must be countered. The United States, however, has little shallow-water ASW detection capability, and, in waters less than 40 fathoms deep, almost all sonar is ineffective. Worse, the United States has limited means to attack these submarines because all ASW torpedoes are hampered in these shallow waters by bottom reverberation and by the physical constraints to acoustic detection.

Second, a new, small cruise missile called the Asp has been developed in Iraq with a warhead that is incendiary, not explosive—a tactic derived from the loss of HMS *Sheffield* in the Falklands when an Exocet burned rather than exploded and put the ship out of action. The skin of the missile is made of a carbon material that enhances the incendiary charge and makes the weapon stealthy. Because Asp missiles are inexpensive and more accurate than the Scud, there are about 2,000 of them in the region.

Aside from the operational challenges, a new multinational television satellite has been launched over the Gulf. Its infrared, optical, and television capabilities enable the world's viewing audiences literally to see the flight deck of the command ship night or day. Attempts to jam the satellite have caused court actions to be filed both in the United States and at The Hague.

And on and on . . . .

* * *

As in other scenarios, these events are invented, although they draw on what has happened in the Gulf. Such scenarios test our readinesss to deal with hypothetical though plausible conditions. The other complementary approach in preparing for an uncertain future is study of the past. Review of the historical record to determine where the future may take us reveals several interesting conclusions about how the proliferation of advanced weapons affects regional, local, and global balances. The following conclusions are partially contradictory and contain some contrarian logic to the scenario that was just painted.

First, although "advanced" military technologies such as submarines, supersonic aircraft, cruise missiles, and smart weapons have been spreading beyond the major powers since the late 1950s, ballistic missiles, chemical, biological, and nuclear agents and truly advanced technology weapons no less modern than those possessed by the superpowers are deployed in growing numbers virtually everywhere on the globe.

Second, although the two military superpowers possess an absolute military advantage over other potential adversaries should they choose to use it, constraints on the actual use, amount, duration, and intensity of force that both the United States and Soviet Union can apply are increasing. This increase in constraints probably is due more to domestic than to international factors and pressures.

Third, despite the proliferation of so-called advanced weaponry, the extensive use of these weapons in local wars, and the grave warnings being posted about their particular dangers by senior U.S. officials, neither the Soviet Union nor the United States has been terribly victimized by this technology to date, either in conflicts where they have been actively engaged or where they have chosen to intervene for the short term.[1] The war with Iraq has not changed that.

From these conclusions, the simplistic argument could be made that the specter of the next round of advanced weapons proliferation is overexaggerated by major powers located outside a particular region. In this time of a diminishing Soviet threat and reduced defense spending, such optimism could become politically attractive and strategically foolish. Three irrefutable points cannot be safely or sensibly dismissed no matter how benign the future may look, and, based on prudence, these points must form the major criteria for future planning.

First, the danger of regional or local states having, and conceivably using, nuclear and other types of weapons—especially biological and, to a lesser degree, chemical weapons and agents—looms so large that even the absolute might of the superpowers cannot assume it away.

Second, the corollary, the express use of so-called weapons of mass destruction by transnational groups, to which we

---

1. Clearly, some observers have argued that the Stinger missile was largely responsible for the Soviet debacle in Afghanistan. Although the Stinger was no doubt very effective, many other factors forced Soviet withdrawal, not the least of which was the Afghan freedom fighters' indomitable will.

in the West apply the sobriquet of terrorists, continues to pose enormous contingent and catalytic dangers to our own well-being and to what has passed as some measure of regional stability all these years.

Third, if future force planning becomes fixated on medium-to low-threat needs, in the mistaken belief that dissipation of a Soviet enemy significantly reduces the technological risks posed by advanced systems elsewhere or that reduced defense budgets do not allow otherwise, the magnitude of the error could be incalculable. Harm's way is not diminished by a decline in Soviet hostile attitudes. Other global trouble spots will become exceedingly dangerous places as this spread of weapons continues and is intensified by political, cultural, and religious strife.

Furthermore, we are dealing in the present tense. The future consequences of superpower and NATO-Soviet arms control agreements will be significant as both superpowers and their (former) alliances move towards major reductions in conventional forces. So, too, the consequences of frozen or shrinking defense spending by both superpowers will impose large reductions in the numbers and/or readiness of their forces to fight. These consequences will add great uncertainty to future considerations of the implications of advanced weapons technology proliferation to regional and local states.

So, what is new? All this discussion has been examined in excruciating detail in the policy debates and classified studies of the 1960s and the 1970s. Aside from Vietnam and Afghanistan, however, there is something *very* new here that affects both the United States and the lesser military states in a fundamental way.

Whether we in America choose to believe it or not, the post-World War II era, which was characterized by the domination and superiority of all or most things American, is over. The authority, influence, and power of the United States have declined despite its absolute strength, and, in some ways, this decline has been dramatic. Although clearly the first among equals, the United States no longer automatically commands universal respect or intimidation by dint of its vast economic, military, political, and ideological capacity and its ability to dominate events. In an approximate way, the Soviets have been buffeted by similar trends, and the Gorbachev leadership is carefully reassessing the utility and costs of the one capacity that ensures the USSR's place as a superpower—its military power.

As the United States' power and authority have diminished, foreign states have skillfully learned how to exploit and manipulate the U.S. political process to their own advantage. The Israeli, Arab, Chinese, Greek, and Turkish lobbies, for example, are the more benign examples of how the U.S. political system can be sucessfully manipulated. Ho Chi Minh and his accomplices in Hanoi vividly showed how a mighty nation's will could be sapped at home, and Ayatollah Khomeni showed great skill at preying on the U.S. political process, whether through American hostages illegally seized from the U.S. Embassy in Tehran, or through the life-threatening censorship of Salman Rushdie's *Satanic Verses*, in which the protection of free speech mandated by the First and Fifth Amendments of the Constitution intensified Khomeni's ploy.

Thus, despite the absolute strength of the United States and whatever international legitimacy the Soviet Union maintains or acquires, this is a new era not only for the superpowers but for the rest of the world as well. A "cultural revolution" has occurred in which the hegemonic aspirations and great influence of the superpowers have been curtailed and the policy instruments of force and its transfer or sale through arms purchases to "client" states have become less acceptable and perhaps less effective. Interestingly, Saddam Hussein's military disgrace will confirm part of this trend as future Iraqi rearmament will be restricted by external suppliers. Furthermore, because the United States operated in this case under a UN charter, the Gulf War is unlikely to be viewed as solely a U.S.-Iraqi conflict.

To be sure, only the superpowers and the advanced military powers in Europe currently possess the panoply of industrial capability for construction and sustained production of many advanced military systems. However, the ability of regional states to play one external power against another and the declining technical difficulty of developing or of "begging, borrowing, or stealing" advanced technology know-how is waxing as indigenous technical proficiency grows.

POLICY GUIDELINES

The key questions that must guide consideration of what to do include the following:

- What's there, namely, who has what advanced weaponry and how much, and what is the record to date vis-à-vis use against the external powers?

- Can these advanced weapons technologies realistically be used against the United States and what actual difference would these systems make if used now and in the future decade?

- What counters or additive military capabilities can the United States afford to develop over the longer term, given the reality of declining military force levels and budgets? Or, put another way, what systems or capabilities can the United States afford *not* to develop should its forces become engaged in conflict in the Third World?

- What constraints or pressures are likely to influence both the regional possessors of these advanced capabilities and the superpowers in the conduct of policy?

- What types of force should the United States maintain to employ in these conditions?

The appendix summarizes current military capabilities for various regional and local states. For the most part, these capabilities are conventional in the sense that, no matter how technologically advanced these local states are, they possess aircraft, ships, tanks, artillery, and smart munitions that presumably could be numerically overwhelmed should either superpower actually undertake conventional military operations. Bear in mind that, outside its littorals, the Soviet Union has far less military projection capability than the United States and, without direct air and ground support from Soviet land bases, the Soviet Union would be in a decidedly inferior position to many regional or local powers if it chose to project power at great distances from home.[1] Desert Storm is the eloquent proof of this conclusion.

Other, nonconventional capabilities, such as ballistic missiles, chemical, biological, and nuclear agents, and their application either through terrorism or under conditions tantamount to surprise must preoccupy us as we enter into new, uncharted political terrain. To be sure, the use of ballistic missiles and chemical, biological, and nuclear weapons is not new. The most recent applications were in the Iran-Iraq war, where Iraq's use of chemical agents was decisive in offsetting Iran's "human sea" suicide attacks and numerical superiority. Local states, however, face some inherent disadvantages in using these weapons against an external power deployed in a regional conflict.

First, ballistic missiles are limited tactically to striking fixed targets that are undefended. Ballistic missiles, as currently possessed by regional states, are inaccurate. This inaccuracy does not mean that the symbolism provided by "demonstration shots" would be devoid of political use even if no military objective were achieved. To be militarily effective, however, either precise and timely locating data on the target must be available or the warheads must carry large amounts of destructive material to compensate for missile inaccuracy. This material would have to be nuclear or biological because the amount of chemical weapons required for wide-area coverage is too voluminous to be delivered by the current ballistic missiles possessed by regional states. Accuracy will improve, however, and today's reality may not apply tomorrow. Generally, the tendency has been to exaggerate the rate at which this type of

---

1. The proof of this assertion requires another chapter. On balance, however, potential Soviet projection capabilities to distant areas show that, at best, they are brigade size or less. The United States has an Airborne Corps (2 divisions), at least 2 MEBs, and perhaps 10 to 12 deployable CVBGs it can send for forceful intervention. Even with large military reductions, the United States should maintain a great advantage.

modernization takes place. Again, Iraq's limited gains in using Scud missiles confirm this conclusion.

Second, the prospects for use of nuclear weapons against a superpower by local powers are virtually nonexistent. In the cases of Israel, India, and Pakistan, each of which is capable of producing nuclear weapons, these weapons have application in regional politics and an undefined context as a deterrent. Use against a superpower is virtually unthinkable unless a crisis of incredible severity occurred. Chemical weapons are readily available but, for the reasons described below, are unlikely to be used against a superpower. Biological agents pose the greatest threat. Not only is their technology available, their use in nonmilitary operations could be devastating and relatively untraceable. Of all the so-called weapons of mass destruction, these biological agents pose perhaps the greatest potential danger for the United States.

Of course, a local state's military or overt use of biological, nuclear, or chemical agents against a superpower poses extraordinary risks without necessarily ensuring any great rewards. Certainly, if the intervening superpower had a portion (or all) of an expeditionary force vaporized by a nuclear weapon or contaminated by chemical or biological weapons, in most circumstances, it would be imprudent to assume restraint would follow on the part of the intervening power. The shock effect would be enormous and the aftermath unpredictable. Given the examples of surprise attack against both the United States and the Soviet Union in 1941, the expectation of a massive response cannot be prudently ignored by local states.

Indirect usage outside the region as a form of terrorism in which the local state can maintain plausible deniability or outright invisibility is, perhaps, a more likely contingency. The logistics of long-distance delivery of these agents in bulk, however, is far from a trivial issue, assuming that the local power proceeded on the basis of attacking the superpower outside the region. For the time being, uses of agents other than biological weapons, directly or indirectly, must be viewed as contingent or catalytic and most likely to occur if, and only if, the local power sees their use as the only option.

To date, the record shows how safe the superpowers have been against the growing array of advanced weapons technologies. Remove Vietnam and Afghanistan from the lists, and the incidents are relatively few. Even in all of Operation Desert Storm, the United States had fewer than 80 killed in action and a third of the casualties were the result of a fluke Scud that tragically fell on a barracks. The United States certainly suffered in Beirut when 241 servicemen were killed by a truck bomb attack. True, the occasional destruction of aircraft and murder of personnel have occurred. The Israeli attack against USS *Liberty* in 1967 and North Korea's blatant hijacking of USS *Pueblo* in 1968 were losses. It was a 1960s vintage Exocet missile that accidentally hit USS *Stark* and a pre-World War I vintage mine that disabled USS *Roberts* in the Persian Gulf, however. The Soviets have had an even safer record. Thus, although history far from guarantees the future, so far only the odd or accidental mishap has occurred.

SHOTS IN ANGER

Suppose, however, that a local or regional state considered using these advanced weapons capabilities against an intervening external power? What might be achieved militarily? For simplicity of analysis, the subject of terrorism is deferred for a moment. The regional and local powers are arrayed into three different groups based on the relative amounts of advanced military capability possessed by each. The first group has the ability to conduct a major battle that takes place over days or even a few weeks. The Arab-Israeli conflicts and the Falklands War are examples, and states like Israel, Syria, India, Pakistan, Iraq, and Iran fall into this category. The second group has the capability to conduct an encounter or engagement situation that would last minutes or a few hours. Libya falls into this group. The third group includes states possessing extremely limited capacity to conduct a skirmish or single-shot effort, after which the state would collapse from technological exhaustion. None of these three categories includes a full-scale invasion or occupation of territory, such as took place in Vietnam or Afghanistan.

Clearly, with highly capable forces designed, equipped, and trained to fight the Soviet Union, U.S. projection capabilities would be hard to counter on a strictly military basis by forces of any regional state. Iraq learned this after "100 hours" of allied ground offensive destroyed its army. This conclusion assumes that neither terrorism nor unconventional attack occurs on a major scale and conflict is kept on a conventional level. Lockerbie types of terrorist acts and the advantages of unconventional or surprise attack constitute the greatest dangers to the United States. The effects of these attacks obviously will be intensified by political or tactical incompetence in which the deployment and disposition of U.S. forces may invite disaster. That was the case in Lebanon in October 1983, where a combination of surprise and terrorism collapsed U.S. policy in the region.

A second weakness, and a corollary of the surprise category, is a skirmish in which the regional state may have advanced weapons capabilities without the superpowers' knowledge. Suppose, for example, that the Grenada opposition had had cruise missiles and surface-to-air missiles (SAMs), or suppose that it had used chemical, biological, and nuclear agents. U.S. forces could have been mauled, casualties could have been extensive, and, worse, the United States could have taken days to mount a response, particularly cleaning up the toxic hazards.

Because the Soviet Union has less worldwide military projection capability than the United States, it has a greater military problem should it get involved. Recall Brezhnev's threat in October 1973 to deploy Soviet airborne units to protect Egypt's Third Army from possible Israeli annihilation; some wags speculated that the Israeli Defense Force would have disposed of those Soviet troops quite quickly. Such an outcome was not an idle risk. Aside from Afghanistan, the Soviets have always been wary of large military deployments far from home, because the ultimate costs of intervention generally outweighed any political rewards by considerable amounts.

In countering the threats posed by ballistic missiles and nuclear, chemical, and biological agents, the United States is faced with several planning constraints. First, the United States has rationalized, planned, and built its forces against the threat of conflict with the Soviet Union. In a resource-constrained environment in which there is perhaps a third or so more programs than future defense budgets can support, adding systems for a nebulous Third World threat will not be easy. Nor will sustaining the rationale for highly capable forces be as easy as it was when the Soviets loomed so large and were the exclusive threat.

Second, the political and bureaucratic pressures within the United States defense decision-making process have resulted in a fixation with buying platforms—high-value ships, tanks, and aircraft for dealing with the Soviet threat—and not necessarily in obtaining all the supporting infrastructure, such as modern battle-management decision aids, effective antichemical and biological clothing, and dedicated surveillance systems for Third World operations.

Third, the United States has legally and premeditatively limited its intelligence, covert operations, and preemptive capabilities—all of which are perhaps among the most effective policy instruments for dealing with aspects of local or regional conflicts. Taken together with the War Powers Act, these constraints are considerable.

Fourth, and most obvious, the American process of government is cumbersome and often awkward in shaping policy actions. It tends to respond rather than anticipate. Responding to perhaps more complex, possibly more likely, and no doubt more diffuse threats requires competence, sophistication, and understanding. With so much public and private oversight, media that are fond of generating more than a few stories based on sensationalism, and internal government bureaucracies that are more often at war with competing agencies and offices than with any external threat, it is a wonder that anything gets done, much less effectively and efficiently. The kidnapping and killing of Colonel Higgins somewhere and sometime in Lebanon and the first failed coup attempt in Panama against Noriega illustrate the frustration and difficulty of any U.S. government coming to grips with these issues.

Fifth and finally, the United States must learn to deal with planning assumptions that are likely to be fundamentally different from those that dictated responding to the Soviet military or naval order of battle. For one thing, the Soviet Union was an excellent adversary. Somewhat clumsy and awkward in its maritime competence as it groped its way to sea in the 1960s and 1970s, it also was relatively predictable. Although the Soviets were able to surprise the United States occasionally with the technical performance of specific new systems like the KY-8 missile, the *Alfa*-class titanium-hull SSN, and the *Tango*-class diesel submarine, collecting intelligence was straightforward because the Soviet Union produced and supplied its own weapons. It could not go elsewhere and stride ahead overnight in a particular category of capabilities. This is not the case in the Third World.

In planning to fight the Soviet Navy, the U.S. Navy was concerned with standoff: long-range AAW at hundreds of miles from the carrier to destroy the "archers" rather than the "arrows" they shot, and deep-water, open-ocean ASW against high-performance Soviet SSNs. Target identification was a lesser problem because few neutral or civilian ships or aircraft were likely to be in remote spots off Kola or elsewhere.

In the Third World, virtually none of these operating assumptions is likely to hold. AAW will become close-in and perhaps point defense in nature because there may not be any sea room for standoff. Deep-water, open-ocean ASW may be nonrelevant in many cases given the geography. The key issue may be target recognition, to avoid repeats of USS *Vincennes'* downing of Air Iran Flight 847. This philosophic adjustment in planning assumptions may be the most difficult step of all to make.

Given these realities, the United States as a nation must take several broad steps. The first step is to define what is meant by the term *low-intensity conflict* and to assign responsibility for the multifaceted tasks across all of government. Indeed, getting a better name than LIC would help. Currently, DOD has been given the task of addressing LIC and has quite properly focused on the military aspects alone. From a national perspective, however, the military option is an incomplete solution and neglects many of the central problems of LIC. Should LIC become a more active threat, this narrow focus could be a prescription for disaster as more than the military instrument will be needed to ensure success. This shortcoming particularly applies to Lockerbie types of disasters.

Second, a strong, legitimate case for using U.S. forces in conditions of local and regional conflict must be made, especially as the sense of Soviet threat appears to be diminishing. Determining what types and levels of forces are necessary will be crucial to this exercise. Third, planning must be more imaginative in deriving contingencies in which advanced technology weapons may be used against us and in ensuring we are prepared to counter or respond effectively to these threats. Fourth, regional surveillance systems like the lightweight satellite, which can detect local ballistic missile launches and provide several minutes' warning time, should be deployed to potential launch sites, either ashore or in ships to permit early-warning detection.[1] Fifth, protective equipment against biological, chemical, and nuclear agents that is easy to wear must be acquired in sufficient numbers and made available to deployed units.

In addition, political initiatives, including enforcement of nonproliferation agreements, missile technology-transfer controls, arms control, limitations on use of toxic materials, and basing-rights issues must be undertaken. No matter what the United States ultimately adds to its current capabilities, any additions will occur as there is substantial reduction, unilaterally or bilaterally, in superpower military force structure.

Given the reality of advanced weapons proliferation, the issue is not what missions U.S. forces must fill in the future but rather what types of forces and capabilities best match the challenge and dangers posed by the spread of advanced weapons systems. In projecting power, the advantages and

---

1. Even a few minutes' detection can allow mobile targets to disperse. In two minutes, a ship at 30 knots will move a mile—a considerable targeting problem for ballistic missiles.

disadvantages of land, air, and sea forces must be carefully balanced. Deployment times aside, the U.S. Army has excellent capability on the very heavy and the very light sides of the conflict spectrum. Heavy forces require extremely large logistical tails of many thousands of tons of daily supplies and cannot be forcibly inserted except through access to friendly and well-protected bases and ports. The time required to deploy heavy ground forces is measured in weeks for division-sized or larger deployments, and the logistics base represents a very large target set. Heavy forces, however, can overcome most conventional opposition in these regions—a crucial advantage.

Light forces, such as the XVIII Airborne Corps and the 7th Division, are extremely mobile and rapidly deployable. Like all light forces, only a few days of ammunition and rations are carried and sustainment through resupply is crucial. Light forces are also not equipped for sustained combat against heavy forces or many types of well-defended forces.

Air power, too, when based on land, is entirely dependent on proximate and friendly access to include resupply for sustained operations. An isolated raid—such as El Dorado Canyon against Libyan targets—is not the same as providing around-the-clock air or ground support; however, in general, small amounts of air power for selected strikes can be rapidly deployed.

Sea forces fit the broad spectrum between achieving much more than light forces and perhaps less than heavy ground forces slugging it out in high-attrition campaigns ashore. Although maritime forces are not always as rapidly deployable as small numbers of light ground and air forces to areas where friendly basing and guaranteed access is assured, these forces have the sustainability, flexibility, and capability to deal with the full array of military capabilities in the Third World.

As advanced weapons proliferate, however, stealthy systems, both air and underwater, raise the greatest military threat to maritime forces of any new and particular weapons technology. Over time, the United States must assume that the most modern technologies will make their way into other hands. Perhaps the most daunting of these new technologies, especially for maritime forces, is stealth. Stealth, with its cloak of invisibility, obviously puts all forces at risk and provides special problems for naval forces because, at sea, the loss of even one high-value unit could compromise the entire operation.

For planning purposes, the United States must assume that not only Soviet weapons but also U.S., NATO, and Chinese-made systems (among others) will constitute the future military threat. In general, the number of advanced systems acquired by the Third World is not likely to be very large, because most regional or local powers can ill afford the price. The use of only a few of these systems could be decisive, however. On the other hand, inventories of tanks, artillery, and aircraft for the land battle are substantial. It is easy to envisage better tanks or aircraft defeating lesser ones in the ground battle. Stealth could remove not only qualitative asymmetries and advantages at sea of technologically superior naval forces, but quantitative ones as well.

For a first cut, U.S. corps-sized operations in regional conflicts [three to four Army divisions and a Marine Expeditionary Force (MEF)], absent the active intervention of the Soviet Union, probably will be the upper limit for contingency planning. Thus, six to eight light and heavy Army divisions (provided there is sufficient lift and protection for logistics) can fill these contingent needs. These forces, however, must be configured to defeat modern threats.

For regional conflicts, sea forces will seemingly fit a broader need, especially where access is limited or unavailable. In addition to the enhancements noted earlier, counters to stealth for air threats and probably for diesel submarine threats must assume higher priority. Although the debate will focus on numbers, the major future technical challenge will be dealing with stealth. Surely by the late 1990s, the United States would be wise to assume that this technology has proliferated in small numbers.

Another point needs to be made independent of the threat posed by advanced weapons. When U.S. force is used, the political reality is that the use of force must be effective, it must work quickly, and losses must be minimal if public support is to be maintained. The spread of advanced weapons magnifies the difficulties of filling these criteria because these advanced weapons, in certain cases, can be more difficult to counter. Perhaps no other problem will be tougher to redress than ensuring that, when U.S. forces are deployed, advanced weapons in the hands of the opposition will be neutralized. For the time being, achieving more than that does not appear politically feasible provided we do not eliminate high-threat risks as the essential ingredient in developing our basic force structure.

The spread of big, bad weapons will continue. As long as their use against the superpowers seems unlikely and mutual fear is self-deterring or self-limiting within a region, however, there will be little political incentive to upgrade the priority to control or deny regional possession or use of these systems. Unless the services can make even stronger arguments as to why planning for these high-threat contingencies is perhaps more important than ever due to the spread of advanced weapons, the pressure will be to cut, cut, cut. Furthermore, the acceptance of fundamentally different planning assumptions will not come easily or quickly. A disaster or a crisis might be necessary to reverse this trend. Unfortunately, we probably cannot afford for that disaster or crisis to occur in the first place. This situation may be the most interesting as well as most fearsome dilemma posed by the proliferation of these advanced weapons.

7

The Cutting Edge: Roles, Missions, and Uses

HARM'S WAY

There is a decisive quality to the term *harm's way* and an implicit naval preference for taking the initiative or the offensive. In reality, that presumption can be misleading because warfare is a mixture of attacking and defending, a compromise between caution and initiative, and, over all, a clash of wills that represents the conflict between the contesting political and policy objectives. Because society is domiciled on land and the sea provides or prevents access by or to society, the exercise of maritime power has inevitably and inextricably been annealed to and wielded over campaigns and battles ashore. Even when navies have been both necessary and sufficient to win a war without a decisive land battle ashore, such as in Japan's defeat of the Mongol hordes in the 13th century, when the "divine winds" obliterated the invading fleet, and in Drake's defeat of Spain's famous armada three centuries later (also abetted by fickle weather), the objective was winning the contest over the shore.

Winning command of the sea, waging economic warfare and blockade, privateering, and attacking or defending the shore were traditional roles that navies performed. Ultimately, the function of a navy was to sink the enemy's ships. The prize, however, invariably extended from the oceans to the shore.

From the Battle of Salamis four centuries before the birth of Christ to Leyte Gulf in 1945, the common naval purposes of dominating or isolating the prize ashore, mutated by technology and the politics of the time, provided the source material for scholars of seapower such as Mahan and Corbett to write convincingly and powerfully on the roles, missions, and uses of navies. Indeed, had Mahan and Corbett seen the Second World

War firsthand, those experiences would have strengthened their collective arguments immeasurably.[1]

ROLES, MISSIONS, AND USES

Roles, missions, and *uses* must be defined so as to accentuate the important differences in the ways navies can be used politically, operationally, and in practice. The division is threefold: *roles* include the exercise of maritime power for political purposes, *missions* address the underlying strategic rationale for navies, and *uses* are what happens in actual practice. *Roles* are the broader political purposes a navy can fill. *Missions* are the doctrinal statements and operational rationale of what the navy is meant to achieve as seen by the respective navy leadership, and *uses* are the actual way naval power is exercised in practice. Clearly, history has demonstrated repeatedly that the relationships among roles, missions, and uses could be coincident (the Royal Navy in the 17th century) or entirely disconnected (the Japanese Navy in December 1941).

Nuclear weapons and then the threat of thermonuclear Armageddon, delivered by supersonic aircraft and hypersonic ballistic missiles, were step functions in transforming what were the traditional roles, missions, and uses for the navy. Sailing in harm's way took on new meaning strategically and tactically, and the link with objectives ashore was far beyond support missions alone. In the past, before the thermonuclear era, wars were usually won or lost (assuming battle was joined) when armies defeated opposing armies and the defeated state had no option but to capitulate or face the unsavory consequences of occupation. If wars were fought across ocean boundaries, navies were essential to, but not always sufficient for,

---

1. The Second World War proved Mahan to be right about the need to win command and the role resources played in conflict. The war also reaffirmed Corbett's *Principles of Maritime Warfare*, which easily could have been updated to account for the new weapons that enhanced the Navy's power.

securing victory. In 1805, at Trafalgar, Nelson effectively eliminated French seapower as a factor in the Napoleonic wars. The wars, however, were not finally over until 1815 when, at the Battle of Waterloo, Wellington finally destroyed Napoleon's army and, with it, Napoleon's last opportunity for controlling Europe.

With the extraordinary destructive power derived from fission and fusion, the presence and threat of nuclear weapons imposed fundamental changes on the superpowers' calculation of military balances. The traditional strategic prerequisites of securing the defeat of the adversary's army to achieve victory mattered less (if at all) as nuclear weapons put not only armies but entire societies at risk. Strategically, nuclear weapons employed in sufficient numbers, for all practical purposes, could theoretically eliminate both an adversary's means and will to fight.

In the nuclear age, as navies acquired significant strategic nuclear weapons capability, they went from possessing only strategically necessary qualities to combining, at least potentially, the political elements of both necessity and sufficiency in achieving "victory" should war occur. Certainly as a strategic reserve or withheld force, protected by the ocean's cloak of invisibility, surviving sea-based nuclear forces could be used in the aftermath of a nuclear first exchange to dictate victory or, in U.S. jargon, to influence the end of conflict on "favorable terms."

On a tactical level, nuclear weapons became the great equalizer. At least in theory, U.S. nuclear weapons were on the ground in Europe to offset Soviet conventional advantages. At sea, at least in the 1960s and 1970s, U.S. nuclear SAMs could knock down flights of Soviet airplanes with better chances of kill than conventional warheads, and nuclear depth bombs could destroy enemy submarines better than conventional depth charges. These same nuclear weapons, however, cut both ways and provided certain advantages to the smaller, less capable Soviet Navy that would otherwise be blown out of the water by the more powerful American fleet. Tactically, nuclear weapons made every surface warship potentially vulnerable no matter how powerful or well protected that ship was.

Because the Soviet Navy acquired roles and missions that sprang from the Sisyphean tasks of preventing and limiting strategic nuclear attack from the sea, the nuclear elements in both navies cut across virtually all their combined roles and missions, strategically and tactically. This nuclear seam became interwoven into the power-projection missions the U.S. Navy would have to conduct in the event of war against the Soviet Union. On the strategic level, the Soviet Navy was required to attempt a nuclear counterforce mission against the United States despite the enormous physical and operational limitations of that task. On the tactical level, Soviet nuclear weapons provided the technological means of overcoming U.S. maritime superiority. In essence, both navies approached the problems of nuclear war like sets of interlocking fingers, with each finger fitting neatly into a doctrinal gap purposely left by the other.

The consequences for harm's way and for commanding or denying control of the sea were profound. Preparations in peace for winning a war that could be victorless had fundamental and obvious limits. Deterrence needed to work; if it failed, preventing rather than escalating the use of nuclear weapons seemed imperative so that society would not be destroyed. These limits, conceptually and operationally, were the hallmark of the nuclear age, and their legacy will extend into the post-Cold War world.

A corollary to the nuclear dilemma, however, rested in the need to take the attack to the Soviet Union. This need meant that the preferred instruments of projecting power were aircraft and missiles, both tactical and strategic, that would directly strike the enemy and his homeland. So, too, forces such as a nuclear submarine fleet that could operate deep in Soviet waters were part of this projective capability.

In all of this, the traditional force for projecting power ashore in the pre-nuclear days—the ground and air forces—was seen as supportive. The role of the Marine Corps, for example, was to reinforce and defend and not to seize or occupy enemy territory in the event of war with the USSR. The vital future question that may dominate debate is whether the traditional ground and air projection forces will reassert themselves as preferred instruments and whether the strike capability of the aircraft and missiles carried by CVBGs will assume the supporting role of pre-1945 days.

As the total number of superpower nuclear weapons decreases and, most importantly, as mutual deterrence becomes less important as the sense of mutual threat dissipates, the practical consequences for the U.S. Navy will most likely rest in the reemphasis of the traditional, long-standing roles and missions of maritime power—achieving and maintaining control of vital sea areas in direct support of objectives and goals ashore—as the key rationale for force structure. The traditional definition of roles, missions, and, indeed, uses in this era, however, are made more ambiguous for two reasons. First, the prospect of the U.S. Navy squaring off against another major navy is extremely implausible, because, absent a Soviet threat, no other navy will be large enough to pose a major threat or rationale for the U.S. Navy for a long time to come. Even if India or Brazil or another regional navy were to become a real or potential threat, visualizing a point in the future where the U.S. Navy could not hold a commanding operational advantage is difficult. Second, objectives ashore are likely to become highly political—preserving stability—and, therefore, not easily defined nor easily matched by traditional policy instruments. Hence, harm's way will have a new meaning.

To be sure, deterring the use or the threat of use of weapons of mass destruction will be of significance as more states acquire these capabilities. Moreover, intimidation or restraint that tempers the would-be hostile actions of powers unfriendly to the United States will perhaps be of more than passing interest in defining future naval roles and missions.

All of this withstanding, the United States would be inviting disaster if it were to assume that powerful and ready, although perhaps numerically fewer, military forces were an unwarranted and counterproductive burden to be shouldered by the nation and its resources. The fact of the matter is that complete demobilization of the U.S. military has never been a permanent condition, and military force, when properly used by the United States, is vital to protect and stabilize our interests. Americans have always accepted the need to defend the nation against "all enemies." The United States fights wars, deploys forces, and takes military action to protect its interests and, more than occasionally, those of friends and allies.

Stability, a well-worn but perhaps not well-understood criterion, could become a chief reason for maintaining future military forces. Stability means achieving a balance or measure in which individual interests can be protected without allowing unfair or decisive advantage to be gained that can be exploited to anyone's detriment. Absolute security for one party means absolute insecurity for someone else. Stability and the condition of stability relieve that imbalance and prevent or neutralize the exploitation of political, military, or economic leverage that could lead to conflict. With the achievement of stability, specific instances of unfair or decisive advantages by themselves are of little or no consequence.

The U.S. armed forces have often been used in stabilizing roles with great effect. In the future, this role should grow. In the case of the Soviet Union, because it is in transition and its future is uncertain, these stabilizing features of U.S. forces perhaps could be put to good use as safeguards and means to influence future Soviet force posture. The U.S. Navy is well positioned to assume this role. In responding to budget reductions, former Navy Secretary John Lehman proposed that a larger part of the Navy should be placed in reserve so that, in the event of a crisis, a big navy could be regenerated quickly. Although implementing his idea may be limited by the costs involved and by the reserve structure itself, the notion of a fleet-in-being could become a powerful future rationale. Specific details on this concept and how it might be structured follow in this and later chapters. Part of this fleet-in-being concept addresses deterrent roles outside the USSR and incorporates what may be needed for the purposes of imposing intimidation and constraint.

One of the other chief stabilizing functions that U.S. military forces have provided has been presence. In Europe, since the end of the war, even though the total number of U.S. forward-deployed forces at any given time has varied by large numbers, the presence of those forces acted as a guarantee or insurance policy to our allies and as a visible sign of U.S. commitment to the Warsaw Pact adversaries. What arose was stability in which both sides were able to pursue their interests without recourse to the clash of arms, based on the reassurance provided by forward-deployed forces.

In the Pacific, a relatively small commitment of U.S. forward-deployed forces, excluding the period of the Korean and Vietnamese wars, has achieved and fostered an extraordinary degree of regional stability. Of course, in the Pacific, the security arrangement is fundamentally different from that in Europe because no multilateral security alliance is in place and no singularly agreed-upon threat exists. Although the presence of U.S. military forces in the Pacific has provoked some controversy and criticism, this presence has unmistakenly and unambiguously contributed to regional peace and stability. For one thing, that presence has proved reassuring. The commitment has generally been viewed as credible by the states in the region. For another, the U.S. assumption of the larger military burden has allowed regional states to forgo acquiring additional military capability that could have proved threatening to the region. Japan is the best illustration of how this mollifying effect has worked.

In the future, as those stabilizing influences of the global U.S.-Soviet competition are reduced or disappear altogether, the implications and consequences for regional balances and potential conflicts are, by no means, clear. Perhaps regional bickering and quarreling could increase or be seen to increase by the decline in the U.S.-Soviet rivalry and a diminishing U.S. military presence. This increase in tension could occur in both the Atlantic and Pacific. Take, for example, NATO and the case of Turkey.

Suppose that NATO's importance and its *raison d'être* diminished. Large troop reductions in the center of Europe would no doubt have matching drawdowns for the European flanks, and large numbers of U.S. forces would also be withdrawn. With the establishment of EC 1992, cheap labor from Turkey will not be welcome by the rest of the community, because such laborers would displace native Caucasian European workers. Therefore, Turkey may be rejected from its European connection and, by default, gravitate towards the Middle East as its cultural and religious heritages are closely attuned to states in that region.

Despite the ancient rivalry between Turk and Arab, a pan-Islamic regime is not out of the question, and, say, a Damascus-Ankara axis or Ankara-Riyadh axis could emerge. Of course, such a connection would not automatically lead to instability. The tendency of this new world to accelerate centrifugal political forces, however, is a possible future outcome.

Thus, the stabilizing influence of U.S. forces, whether deployed overseas or in the United States, will be a central rationale in determining future maritime roles, missions, and uses. This rationale does not mean that overseas U.S. presence cannot and should not be reduced. Rather, careful assessment of what level of presence is necessary must be accomplished on a regional and state-by-state basis. This assessment follows in the text. Nor does this mean that U.S. forces stationed in the United States cannot be used or placed in a different status, whether as a fleet-in-being or in some other posture.

Traditionally, maritime forces in the United States have filled roles and missions that range from peace to war and from power projection to sea control. When Admiral Elmo R. Zumwalt, Jr., was CNO from 1970 to 1974, he argued that the Navy had four functions: deterrence, power projection, sea control, and peacetime presence.

In this construct, the nuclear case was largely confined to the deterrence role. Admiral James L. Holloway, III, Zumwalt's successor, compressed these four missions into power projection and sea control. Nuclear deterrence was clearly part of power projection. Admiral Thomas B. Hayward and Admiral James D. Watkins, the successor CNOs, dwelt on *maritime superiority* as the linchpin for the Navy's missions and further defined the term as being able to operate, if necessary, deep in enemy homewaters. Watkins, with the aggressive and partisan support of Navy Secretary John Lehman, carried the rationale a step further by having one of the Navy's key missions and roles be to specifically threaten the enemy's sea-based nuclear retaliatory forces. This mission became a central part of the maritime strategy. Admiral C.A.H. Trost, in light of the fundamental changes occurring in the USSR, delinked maritime superiority from specific wartime scenarios and argued, much as his earlier predecessors had, for strong and flexible maritime forces. Throughout this period, aircraft and missiles projected power, and Marine Corps ground forces played a supporting role against the primary threat.

It is interesting that, whether one agreed or disagreed with the case for the maritime strategy, as a mission statement and rationale, it became a powerful marketing tool with Congress in underwriting the 600-ship Navy. Any future mission statement will have to overcome that success in two ways. First, a new mission statement must be credible and relevant. Second, because the force structure will rely on the capabilities needed to counter Soviet threats, the new mission statement must either prove the relevance to other threats or make appropriate changes in the shape of the Navy.

Clearly, the actual and potential use of maritime forces weighed heavily in this rationale. Whether Zumwalt's four roles or Holloway's two are used, both provide a good foundation on which to build. Because of the changes in U.S.-Soviet relations and the many uncertainties ahead, drawing a distinction between Soviet and non-Soviet roles, missions, and uses is important. One of the new roles for the Navy may be providing the instrument, incentive, and means to influence this transition to a more stable, lower level of maritime forces, a requirement mandated by economics if not by strategic assessment.

The principal roles and missions of the U.S. Navy must be to continue to prevent war that could become nuclear, to project power to protect or promote U.S. interests, and to contribute to achieving conditions of stability that advance the well-being of the United States and its friends. Put another way, the interests of this nation demand free and unfettered use of the seas and its resources subject to the rule of law. The ultimate purpose of the Navy is to gain, protect, or permit that use, and the roles and missions go about achieving that purpose. As Soviet posture becomes less threatening and nuclear deterrence less visible a role, the Navy is likely to return to its pre-nuclear rationale of providing a broad range of combat and support capabilities to the battle ashore. This means that ground- and land-based forces could again become the principal instruments for projecting power, especially for reasons of stability.

For the USSR, these general roles and missions have been and will be translated by the Gorbachev leadership into specific uses of maritime power. First and foremost, the Soviet Navy contributes to nuclear deterrence in two ways: (1) the destructive, offensive power of sea-based nuclear forces provides deterrence through retaliation, a strategic reserve through survivability, and a warfighting capability through hard-target kill potential, and (2) the antisubmarine capability protects Soviet sea-based nuclear forces and threatens those of the adversary. Second, the Soviet Navy has local sea-control qualities that will permit resupply and reinforcement in wartime. Third, it provides power projection through amphibious forces and direct, nonstrategic nuclear strikes against the shore. Fourth, in terms of crises and routine diplomacy, the Soviet Navy offers a highly flexible means of signalling intent.

As the Soviet threat recedes, how will the Soviet Navy's future roles and missions be affected, especially since the Soviet Navy will shrink numerically and no doubt be altered qualitatively as well? The change in Soviet strategic purpose has not yet been translated into force structure. There is every reason to believe, however, that emphasis will remain on strategic nuclear deterrence. To the degree that out-of-area forces are required, this requirement is likely to diminish and, indeed, the Soviet Union may conclude that its resources are better spent elsewhere.

THE NEXT CENTURY

How, then, should the United States structure the roles, missions, and uses of its Navy for the next century?

First, Secretary of Defense Dick Cheney and Chairman of the JCS General Colin Powell have outlined what is likely to become, over time, a sweeping change in the overall military strategy of the United States (figure 3). The Navy should begin using this outline and concept for developing and considering future strategic rationale. Clearly, in each of the four categories noted for force structure, the Navy will play crucial roles.

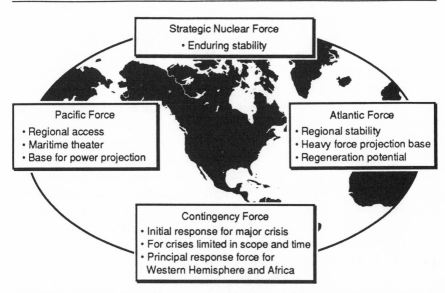

SOURCE: Posture statements made by the Secretary of Defense and the Chairman of the JCS to Congress, January 1991

Figure 3. Force structure concept

Much of the current American rationale and conventional wisdom about maritime forces naturally arises from geography and the island-nation realities of the United States. Outside the Soviet Union, however, no significant threat exists that could seriously challenge American access to and use of the sea or dislocate and interrupt that access militarily. Thus, two minimum conditions must be met by U.S. maritime forces. First, the U.S. Navy must serve as a counterweight to and a safeguard against the Soviet Union until such time as that threat disappears. This role conforms to Cheney and Powell's Strategic Nuclear Force (enduring stability) and Atlantic Force. Second, the U.S. Navy must be prepared for a variety of contingent uses outside the USSR in which the threat environment poses different and, in some cases, more exacting operational demands on maritime forces. This role conforms with the Pacific Force and Contingency Force categories. These missions set the groundwork for the future principal political roles to be filled by the Navy and Marine Corps.

Against the prospect of a continuing although (greatly) diminishing Soviet threat, the U.S. Navy must be seen as having the residual role and the actual capability to defeat or neutralize the Soviet Navy in conflict. This role must be achievable whether at current or even significantly lower force levels or when arms reductions and unilateral cuts in force structure occur. Because of the great flexibility in U.S. naval forces, defeating or neutralizing Soviet naval power can take one of several forms.

The U.S. Navy could steam directly in harm's way, bearding the naval lion in its den, deep in Soviet homewaters. That, in all likelihood, would entail certain risks and rewards that future leaders might find too potentially costly in peace and war. Alternatively, the U.S. Navy could either blockade the access points for Soviet egress, making it exceedingly difficult and costly for Soviet forces to break out of homewaters, or wage a battle of attrition in which Soviet naval forces were hunted down and sunk on the high seas. In each case, the goals of destruction or neutralization would dictate the use of the fleet.

Concurrently, the fleet-in-being concept should be applied in influencing future structure and use of Soviet maritime forces. Assuming the United States concluded that Soviet maintenance of a sea-based nuclear deterrent within the context of START was in our mutual interests, the major systems the United States would want the USSR to cut back on would be Soviet nuclear and conventional submarines. Conversely, the Soviets would argue that concomitant reductions in U.S. CVBGs take place. Perhaps a tradeoff of 50 (modern) SSNs for a CVBG would be a starting point for negotiation, with the prospect that a portion of those units might be stood down as part of a fleet-in-being. Then, as future relations played out, the final disposition of these forces could be made permanently to either a fully deactivated or activated status. Because, for the time being, the U.S. Navy has sound reasons to oppose naval arms control, this initiative cannot and should not be taken immediately. As argued later, however, the Navy would be wise to begin serious reexamination of this approach.

In all circumstances, this argument fully supports the "enduring stability" rationale and the "regional stability" and "regeneration potential" specified by Cheney and Powell.

In non-Soviet conflict, the roles that the Navy must play are several-fold. First, the Navy can certainly deter the use of nuclear weapons and probably deter the use of chemical and biological weapons through the threat of or actual retaliation. These roles are likely to be subsumed under the capabilities to provide continued nuclear deterrence against the USSR.

Second, by having the ability to project power quickly, massively, and with great effect, the Navy can physically constrain and even psychologically intimidate states and leaderships that might otherwise seek to harm U.S. interests. In the future, this type of force will have to be applied with greater discretion and precision than ever before. The politically imposed requirements of minimizing collateral damage and civilian or excessive military casualties and the need for rapid success will weigh more heavily than in the past. The Gulf War is the clearest example of the model conflict in that regard.

Third, the Navy will play a stabilizing role by virtue of its presence and the political symbolism underscored by that presence. Unfortunately, the metaphor of the policeman on the block was put in disrepute by the Vietnam War, and the hint of a world gendarmerie role, however valid, will be partially reinforced by the war and now the peace in the Persian Gulf. This role will mark a return to the pre-nuclear era when the Navy contributed to events ashore.

Fourth, the Navy must continue its role as an instrument of foreign policy to be used in contingencies or crises. The use of U.S. forces in Beirut from 1982 to 1983, in Grenada, in strikes against Libya, in escort roles in the Persian Gulf, in Panama, and, perhaps most significantly, in the Gulf Crisis of 1990 and the Gulf War in 1991 bounds the bulk of the scenarios likely to be visited in the future.

Fifth, naval roles will be required to incorporate broader tasks, including antidrug operations, LIC responsibilities, and, perhaps increasingly, humanitarian-related assignments. Defining what is required and meant by each role is crucial, and, at the least, determining what should not be expected will contribute to increasing the chances for success. More will be said about that in chapter 11. In each regard, these roles fit what was intended under Cheney and Powell's Pacific Force and Contingency Force requirements.

Translating these political roles into naval statements and rationale for missions is a more difficult task. Because the nature of these roles is political and, in some ways, highly sophisticated and complex, expressing those subtleties succinctly and directly will be difficult, particularly if one of the roles is to help shape and influence the transition of the Soviet Navy. Without a concise, precise threat to design against, the ambiguities and uncertainties about predicting the future can be formidable and can dilute an otherwise valid but not entirely obvious argument.

For example, it is easy to confuse naval qualities, such as flexibility and promotion of stability, with specific missions. Naval missions are achieved through the application of combat capabilities and qualities of maritime forces such as flexibility and power projection. Missions, however, cannot and should not be confused with capabilities. Broad mission statements like deterring war, protecting interests, and carrying out crisis-management tasks will be perceived as hollow and vacuous if no reason is given for such missions.

The principal missions of the Navy are, of course, to achieve those broad objectives; therefore, the first mission must be to defeat or neutralize Soviet maritime power at all levels of potential conflict. As the degree of Soviet threat shifts up or down, the U.S. Navy can respond accordingly. Given the U.S. Navy's current position of superiority, however, maintaining those absolute and relative advantages should persist into the future.

Second, the Navy must be able to defeat or neutralize non-Soviet maritime threats wherever and whenever they may arise. Because the cumulative nature of these threats is less than the collective strength of the USSR (although the geographical boundaries may be greater and response time shorter), the U.S. Navy could deal with these other requirements with a smaller navy if there were no Soviet threat at all.

Third, the Navy should serve as a transition tool to encourage the Soviet Navy to adopt a less-threatening force posture and to deter and constrain would-be non-Soviet adversaries. During such a transition of missions, the Navy must be prepared to undertake new missions, including humanitarian assignments as well as the battle against drugs.

To accomplish portions of each of these tasks, the Navy should undertake a fifth mission—that of a fleet-in-being or a national insurance policy. The reasoning is as follows. Because of the great uncertainties ahead and the possibility that political events could occur quickly, the United States needs to be able to reconstitute power on a relatively short basis. Reconstitution becomes the centerpiece of a fleet-in-being.

In the event that tensions and hostilities with the USSR resume and produce a new and hostile cold war with renewed emphasis on military power, this fleet could be reconstituted quickly to guarantee that, in all conditions, we will be able to maintain access to our overseas allies and interests. Reconstitution could also be central to the missions of the other services. This concept is translated into specific force alternatives in chapter 10.

Despite the political roles and rationale for missions of navies, perhaps the more interesting and speculative question is how the U.S. Navy is likely to be used in the 21st century. The answer to that question obviously rests in the nature of the international environment and the future consequences of domestic politics on using force in whatever contingency, crises, or routine instance arises.

Using the base case outlined earlier for defining international and domestic politics as the starting point and introducing a few wild cards along the way, the U.S. Navy of the 21st century is likely to be used as follows.

First, if the Soviet strategic and theater threat to the West recedes, the need for traditional wartime uses to project power and control sea routes against the USSR will likewise decline. The U.S. Navy's posture and use as a strategic deterrent will have declining emphasis vis-à-vis the USSR, but will have general applicability to states and transnational groups with potential access to weapons of mass destruction. In this future, U.S. SSNs would be assigned the nominal task of protecting the SSBN force that would usually be deployed near the continental United States (CONUS).

Second, if and as the anti-Soviet missions become less important, the U.S. Navy will be used to maintain global presence, at reduced and selected tempos, to provide reassurance and stability to regions and friends that require it. Part of this presence may be put to use in the drug war in which the Navy has an obvious surveillance mission. Measuring effectiveness of presence, however, is difficult and, in some ways, politically counterproductive because the political expectation for determining cause and effect is frustrated by the inability to measure and to prove an incontrovertible relationship.

Third, the Navy will provide important capability in future crises where U.S. force must be projected to protect U.S. citizens and interests.

Fourth, the Navy's use as a fleet-in-being would serve two principal insurance functions. By keeping sufficient numbers and capability in a posture that could be regenerated or reconstituted as threats developed, the nation can hedge against these vast future uncertainties. Assets could then be disposed of accordingly as the passage of time naturally clarifies some of these uncertainties. As the defense industrial base continues to shrink, an investment strategy that favors development and testing of new systems rather than full-scale production and that applies a similar approach to procuring logistics and ammunition might be adopted. Although it is too soon to tell whether these alternatives will be fully feasible, a fleet-in-being concept provides a national insurance policy that protects the economic health of the nation by reinforcing the technical strengths and conforming to the likely budget realities. All these possible uses are summarized in table 1.

Finally, as the future environment clarifies, the bulk of naval capabilities that formed the principal power-projection instruments may assume a supporting role and the Marine Corps and ground forces that supported the naval campaign against the USSR may become the new principal projectors of power. Should this transformation take place, the consequences for future force design and use will be profound. One small example would be in the resurgent need for minesweepers and assault ships, which frankly lacked justification when the Soviet Union was the threat.

Table 1. Actual uses of maritime forces against past threats and possible uses against future threats

	Actual uses against past threats				Possible uses against future threats	
	1970-1980		1980-1990		2000	
Action	USSR	Other states	USSR	Other states	USSR	Other states
Nuclear war						
Strategic, theater	No	No	No	No	Highly unlikely	Possible
Offense, defense	No	No	No	No	Highly unlikely	?
Nuclear deterrence (Fleet-in-being)	Yes	No	Yes	No	Yes	Possible
Deterrence of chemical, biological, other weapons of mass destruction	—	—	—	—	Possible	Possible
Major conventional conflict						
Navy vs. navy	No	No	No	No	Highly unlikely	?
Strikes against the shore	No	Yes	No	No	Highly unlikely	?
Amphibious operations	No	Yes	No	No	Highly unlikely	?
Direct defense of the U.S.	No	No	No	No	Highly unlikely	?

(Continued on next page)

Table 1. (*Continued*)

Action	Actual uses against past threats				Possible uses against future threats	
	1970-1980		1980-1990		2000	
	USSR	Other states	USSR	Other states	USSR	Other states
Local interdiction/ protection						
Escort	No	No	No	Yes	No	Likely
Reprisal/ punitive strikes	No	Yes	No	Yes	No	Likely
On the ground	No	Yes	No	Yes	No	Likely
Crisis management	Yes	No	No	Yes	Uncertain	Very likely
Intimidation/ constraint	Yes	Yes	Yes	Yes	No	Yes
Routine diplomacy	Yes	Yes	Yes	Yes	Yes	Yes
Political support	No	Yes	Yes	Yes	Uncertain	Yes
Nontraditional						
Counterterrorism	No	No	No	Yes	No	Yes
Counterdrugs	No	No	No	Yes	No	Yes
Humanitarian	No	Yes	No	Yes	Possible	Yes
Fleet-in-being	No	No	No	No	Possible	Possible
Maintaining industrial capability should more forces be needed	Yes	Yes	Yes	Yes	Possible	Possible
Insurance policy	No	No	No	No	Possible	Possible

To use the newer language of the day, as defined by the current force structure concept, the Department of the Navy (DON) must play a crucial role as part of the Strategic Force to ensure enduring stability; as the central part of the Pacific Force which, by virtue of geography, must be a maritime theater; as part of the Atlantic Force, particularly in force regeneration, resupply, and surge in crisis; and, finally, as part of the Contingency Force, as future crises are likely to be in regions most accessible and sustainable by maritime power.

8

Running on Empty: Money, Resources, and a Fraying Infrastructure

The most painful irony for the United States today is that, although it is the richest country in the world, it cannot get its fiscal and economic house in order. All things being equal, if this condition does not improve, at best the nation's standard of living and quality of life will continue to erode. At worst, catastrophe is not out of the question. As a result, the competition for and the scarcity of resources will dominate political debate and decision over where government chooses to spend its money. Despite the rigor and intensity of the parallel debate over strategy and policy, at the end of the day, budget and resource allocations are the clearest expressions and surrogates for the strategic choices and priorities that set the nation's defense.

Further, without a clear and present danger to coalesce public opinion, deriving a relatively unspecific strategy to hedge against the unknown and unpredictable threat will be subject to controversy and, possibly, derision. A strategy is dependent upon objectives. Objectives are dependent upon a certain understanding of and consensus on what needs to be achieved. This consensus, therefore, must be specifically declared. Then, that specificity can be translated into actions that set priorities and allocate resources authoritatively.

In World War II, allied objectives were to win first in Europe by defeating Hitler and his army unconditionally. Our objectives for most of the Cold War were to deter Soviet aggression and attack; if deterrence failed, we were to "prevail" on terms acceptable to us and at the least cost or lowest level of violence possible. In the post-Cold War era, our objectives are likely to become even more ambiguous and vague and, hence, more difficult to articulate into a cogent, comprehensible, and supportable strategy.

THE ECONOMY AND THE BUDGET

Then there is the matter of the economy, the federal budget, and the share of GNP that will go to defense. The reality is that, as long as deficits loom large and virtually all claimant programs for federal spending have built-in escalators that require more money each year, the pressure to cut defense will become excruciating. A slowdown or economic recession that limits or reverses growth in GNP will obviously exacerbate the fiscal problem for defense.

Due in largest measure to the Gulf Crisis, the 1990 Budget Reconciliation Act was favorably disposed to defense, and the upper spending limits for outlays for FYs 1991, 1992, and 1993 were, respectively, $297.7 billion, $295.7 billion, and $292.7 billion. The legal debt ceiling, however, was raised over $1 trillion through September 1993, from $3.1 to $4.2 trillion, which virtually mandates that deficits continue and that the Gramm-Rudman-Hollings Deficit Reduction Law be adjusted to meet these realities as indicated in table 2.

Table 2. Adjustments to Gramm-Rudman-Hollings Deficit Reduction Law (in billions of current-year dollars)

Fiscal year	1987 limits	1990 revision
1990	100	220 actual
1991	64	327
1992	28	317
1993	0	216
1994	Surplus	108
1995	Surplus	83

For FYs 1991 through 1993, three sublimits for spending sequestration under the law were set for defense, international, and domestic programs so that the previous 50-50 split in assigning outlay cuts between defense and nondefense programs mandated by Gramm-Rudman has been held in abeyance. In practical terms, the sequestration power of

Gramm-Rudman has been neutralized. The huge deficits, however, mean that cuts must and will be taken in the coming years despite the 1990 Budget Summit. Defense will be hostage to these budget pressures, even though the Gramm-Rudman axe has been temporarily sheathed.

The most likely outcome is that, over the next few years, the defense budget will be in a free-fall, propelled downwards by deficit, debt, and the irresistible and built-in growth in non-defense programs. Nondefense programs account for about three-quarters of the federal budget. Although predicting what the floor, ceiling, or steady state for future defense spending may be is impossible, clearly, examination of a wide range of possibilities is essential. This examination occurs later in this chapter.

The consequences of this strategy-budget quandry are several. First, breaking the budget's strangle hold on strategy will be extraordinarily difficult without the rallying point of a principal threat and may perhaps be impossible given the likelihood, indeed the certainty, that the defense budget will be driven even lower by economic necessity and scarcity.

Second, without clear, crisp, and enforceable strategic direction and policy objectives, the cumulative effect of the budget cuts, if the past is any guide, will be to exacerbate and magnify the diminution in aggregate military capability.

COST CREEP

To compound these already tenacious problems, built-in pressures inherent and internal to the workings of the acquisition process place enormous and irresistible upward pressure on costs each year and impose even greater demands on a constrained budget. These pressure-builders include cost creep, costs of regulation and oversight, and the pernicious effects of program instability, that is, changing the procurement budget or the number of items that ultimately are bought.

Consider the cost creep, in real terms, of acquiring the goods and services for defense over these years. The trends between annual defense spending and military personnel over the past four decades are revealing (table 3).

Table 3. Annual defense spending vs. endstrength[a]

	1955	1965	1975	1988
Defense outlays (in billions of FY 1988 dollars)	$208	$199	$190	$290
Active-duty strength (in millions)	3.0	2.7	2.1	2.1
Selected reserve component (in millions)	1.0 (estimated)	1.2	0.9	1.2

a. Figures taken from National Defense Budget Estimates for FYs 1988-89 and The Secretary of Defense Annual Report to Congress for FY 1989. The years represent peacetime spending and, before 1970, the draft.

The upshot is that, over the past 35 years, although defense spending increased by 50 percent in real terms, the total number of personnel in service declined by 30 percent. Although the end of the draft in the mid-1970s and the establishment of the all-volunteer military certainly were factors in this budget-personnel interaction, consider the replacement costs and the cost creep of like platforms—that is, tank for tank, ship for ship, and fighter aircraft for fighter aircraft. Using FY 1988 dollars in all cases, table 4 compares 1965 and 1988 prices.

The same trend applies for the next-generation systems. Hence, the B-2, SSN-21, and ATF can be expected to be priced at greater real-cost multiples than their predecessor platforms. The reasons relate to the costs of advanced technology. At the so-called knee of the curve or point of diminishing returns, where achieving more capability requires multiple or order-of-magnitude cost increases, systems will be more expensive in real terms after accounting for inflation. With increases in the technological level of the threat, pursuit of more capable and therefore more expensive weapons systems is not an end in itself, but a legitimate military need.

Table 4. Comparison of 1965 and 1988 prices for weapon platforms

	Price (in FY 1988 dollars)	
Platform	1965	1988
Tank (M-60 vs. M-1A1)	800,000	2,300,000
Fighter (F-4 vs. F-15C/D)	7,000,000	40,000,000
Submarine (594-class vs. 688-class)	250,000,000	700,000,000

The overhead costs of administering the government's system of oversight and regulation of acquisition also put pressure on the budget. Recent studies have shown that between 15 and 25 percent of the total defense procurement budget may be spent on this overregulation.[1]

As a result, even as the threat declines and defense spending is reduced dramatically, the replacement costs of new systems, in real terms, will increase perhaps several-fold, and the costs of managing and overseeing the acquisition process will likewise continue to grow substantially if not geometrically. Similar increases will occur in manpower costs and in training, maintenance, and operations costs. Thus, the double pincers of declining budgets and escalating real costs will close in on the force structure. Furthermore, the above costs do not consider the inefficiencies of a process in which program instability and budget myopia of a short-term bias introduce the lion's share of unplanned cost growth.

PROGRAM INSTABILITY

Consider program instability. The general effects of program instability (and the costs of oversight on the DOD budget) are surprisingly profound, especially to the uninitiated.

---

1. See the CSIS study entitled *U.S. Defense Acquisition: A Process in Trouble* (1987) and the Presidential Blue Ribbon Commission Report on *Improving Defense Management* (1987).

Program instability occurs every year when unplanned changes to programs occur, either through increases or decreases of total program allocation or number of units to be purchased. The effects are manifested in unit costs and, in almost every case, lead to cost increases. Tables 5 and 6 show the changing relationships between programs and unit costs based on changes to the overall defense budget and the historical effect that has had on the acquisition budget in a period of declining defense spending.

Table 5. Changes to total defense procurement spending and the effect of program stability when spending begins to decline

Unplanned budget change (percent)	Effect on acquisition budget (percent)	Effect on non-major weapon systems portion (percent)	Quantity change (percent)	Unit-cost change (percent)
+12	+22	+22	+24	− 3
+ 8	+14	+14	+14	0
+ 4	+ 6	+ 5	+ 4	+ 4
+ 2	+ 2	+ 1	− 1	+ 5
0	− 2	− 3	− 6	+ 8
− 2	− 6	− 8	−11	+ 9
− 4	−10	−12	−16	−12
− 6	−14	−17	−20	+14
− 8	−18	−21	−25	+16
−10	−22	−25	−30	+19
−12	−26	−29	−34	+22
−14	−30	−33	−39	+25

SOURCE: *U.S. Defense Acquisition: A Process in Trouble.* Washington, D.C.: CSIS, 1987, p. 56.

NOTE: The relationships are based on a review of 150 defense programs for FYs 1979 through 1986 that were covered under the Selected Acquisition Review (SAR) program mandated by Congress.

Table 6. Changes to total defense procurement spending and the effect of program stability when spending begins to increase

Unplanned budget change (percent)	Effect on acquisition budget (percent)	Effect on non-major weapon systems portion (percent)	Quantity change (percent)	Unit-cost change (percent)
+12	+22	+22	+26	− 2
+ 8	+14	+14	+14	0
+ 4	+ 6	+ 6	+ 4	+ 2
+ 2	+ 2	+ 2	− 1	+ 3
0	− 2	− 2	− 6	+ 4
− 2	− 6	− 6	−10	+ 5
− 4	−10	−10	−15	+ 6
− 6	−14	−14	−19	+ 7
− 8	−18	−18	−24	+ 8
−10	−22	−22	−28	+ 9
−12	−26	−26	−32	+10
−14	−30	−30	−35	+11

SOURCE: *U.S. Defense Acquisition: A Process in Trouble*. Washington, D.C.: CSIS, 1987, p. 56.

NOTE: The relationships are based on a review of 150 defense programs from FYs 1979 through 1986 that were covered under the SAR program mandated by Congress.

Although specific programs may not follow this pattern exactly, the point is that program instability, through unplanned changes in unit buys or budget allocations, is enormously expensive, especially when large cuts are made. Thus, in a declining budget environment, the net effect is to induce rather large inefficiencies.

Inefficiencies aside, possible savings as a result of changes to the regulatory and oversight process could be substantial, as indicated in table 7.

Table 7. Potential defense acquisition savings

Category of cost savings[a]	Amount of budget affected[b]	Percentage of budget affected	Ranges of realistic improvement (percent)	Maximum annual savings realized[b]		
				Near term	Medium to long term[c]	Total
Oversight, auditing, and regulations	200	5-10	2-8	6	10	4-16
Program instability, poor estimates	100	10-40	5-10	3	7	5-10
Requirements, excesses	100	20-40	10-15	1	14	10-15
Overspecs, errors	150	5-15	4-6	2	7	6-9
Totals	$200	24-61[d]	12-25[d]	$12	$38	$25-50

SOURCE: *U.S. Defense Acquisition: A Process in Trouble.* Washington, D.C.: CSIS, 1987.
a. Based on a constant $200-billion acquisition budget.
b. In billions of FY 1988 dollars.
c. The near term is one to two years; medium to long term extends to ten years.
d. Percentage figures reflect average ranges of impact or realistic improvement.

SPENDING, AFFORDABILITY, AND TRADEOFFS

Finally, before examining future resource limits and potential consequences for the Navy, what the nation can afford to spend on its defense and what it will choose to spend are clearly two separate considerations. During World War II, the United States spent nearly half its GNP on armaments. In the last 45 years, spending has fluctuated between 4 and 12 percent of GNP (figures 4 and 5).

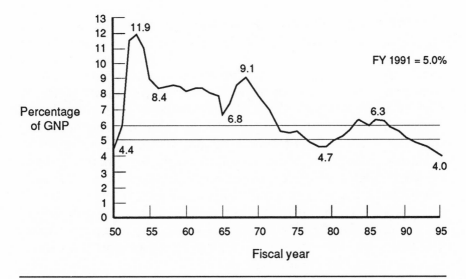

Figure 4. Defense outlays as a share of GNP

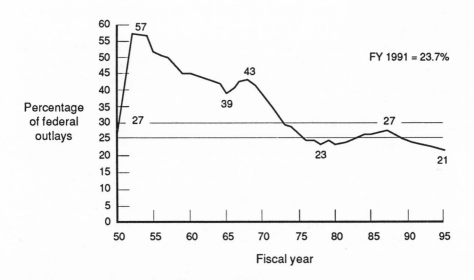

Figure 5. Defense as a share of federal outlays

The hidden element in this interaction of strategy, force capability, and budget is the infrastructure that supports the defense establishment. Much has already been said about the weapons acquisition process. The remaining part of the defense infrastructure cannot be separated from the military forces that it must support. Thus, the first order of business is to 1) examine a plausible range of future defense levels of spending, 2) specify different shares of that spending for the Navy, 3) derive the force structure and maritime capability that would be yielded from those shares, and 4) evaluate how each force can or cannot carry out assigned tasks and objectives and what each force requires in terms of a supporting infrastructure. Then, the defense industrial base, the manpower base, the shore establishment and basing facilities, and the intelligence base can be examined.

In setting a range of possible levels of defense spending, the future economic prospects and projections for the United States do not need to be forecast. Although recession, depression, or boom would have powerful consequences, the effects of the future performance of the economy are registered through the various levels of defense spending that are posited. Thus, this method of examination is independent of the boom or bust performance of the economy.

The administration's request for FY 1991 was $306 billion in total budget authority for national defense, of which $295 billion was for DOD. The breakdown for DOD was as follows:

- $25 billion for nonservice programs

- $100 billion for the DON

- $95 billion for the Department of the Air Force

- $75 billion for the Department of the Army.

The Navy's share under this distribution is 37 percent.

Unless a crisis occurs, obvious political or economic pressures will drive down defense spending. The question is by how much. Using possible future levels of budget authority of $270, $250, $225, $200, and $150 billion (FY 1991 dollars), and possible Navy shares of 33, 37 (today's share), 40, 50, and

60 percent, table 8 shows the fiscal consequences for the Navy.

Table 8. Defense budget authority (in billions of FY 1991 dollars)

DON share (percent)	Likely range for FYs 1991-1993			Likely future range	
	270	250	225	200	150
33	90	83	75	67	50
37	100	93	83	75	58
40	108	100	90	80	60
50	135	125	112	100	75
60	156	150	135	120	90

NOTE: Not all budget authority goes to the services. Usually, 10 to 15 percent is assigned to nonservice programs. Budget authority is reduced by 10 to 15 percent to reflect nonservice programs. For FY 1991, the total DOD budget of $295 billion resulted in $270 billion going to the services.

For the near term (FYs 1993 through 1995), the DON budget authority is most likely to be in the $70- to $85-billion range. Over the longer term, those boundaries could decline to the $50- to $70-billion level or even lower depending on the state of the economy and our relationship with the USSR.

Of course, associating the size and shape of a future Navy with fiscal boundaries is risky. Such a connection could erroneously create the impression that a direct relationship exists between budgets and force structure that is readily translated into a particular formula. That is not the case. For example, a 600-ship Navy could be maintained on a budget of $50 billion a year, but, to cite two polar extremes of what that Navy could be like, it could be a force of 600 de-manned ships that are largely in either standdown or cadre status, incapable of performing most missions in the short term, or it could be a force of 600 small, inexpensive ships with limited capabilities.

Similarly, because ships' lives can be extended and replacement or modernization points can be stretched out, there is also the risk that an expectation of false savings can be created and a lower-cost Navy made to look more affordable and attractive when, in fact, that Navy would be "hollow" and unable to perform its missions.

Finally, although the impression that adequate tradeoff analyses have been conducted can be created by comparing the costs of CVBGs, SSNs, and land-based tactical aviation, this simplistic approach ignores the combat capabilities that are retained or forgone. For example, one carrier with its air wing may cost the same to procure as three or four SSN-21s. Such a tradeoff, however, is a nonsequitur without a good idea of what roles and uses that carrier or those submarines are to play.

Table 9 gives an approximate idea of what the Navy might be like at the turn of the century. This table was created by projecting historical cost data and assuming four fiscal scenarios, a Navy configured more or less along the lines of today's Navy, and readiness and training at today's standards. The scenarios reflect the budget authority shown in figure 6. Thus, in this analysis, the approximate range in the future size of the Navy varies from a total of 568 to 345 ships, depending on which fiscal level is used.

Using a second type of analysis with lower boundaries for future spending that vary from $45 to $85 billion per year, table 10 shows the approximate force levels that the given budgets will sustain over a longer term.

For the moment, if current DOD plans hold, the Navy of the next five years will be a smaller version of the current 600-ship Navy, the overall reductions being about 20 to 25 percent. Thus, if current DOD cost figures are correct and funding can be maintained at about $85 billion or more per year, the Navy will be built around 12 CVBGs, 130 surface combatants, probably 70 to 75 SSNs, and just under a MEF's amount of lift.

That Navy, at about three-quarters of its current size, represents quite a dramatic change by itself.

Table 9. Four possible Navy configurations through FY 2004

Component	FY 1989	Scenario 1 (+2% growth)	Scenario 2 (No growth)	Scenario 3 (−2% growth)	Scenario 4 (−4% growth)
CV/CVN	14	12	10	7	5
BB	4	2	0	0	0
CGN/CG	40	27	27	27	14
DDG/DDG-X	37	52	49	47	35
FF/FFG	76	20	0	0	0
SSBN	36	25	23	21	18
SSN	97	85	83	81	75
AUX	125	148	141	136	110
Amphib	64	61	57	42	34
Other	75	70	70	64	54
Total	568	502	460	425	345
Personnel (Navy only)					
Officers	72.6	65.7	61.8	58.3	54.0
Enlisted	515.8	473.9	446.0	417.0	380.5

SOURCE: Harlan Ullman and Thomas Etzold. *Future Imperative: National Security and the U.S. Navy in the Late 1980s.* Washington, D.C.: CSIS, 1985. The cost model demonstrated on pages 26-28 was updated and projected into the next decade.

The crucial assumption is about readiness and training. Clearly, there can be a larger, less ready Navy; however, the range of permutations is impossible to sketch because it comprises nearly an infinite set. Given that fact, what is needed most is an approximate idea of what size and shape Navy may be affordable and sustainable at various assumed arbitrary levels of spending, what the capability of those navies will be in a variety of operational scenarios, and what all that means for broader U.S. commitments and national security policy objectives. This evaluation is made in chapter 11.

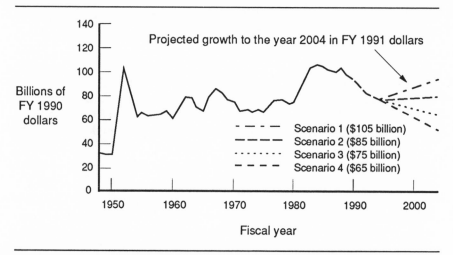

Figure 6. Historical and projected growth in Navy budget authority

Table 10. Approximate combat force levels for a given budget

DON budget (in FY 1991 dollars)	Nominal CVBG [a]	Amphibious ships	Submarines (SSN/Trident)	Surface combatants	Total ships
$45 billion	4-5	10-15	40-45	55-60	250
$55 billion	5-6	25-30	45-50	65-70	300
$65 billion	7-8	25-30	55-60	75-80	350
$75 billion	8-9	40-45	60-65	90-95	425
$85 billion	10-11	40-45	65-70	110-115	480

NOTES: Annual operating cost for one CVBG is $550 to $650 million. Using the current Navy budget and naval estimates for replacement costs as well as projected costs for operations, maintenance, and personnel, approximate-size navies were derived for each budget level. These estimates were confirmed by other projections unofficially made in the Navy and conform to the future planning estimates displayed earlier. The shipbuilding and conversion share of Navy total obligational authority (TOA) is computed with the assumption that infrastructure will be reduced proportionately with TOA. Figures shown are the results of long-term steady-state construction and assume readiness and training remain at today's levels. Force structure, in this case, favors CVBGs over SSNs.

a. A CVBG has one carrier, one air wing, and eight to ten escorts. The logistics and support ships are not shown as an individual group and are included under total ships.

THE INFRASTRUCTURE

Defense Industrial Base

At the same time that the Navy is contracting, the defense industrial base is also shrinking. Predicting what that base will look like in the future and how the compression in size will affect the ability of DOD to acquire goods and services at a reasonable and affordable cost is extremely difficult. Presently, there is perhaps a third more civilian defense industrial base than the defense budget can sustain.[1]

Figures 7 and 8 show the quantitative decline in the number of defense firms. Although nothing in the numbers themselves is inherently negative, they are accompanied by a compression in the overall technological capacity of the base. Of course, more data will be needed to confirm the validity of these trends.[2]

There are two dramatically opposed arguments as to how the government should deal with the consequences of a smaller defense industrial base. The first argument is market driven and based on the private sector responding to economic forces alone without any government intervention. This argument assumes the government cannot and should not influence or shape the dimensions of the future defense industrial base because such intervention would only worsen rather than help this transformation and because competition, cost, and quality performance can come only from market-generated forces.

The opposing argument maintains that it is fanciful to believe that defense is truly a private market in which market forces operate in unrestricted, economically rational ways because there is only one buyer (the government), there are irrational laws of supply and demand, and there is no free-market mechanism to determine price or value. Therefore, someone must intervene, if only to perform triage, to ensure the necessary or crucial parts of the defense base are protected.

---

1. *U.S. Defense Acquisition: A Process in Trouble.* Washington, D.C.: CSIS, 1987.
2. *Deterrence in Decay: The Future of the U.S. Defense Industrial.* Washington, D.C.: CSIS 1989, pp. 30-31.

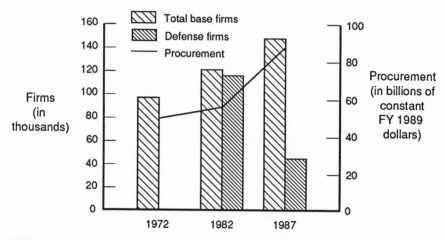

SOURCE: Bureau of the Census, *1982 Census of Manufacturers,* Washington, D.C., 1986; Defense Logistics Agency, *DOD Contract Database,* Washington, D.C., 1988.

Figure 7. Structure of the defense industrial base from 1972 to 1987

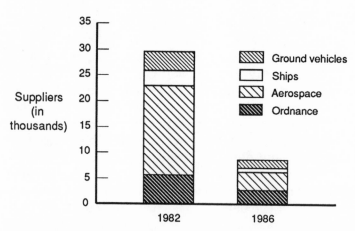

SOURCE: Defense Logistics Agency, *DOD Contract Database,* Washington, D.C., 1988.

Figure 8. Weapons defense suppliers by product type

The weakness of the first argument is that, in the true economic sense, no free or open market really exists. Hence, a laissez-faire approach cannot work. The weakness in the interventionist argument is that government does not have a good record in that regard and probably never can determine what fair criteria for triage are, given that Congress and the political process will distort any attempts at objective corrective intervention. Thus, there will be deadlock.

Depending on whether an interventionist or laissez-faire approach is taken, three derivative resource strategies are possible. One is to favor readiness at the expense of procurement. This strategy entails keeping a ready, perhaps larger, force but diminishing the rate and scope of the modernization and replacement of systems. The operative assumption behind this strategy is that near-term use of the forces is likely and, therefore, readiness counts. The negative sides are that large outlay cuts in this strategy will eviscerate the procurement accounts, and, although the force will be ready, it will fall behind the competition in advancing and improving its weapons.

The second strategy is that of investment, in which the forces will be cut to maintain a healthy defense industrial base. This strategy favors research, development, and testing over procurement so that the capacity for maintaining technical superiority remains. Because declining budgets are likely to preclude large-scale procurement of many systems, only a "tepid" manufacturing capability may be needed. The advantages of this strategy rest in maintaining technical competency where it counts. The disadvantages rest in the inability of the government's cost accounting system and acquisition process to absorb such an approach. In practical terms, developing contracts with sufficient incentives for an industry trained and required to make profits on production and not on research would be exceedingly difficult.

The third strategy is to split the difference and move to a smaller, still ready force while attempting to maintain technical supremacy. Although this strategy is the most politically attractive of the three, the national budget may require starker choices. If that is the case, this strategy will not work.

In the case of the Navy, the decline of the shipbuilding industry may be the precursor of broader trends in industry. Furthermore, within the shipbuilding industry, the possible contraction of the Navy's private-yard nuclear capability could impose the need for new ways of conducting business if and as those two facilities face downsizing.

One possible alternative is a return to a modified arsenal system, wherein the government becomes the owner if not the operator of the means of production. In this case, the government would acquire, possibly in an innovative way, crucial production capabilities and either operate them or contract out their operation [i.e., establish government-owned, contractor-operated production facilities (GOCOs)]. Past problems with

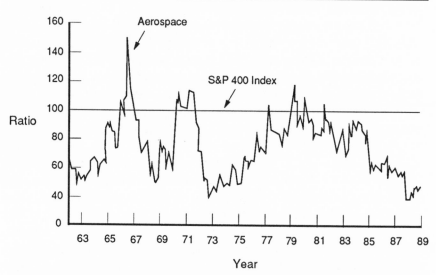

NOTE: This composite indicates how the market views the financial health of the aerospace industry. Aerospace performance in the chart is the average of the 40 largest DOD contractors (determined by yearly revenues) for aircraft, missiles, and space, electronic, and advanced weapons systems, or about three-quarters of the procurement and research and development account.

Figure 9. Standard and Poor's (S&P) Aerospace Price/Earnings Composite relative to the S&P 400 Index from 1962 to 1989

the arsenal system have included high overhead costs of maintaining the facilities, inefficiency, and difficulty in ensuring competition and innovation. Depending on how quickly the industrial base contracts, however, an arsenal approach may become mandatory.

Another bleak and perhaps distant consequence and danger is the actual collapse of a large segment of the defense industrial base. Because of the realities of the defense budget, the aerospace industry is in difficulty (figure 9), which means that further contraction and compression is likely.

Should one or two major corporations fail and, unlike earlier periods when government intervened to assist Chrysler and Lockheed, should the government not intervene, the industry could suffer a massive loss of confidence. In other words, the actual shrinkage could be dangerously magnified in terms of its effect on the private defense sector.

The unsatisfactory conclusion is that we have not given enough serious thought to the issues of the declining capability in the industrial base and an assessment of the likely consequences for the Navy. This assessment should be a high-order priority and should be carried out over the next year.

Manpower Base

Unquestionably, the most crucial defense resource is people, a point John Paul Jones underscored two centuries ago with his dictum that "men are more important than guns in the rating of a ship." The manpower base is changing. During the 1980s, there was the growing concern that manning the active force of 2.1 million would be made extremely difficult by the shrinking demographics of the 17- to 18-year-old population base available for service. That base will continue to shrink through 1992. Figures 10 and 11 give demographic projections for the United States.

With an active-duty force of 2.1 million, the problem was that, as a result of the contraction in the 17- to 18-year-old population and the need for DOD to acquire over 300,000 new accessions a year, there simply were not enough physically and mentally qualified personnel available to continue the all-volunteer

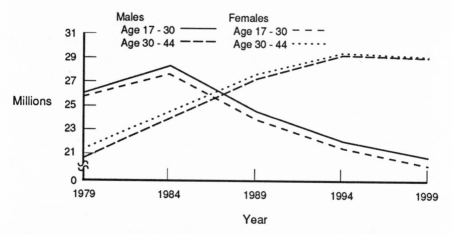

SOURCE: *The Military Balance, 1983 - 1984.* London: International Institute for Strategic Studies (IISS), 1984, pp. 145 - 148. Based on *UN Demographic Yearbook 1988.* New York: UN, 1988.

Figure 10. Demographic projections for the United States

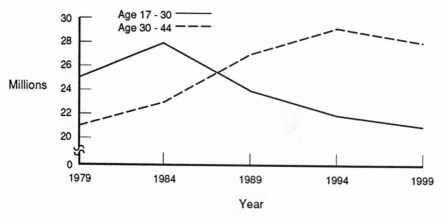

SOURCE: *The Military Balance, 1983 - 1984.* London: IISS, 1984, pp. 145 - 148. Based on *UN Demographic Yearbook 1988.* New York: UN, 1988.

Figure 11. Demographic projections for the United States for males only

force without major modification. Now, the reality is that, although the supply side remains constant, the demand side is shrinking. This change is a fundamental shift and will require fundamental adjustment of personnel plans and policies.

In its FY 1991 action, Congress reduced the size of the future Navy to just over 500,000 sailors, a 10-percent decrease. That level may not be sustainable, however, and future budgets could drive that number down dramatically. Getting down to this smaller Navy will be no easy matter.

In the past, recruiting and retaining personnel were the service watchwords and objectives. In the future, separating and screening personnel are going to be the dominant needs. With an all-volunteer force, each sailor has a legal contract with the government. Involuntary separations will be required. How does the government, in good faith, willfully breach a contract when the service member wishes to stay in service and there are no grounds for discharge other than fiscal cuts?

On the other side of the coin, the services will still require qualified personnel because future weapons systems will continue to demand capable, skilled operators and maintenance personnel. Given the fighting orientation of the services, the largest category of qualified recruits the services prefer to enlist are male, high-school graduates. This preference means that a smaller force and lessened demand could lead to a form of discrimination against minorities, who make up a high proportion of those students who do not graduate from high school, and women, who are less eligible for combat billets. Recourse to the courts, both by those who are separated involuntarily and by those who are not permitted to enlist, is a likely outcome.

This shift in manpower emphasis from recruiting and retaining to separating and screening will be difficult to manage and is indicative of the different nature of the challenges posed by the post-Cold War era.

Basing and Logistics Facilities

As was demonstrated by the 1989 Congressionally mandated base-closing commission, reducing the shore establishment and base support facilities for stationing, maintaining, and training a smaller Navy is a tortuous political problem. In 1990, the Navy owned nearly 600 pieces of real estate worldwide, of which just over 500 are in CONUS and 85 are overseas. That is more than one piece of property per Navy ship. Despite good intent, Congress largely foiled the base-closing commission's attempt to downsize support facilities in a rational and coherent way consistent with the needs of a smaller force structure.

The fundamental problem in rationalizing and streamlining this basing and support structure is the political nature of U.S. constituent politics. Members of Congress represent their constituents, and bases in home districts equate to jobs. Because this problem is an old story and a reality unlikely to change much in the future, the risk of having relatively few ships and a fat shore structure must be taken seriously.

One of the difficulties in rationalizing the basing structure is that no comprehensive approach for relating that structure to alternative military force structures has been presented to Congress. Nor is the basing structure assessed against the remainder of the defense infrastructure to identify what is being forgone to maintain those bases. Although eliminating politics from the future of military bases is impossible, a systematic comprehensive method for equating a streamlined base structure with strategic and force-structure needs must be developed. Because closing bases costs money and the government must often spend money to save money, this methodology must include an accurate forecast of what savings, if any, will be achieved and when they will be achieved. Finally, this methodology must identify many of the satellite commands, units, and organizations that have proliferated to these bases, which, if inadvertently decommissioned, could have highly negative effects on the Navy's ability to support the forces.

Both a zero-base, top-down study to determine what an ideal base structure should look like and a bottom-up, highly practical review to make the best of what we have in streamlining and rationalizing these facilities must be carried out. Comparison of these two basing studies will go a long way in making an effective case for matching the basing structure to actual military needs. Without such an approach, a future defense builddown could easily lead to a bloated, redundant shore establishment that hampers rather than helps U.S. fighting capability.

Intelligence Base

The final category of defense infrastructure is the intelligence base. Throughout the Cold War, the intelligence community purposely focused on the principal threat, the USSR. As political emphasis shifted from human intelligence collection assets and operations to overhead and other surveillance systems, the result was largely to field advanced, very expensive reconnaissance capabilities designed principally to target the USSR. That these systems can be used elsewhere is obvious. Given the reality of costs and budgets and the uncertain nature of future threats, however, the intelligence community is seeking new ways to deal with these requirements. Just as other components of the defense infrastructure have been swept up by this sea change, so has the intelligence community.

Future reliance on personnel who are highly knowledgeable about certain regions and on so-called less expensive, lighter-weight surveillance systems, and a shift in emphasis from collection to evaluation and forecast are likely directions. In this uncertain future, no matter how well the acquisition process, industrial base, manpower base, and shore establishment may be modified, similar levels of adjustment will need to be made across the entire intelligence community.

MAXIMIZING EVERY DROP

Our national fuel tank for defense is running on empty even though plenty of gasoline is available. It will be absolutely vital to maximize every drop of available resources. That need is not new. Unless it is taken far more seriously than in the past, however, the decline in force structure and the decompression of the defense infrastructure could have the pernicious effect of weakening the level of military capability that we choose to obtain.

9

A Strategic Compass

A compass needs cardinal points if it is to be of any use to the mariner. The first cardinal point on this compass for charting future uncertainties must be fixed in terms of responding to the consequences of profound change and a perhaps radically different security environment. These changes are ending the Cold War and are reverberating across every naval consideration from lofty levels of strategy to basic needs for recruiting and retaining sailors and marines. In these turbulent times, anticipation of future demands must account for adversaries who are not likely to have big and powerful navies. The Navy is shrinking from "600 ships" to no more than 450 ships and is likely to decline further in size as defense budgets continue to be squeezed. The operational environment will make close-in AAW, shallow-water ASW, probably mine countermeasures, and explicitly joint and combined operations new and exacting demands. Maritime power may well be returning to its traditional role of influencing and supporting campaigns ashore in conditions of war and crisis and promoting regional stability. The defense industrial base will compress and could implode, especially if the political irrationalities of a system of divided government are not held in check. Furthermore, even manning the services is liable to enter a new and fundamentally different environment.

Perhaps at no time in its history, short of war, has the Navy been faced with such a wide-ranging array of simultaneous challenges, each stemming from the consequences of change and transition in national and international conditions. Thus, "true north" is the realization that the Navy must make do with far less in a strategic environment where the basic assumptions and solutions of the past will no longer be sufficient for defining many future tasks. This realization must permeate all efforts to deal with these changes and serve as a reference point in defining the future status of the Navy.

The second cardinal point must be defined by the result of credible tradeoff analyses between and among commitments, force levels and force postures, and budget allocations to focus on the policy consequences driven by changing resource allocation patterns. We need to know the range of things certain levels of maritime power can and cannot achieve. Further, this comparative analysis must also deal with the defense infrastructure and relate infrastructure to force structure so that both areas can be dealt with comprehensively. Indeed, a comprehensive, interactive tradeoff analysis may be the most important function to be performed in the post-Cold War world so the public and Congress can better understand what should and should not be achievable operationally and strategically for the dollars spent, and what capability may be forgone.

A NEW SECURITY FRAMEWORK

Since the end of the 1939-1945 war, containment of the Soviet threat has been the central tenet of America's strategic policy. Now that the Soviet threat is changing decidedly (even though uncertainty abounds over what all this change will mean for the future), a new strategic framework needs to be fashioned if we are to be able to respond decisively and appropriately to this different environment. The situation was similar in early 1969 when the Nixon administration conducted a sweeping and successful strategic review. Although such a reassessment is imperative, the political signal sent by that review could reverberate intensely. In 1977, for example, the Carter administration embarked on a zero-based analysis of U.S. security policy that unintentionally unleashed a political firestorm that ended whatever use the exercise might have had in the first place. A similar political earthquake is not out of the question if a future review were to be handled incorrectly.

At the outset of any review, there is no need to change the traditional and basic American security objectives and purposes. Preventing war that could involve weapons of mass destruction, promoting regional stability, and protecting the interests of the

United States and its friends are sound and traditional aims transcending the level of any given threat. Indeed, these objectives, with minor modification, could have served this country well in the modern era whether in 1917 or 1941. The difficulty rests in taking valid objectives and translating them into action when the sense of threat has been alleviated and become more ambiguous. Hence, determining the means of ensuring an orderly and stable transition from one era to the next could be as important as the actual framework itself.

Clearly, if this strategic framework is to be effective, it must provide sufficiently rigorous and enforceable guidance and direction for the military departments to follow and must outline the role that the Navy will play within this security framework. Defining the Navy's role absent that broader context and guidance and in isolation from political reality would be an invitation to disaster. Indeed, it is probably as much or more in the Navy's interest for this broader construct to come forward, regardless of whether maritime or ground and air capabilities are emphasized.

Although these traditional and overarching objectives for U.S. security are unarguable, they are not necessarily sufficient in themselves or sufficiently broad enough to deal with this coming era. As the national security framework must expand to accommodate broader economic, social, and environmental factors that constitute important facets of this new world, so too, the broad national security objectives must also reflect these changes. Therefore, promoting and protecting the interests of the United States and its friends must be expanded to include the relevant economic, social, and environmental issues that are obvious security concerns. As the distinctions between internal and external national security challenges disappear, the overall security objectives must reflect these realities too.

In arriving at a new security framework, six national "deficits" should be considered: the economic, infrastructure, social, defense, conceptual, and governance deficits.

The economic deficit incorporates all aspects of national debts incurred or owed by both the private and public sectors. The public debt, now over $3 trillion and increased by law in 1990 by another $1 trillion, has doubled in real terms in a decade, and the annual cost of servicing this debt will soon exceed annual defense spending. The annual federal budget shortfall is headed for record levels, even after the receipts of the annual Social Security surplus ($200 billion per year) are added. Furthermore, this shortfall does not include all the costs of indemnifying the savings and loan industry (estimated between $200 and $500 billion total), which are handled "off budget," and all the costs of Desert Storm beyond those made good by our allies. The trade deficit is about $100 billion per year, and total public and private U.S. debt has risen to about two-and-a-half times GNP, or $12 trillion, which means about a quarter of GNP goes to service the debt. The only bright spot is the increase in the national savings rate, which could mollify some of the more pernicious effects of these trends.

Once the dust settles in the Persian Gulf, the upshot of this economic deficit for defense is clear. Given all the competing demands for national spending and the large percentage of GNP already going to service debt, the defense budget can only go down. The only question is how quickly the decreases will come and how rational they will be. Table 11 illustrates the debt driving this decrease.

The social deficit concerns, among other issues, the gaps between rich and poor, the enormous drug epidemic, the growing underclass, and the need to deal with the nation's aging population.

The infrastructure deficit applies to the decaying network of roads, transportation systems, public works, medical care, and education. Rectifying this deficit will require huge influxes of human and capital resources.

The defense deficit rests on the paucity of threat and resources. A reassessment of the basic underpinnings of defense needs to be made as the Soviet threat is in transtition. As has been amply noted, threat and defense resources are directly related.

The conceptual deficit stems, in part, from the changing international and domestic environments and changing threat perceptions. These changes are creating a vacuum in the national security atmosphere. That vacuum must be filled or, as in nature, there could be an implosion.

Table 11. Debt and GNP: the drivers (in billions of then-year dollars)

Calendar year	GNP	Total federal debt	Total U.S. debt[a]	Ratio of federal debt to GNP (percent)	Ratio of U.S. debt to GNP (percent)	Debt service/ GNP[b] (percent)
1970	1,015.5	300.8	1,596.9	29.6	157	8.4
1982	3,166.0	991.4	5,630.9	31.3	178	7.23
1985	4,014.9	1,600.4	8,243.1	39.9	205	18.5
1989	5,233.2	2,267.6	12,385.7	43.3	237	23.4[c]

SOURCE: Figures taken from the Economic Reports of The President and Statistical Abstracts of the Federal Reserve System.
a. Total debt includes total credit market debt outstanding from the U.S. Government, all state and local governments, households, farms, corporations, and mortgages.
b. Debt service calculated on indexed average among bank interest rates and Federal Reserve Discount and Federal Funds Rates.
c. In 1990, debt service has been estimated to be about 30 percent of GNP.

Finally, there is the governance deficit in which the gap between the need for good government and the actual performance of divided government could become a chasm.

Clearly, in the future, the concept of national security will have to address some, and possibly each, of these deficits, particularly if the strategic locus shifts from military to political, economic, and social issues. Figure 12 shows the components of this new national security framework.

Perhaps the greatest difficulty in constructing any such framework is the lack of a uniformly accepted standard of measure. Without the means to discuss or conduct tradeoffs between each of the deficits, establishing useful priorities will be a daunting task. Put another way, there may be few fungibles among the deficits. For example, in the past when we had difficulty in structuring tradeoffs among the military services and priorities for regional contingencies, we at least had a common language to express the combination of military capability, political risk, and actual commitment. Today, however, no readily apparent vocabulary exists for evaluating how much a reduction, say, of part of the economic deficit equates with forgoing resources in the social or defense deficits and what this does for national or individual well-being. Determining what effect the diversion of $1 billion or $100 billion from one deficit to another will have on national security is difficult.

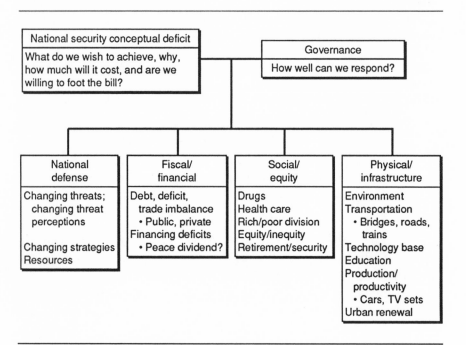

Figure 12. The national deficits

To relate each of these competing deficits and their demands on the nation's resources to this new national security framework requires a comprehensive approach that incorporates both top-down and bottom-up analyses. From the top down, the nation's wealth can be expressed in terms of GNP, which now approaches $5.5 trillion. Determining and distributing the government's share of GNP becomes the clearest expression of the top-down approach.

Figure 13 illustrates the bottom-up approach using the defense portion of national security. Assuming that a floor for these military capabilities can be projected, the first task rests in translating that level into the specific types and numbers of forces to be maintained by the United States. As noted, this floor is estimated to be 750,000 to 1,000,000 active-duty service personnel and an annual defense budget of $150 to $200 billion (FY 1991 dollars); however, considerable effort should go into verifying this estimate. The second task is determining what forces above that level are necessary to counterbalance and deter Soviet military power, and the third task is to relate these force postures in a transition strategy that will safely and securely allow the current configuration and disposition of U.S. defense capability to be reconfigured at lower levels.

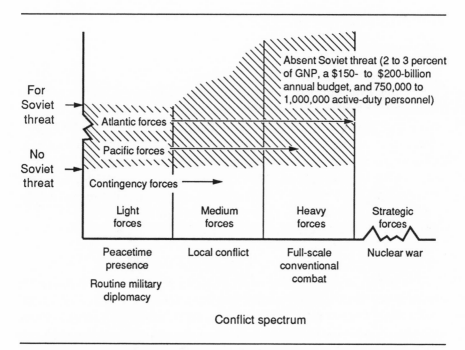

Figure 13. Required U.S. military capability

From the top down, there are two crucial tasks. First, an international framework for shaping the transition to what the Bush administration calls the post-containment era or new world order must be created. That framework must incorporate traditional American security objectives in Europe and the Pacific with the new and changing realities, most dramatically in the post-conflict Middle East region. Second, a domestic framework must be put in place that will help government make some of the cross-deficit tradeoffs that are so crucial and will reduce some of the major choke points in the process that impede our ability to take and implement necessary policy actions. By establishing these cardinal points as references for exploring the future, the Navy can then box its strategic compass in preparation for steering future courses and allocate its forces for the Strategic, Atlantic, Pacific, and Contingency missions outlined by Cheney and Powell.

International Framework

In Europe, the United States must become more aggressive in encouraging or challenging the USSR to embark on even more dramatic arms-reduction initiatives. The reasons are straightforward. This great moment may not continue forever as an unlimited, open-ended opportunity. Therefore, prudent speed is important. The Soviet Union has indicated a particular bent for embarking on sweeping change. The result should be to test that resolve now rather than wait for a future date when that receptivity may be gone. Furthermore, the nature of the Soviet response will encourage the NATO alliance to choose its future course as well as provide strong rationale for whatever that decision may be. All this should be pursued even as unrest and violence sporadically occur within the USSR.

Second, NATO should become the primary instrument for defining the future security environment in Europe, at least regarding the 16 member nations. As the military threat posed by the Warsaw Pact declines, NATO should be advancing the next-generation arms reductions proposals, a CFE II perhaps, advancing confidence-building measures, and outlining verification functions it could fill to oversee arms reductions.

Because the pressure to cut defense spending in NATO will be irresistible, NATO should be investigating alternative force postures that emphasize the themes of reconstitution and regeneration of forces as suggested under the Atlantic Force rationale. This investigation should be conducted before flexible response is replaced as the operational doctrine (if it is replaced). In other words, because warning time will be lengthy in the future, maintaining a forward-deployed infrastructure and a force posture that could be reconstituted over a period of months and redeployed as required has excellent political value as a basis for future planning.

Depending on how CSCE and EC 1992 evolve, NATO could integrate its future with those developments in a broader European framework for security. Through the 21st century, maintaining NATO in its central role is the most likely course of action; handing off its military responsibilities to a new security framework within CSCE or EC 1992 is another; and there may still be others. Inviting Japan and perhaps a few other Pacific Rim states to sit in as observers in CSCE would be advisable, because much of Europe's future security will have an enhanced economic component that will require Japan.

In the Northwest Pacific, a multilateral framework for security should be established around the notion of enhancing regional stability. CSCE and the EC 1992 framework provide rough analogs for the Pacific. The United States, USSR, Japan, China, and both Koreas should form the nucleus of such a group. The initial focus should be on initiatives to reduce the chances of crisis or conflict in the Korean peninsula, where regional war is most likely to occur. Confidence-building measures, arms reductions, and even some discussion of Korean reunification would form the agenda. The broader issue would rest in defining regional stability and what that means in terms of security relationships and mechanisms that could downsize the military components in a stable way. Furthermore, as the bilateral U.S.-Japanese relationship is stressed by economic, cultural, and other tensions, this multilateral approach can absorb some of the future shocks that will arise between these two countries.

Obviously, Asia is not Europe, and what has happened, for example, with the two Germanys could not automatically be replicated in the Koreas. A driving factor for establishing a multilateral framework for Pacific security, however, rests in the shift of Moscow's control over Eastern Europe and the obvious decline in military threat stemming from the political dismemberment of the Warsaw Pact. Reverberations will be felt in the Pacific, and, because the Soviet Union is an Asiatic power as well, there must be a response to these tremors.

The most uncertain region for the immediate and perhaps long-term future is the Persian Gulf and Middle East. The consequences of the Gulf War will be profound and unpredictable and will probably involve United States' presence, commitment, and economic largesse for the foreseeable future. The duration and costs of the war, as well as the performance of our forces and equipment, will hold potentially overriding significance for the design and force structure of the future U.S. military. Two obvious areas come to mind.

First, the ability of maritime forces to deploy quickly to a crisis area carrying personnel and sustainable, highly capable, and plentiful combat equipment has been reaffirmed by the crisis in the Gulf. Naval and Marine Corps forces dispatched to Saudi Arabia and the Gulf formed the first wave of defense. There is no dissent on this account or on this capability.

Second, it is almost unimaginable that maritime deployments to the Gulf region after the war will not be required. It is plausible, although not necessarily practical, that a need not entirely dissimilar to the 40 years of deployments to NATO Europe will be created in the Gulf. Maritime forces along with ground and air forces of some configuration are therefore likely to find long-standing presence in the region a mandatory requirement.

The role of the United States in each of these regions must be as the insurer of stability and the guarantor of a stable transition. We must assume this role because it is in our basic interests to do so. Thus, in Europe and vis-à-vis the USSR, the U.S. strategic nuclear guarantee would remain, admittedly with fewer nuclear forces as START plays out, and with a strong but smaller forward-based presence. As the number of U.S. forces overseas is reduced, however, the United States must maintain a credible reconstitution and regeneration capability for its military power. Much of this power will be through strong maritime forces to maintain or regain ocean access to key littorals. Some of this power will be through innovative uses of CONUS-based, rapidly deployable air-ground capabilities, and some of this power will be through imaginative ways of altering the defense technical-industrial base to accommodate longer warning times and lower procurement budgets. The time to start these approaches is in the next year or so, after the current round of arms negotiations between the United States and USSR has been completed and after the initial effects of changes in Eastern Europe and German reunification clarify.

Domestic Framework

The second task is to develop a domestic national security framework. This task may be more difficult. Incorporating all the deficits will be impossible initially because each requires resource allocations that either cannot or will not be made available. The government is not and may not be able to be organized to incorporate this broader agenda, in which security becomes far more than defending against Soviet or Soviet-inspired threats. Although the Navy is not responsible for designing these broader views, it cannot afford to ignore them either.

Political debate over the domestic agenda and domestic deficits is perhaps intractable and unresolvable. As a result, future federal budgets will be products and hostages of this political termoil. Clearly, defense spending will fall victim to the excruciating pressure to cut. Furthermore, new meaning and new tasks will be assigned to what were formerly traditional national security roles. All the while, steps to improve the process of governance should not be halted and must point towards more visible and implementable solutions. The defense-resource decision-making process and the defense acquisition process are two crucial targets for immediate improvement, and strengthening program stability while streamlining procurement are two vital objectives for this reform.

The Navy, through DOD, should make a strong case for a pre-budget agreement between Congress and the White House on several crucial planning factors. A two-year line for budget authority and outlays should be set and kept, and perhaps a 1- or 2-percent margin could be included to give reasonable flexibility in setting the top line. Although two-year spending levels were used in the October 1990 Budget Summit agreement, it remains to be seen how long that agreement will last. Second, general agreement on the levels of readiness for particular forces must be reached in advance. Third, a consensus should be reached on the relationship between modernization through replacement and upgrade and the size of procurement and research and development budgets. With these broad guidelines, DOD and the Navy will be better able to develop and implement future programs.

In addition, the areas of acquisition, including the defense industrial and technical base and research and development, must be improved and reformed to break the logjam that blocks the process. The following are summaries of recommendations made in chapter 3:

- First, Congress must streamline and codify the procurement rules, regulations, and oversight laws. The new code must be understandable, compact, enforceable, consistent, and fair.

- Second, redundant layers of oversight must be eliminated and the penalties for genuine abuse and outright fraud must be increased. Committee jurisdiction must be rationalized and redundancies reduced.

- Third, pre-agreement between the two branches of government over budget levels and the specific guidelines for force structure must occur before budget guidance is sent to DOD.

Until the domestic side of the house is put in better order, any strategic compass will lack the means to correct for political deviation and variation and, hence, will be incapable of determining an accurate or even an acceptable course. Such a situation would be a prescription for disaster.

FORCE STRUCTURE AND RATIONALE

Against that context, the Navy can calibrate its roles. First and foremost, the Navy's rationale must rest on its flexibility, deployability, and forward-based qualities. These determinations must relate to defining future U.S. commitments, however, because commitments give rise to the operational requirements for sizing and using the force. The first step is to determine the force-level floor based on virtually no Soviet threat, and then build upwards to incorporate the requirement to deter the USSR.

Other Than Soviet Threats

At a minimum, given the uncertainties outside the Soviet Union and assuming no Soviet threat, the United States will probably need, on a continuous basis, an immediately deployable (if not deployed) CVBG on both coasts as insurance policies. These carriers need not always be deployed, but they need to be instantly deployable. This posture would also assume continuation of an additional and forward-deployed carrier in Japan as the most visible sign of maintaining the sound security relationship with that country. To keep one carrier in a fully deployed or immediately deployable status, history and practice have shown that three other carriers are required. These ships would be in some form of refit, overhaul, or workup. Because a full-time training carrier is required for pilot qualification, a ninth ship would be required if the other carriers could not be made available to fill this essential mission. Commitments would be tailored accordingly, and eight to nine CVBGs would become the future minimum level *absent* a Soviet threat.

Because high-threat operations demand two and usually three carrier groups in a battle force, this force structure would allow prompt constitution of a two-carrier battle force and slightly longer generation time for a three-carrier force from each coast. In the Atlantic, the deployed carrier group and the training carrier supported by the "working-up" carrier would be available. To be sure, changes in how the training carrier operates and assignment of a ready air wing will be required and will no doubt have to be done innovatively and imaginatively.

In the Pacific, the deployed CVBG and the Yokosuka-based carrier would be supported by the working-up carrier. This means that, in all cases, a two-carrier battle force is immediately available on both coasts.

It is difficult to determine how the Navy's carrier force could safely descend below that floor in this century. One deployed or readily deployable carrier on each coast seems an absolute minimum. Furthermore, removing a carrier from Japan seems politically unwise, at least in 1991. Given the lengthy period required for SLEP, eight or nine carriers (and therefore CVBGs) constitute the long-term minimum level.

The number of carriers establishes the requirements for escorts and logistics ships. Assuming that 2 to 3 Aegis ships, 2 to 3 other escorts, and 2 SSNs are assigned per carrier, 9 carriers will require 36 to 54 surface combatants and 18 SSNs. Similarly, about 60 to 80 logistics ships and their escorts will be required, assuming 1 major replenishment group per CVBG.

Nuclear deterrence will remain a bedrock function. The United States is unlikely to have fewer than ten Trident SSBNs even with no Soviet threat. Five would be based on each coast and deployment could be in homewaters. Nominally, two to three SSNs would protect each SSBN as a contingency against a resurging Soviet threat or some unforeseen challenge to the integrity and safety of the future SSBN force.

Using the same type of floor analysis for the Marine Corps, the minimum force that would be politically acceptable would probably be a MEB on each coast. These brigades would include forward-deployed units.

Based on an absence of Soviet threat, what emerges is a floor Navy in the year 2000 that consists of no fewer than 8 or 9 CVBGs, 50 to 60 surface combatants, 50 SSNs, 2 MEBs, 10 Trident SSBNs, and an overall Navy of about 300 ships. The assumption is that this would be a ready and highly capable Navy and could include a portion in reserve or in cadre status as a fleet-in-being or insurance policy. Clearly, replacement ships, whether of a revolutionary nature or with major evolutionary advances, would be coming on line. This Navy would be manned by about 350,000 officers and enlisted and would cost the taxpayer about $70 to $75 billion a year (in FY 1991 dollars).

All this assumes a smooth transition with the Soviet Union and either bilateral or unilateral arms reductions that minimize our fears and concerns over Soviet military power. In parallel, the Army and Air Force would be much smaller as well, and the Navy would be receiving perhaps three-eighths of the defense budget, about the fraction it received in 1990.

The Soviet Case

Whether the USSR can be influenced, persuaded, or cajoled into following, from a Western perspective, a benign track is debatable. Hence, the "delta" or difference in U.S. maritime forces between the non-Soviet floor and what we have today and are likely to have in the future is crucial. In 1991, that delta equates to 4 or 5 CVBGs, 100 surface combatants, 40 SSNs, 6 underway replenishment groups (URGs), and nearly a MEF. In other words, a 12-CVBG Navy is essential today.

As budgets contract and force reductions follow, the Navy's role as a fleet-in-being could increase. The Navy will serve as a national insurance policy and as a bargaining chip for influencing future Soviet actions. Instead of scrapping or mothballing the big-deck carriers, these ships could be turned into large assault or lift ships capable of transporting, say, part of a Marine Air Wing and assault troops—a modern version of the *Arapaho* concept. Another option is to place several carriers in a reserve or even a stood-down status. Hence, smaller crews would be required. These ships would be capable of returning to full carrier duties perhaps within three to six months, depending on how long it takes to refit and train the air wing. Despite the enormous technical problems dealing with maintenance, normal deterioration even in cold-plant status, and the great skill required in operating aircraft that can be developed over time only with practice, these options for preserving carrier strength should be carefully investigated. The notion is to rely on a fleet-in-being to influence Soviet actions and serve as an insurance policy if the strategic situation deteriorates.

Rather than decommission or destroy the remaining SSNs, these ships could be placed in cold-plant status, either in commission or in reserve, with cadre crews for security of the ship and the nuclear reactor and for minimum maintenance. In crises, these SSNs could be reconstituted. Unlike the obsolete mothballed reserve fleets following the Second World War, the 637-class and even 688-class submarines that might be placed in this status would still have a long operational life if called upon in the future.

Maintaining the remaining assault lift and even the URGs in reserve might be too expensive, and these ships might have to be "mothballed." The alternative of renting these ships and perhaps other obsolescing combatants to other states is an interesting possibility, although the Calvinist ethic of the American people eschews mercenary roles. Consequently, the alternative of maintaining a "rent-a-navy" may be far-fetched.

If the USSR cooperates, bilaterally or unilaterally, these extra forces could be decommissioned and scrapped. The point is that, even if these units are not kept fully operational, they still serve a vital political purpose as part of this national insurance policy.

In the case of the USSR not cooperating or reasserting its long-term belligerence and hostility, the Navy could be regenerated back to a strong posture. Given that modernization instead of replacement would have probably been the result of budget reductions and program stretch-outs and cancellations, the Navy would have to shift its focus to replacing all of its forces. Replacement options are discussed in the next chapter.

Clearly, none of this will happen easily, smoothly, or cheaply. As in closing bases, assuming this transitional role will cost money. Furthermore, the uncertainty of the future complicates our choices. The new and emerging future security environment simply raises too many direct challenges and uncertainties for it to be otherwise. At one level, the Navy may have to swallow hard and consider using arms negotiations as a policy tool to its advantage. At another level, responding to non-Soviet threats will directly challenge previously dominant and heretofore sacrosanct bastions within the service. For example, in Third World operating conditions, SSN-21s and ASW aircraft have less operational impact. Lift for one-and-a-half MEFs is more than apparently would be required and more than could be sustained by future budgets. Furthermore, expensive intelligence-collection assets have less relevance against a less well-defined, non-Soviet threat. These realities challenge bureaucratic strongholds and long-standing divisions of authority within the Navy.

On the other hand, the traditional carrier battle force will appear as a more dominant force. Without Soviet opposition, in a fair fight, no regional power for the foreseeable future realistically will be able to challenge a carrier battle force, short of using weapons of mass destruction. Amphibious forces up to a MEB seem well configured for future non-Soviet threats. Lastly, refocusing research and development on these new operational requirements does not seem an insurmountable problem.

Thus, as far as the Navy and Marine Corps are concerned, inventing a new strategic compass to chart future courses is to the benefit of both the nation and the service, provided new ideas and innovative options can be freely ventilated. The larger problem may rest in applying the strategic compass to chart the future of the commercial infrastructure and industrial base.

A distinction must be made between commercial shipping and ship building. Although the U.S.-flag fleet of merchant ships has largely disappeared, the strategic consequences are not particularly damaging. Merchant ships are available in large numbers, and they all need not have U.S. flags. In crises, ships can be commandeered. If we are engaged in support of allies, it is inconceivable their ships would not be used for transport. Although we can mourn the passing of the U.S.-flag fleet, we need not be strategically harmed by that reality.

The same is not true on the production side. Production includes shipbuilding, aerospace, electronic and weapon systems, logistics, and service industries—commercial businesses that provide goods and services necessary for the common defense. This sector is in trouble. Shipbuilding has been in the van of shrinking industries. Others will follow. Although a term like *industrial policy* has such political volatility and divisiveness to render it useless, clearly, some kind of defense-industrial base strategy is imperative.

The recommendations for repairing the acquisition process, made earlier, must be enacted with haste. The best policy is to remove the constrictions and obstacles that prevent the process from functioning, but that may not be enough. Indeed, the notion of structural disarmament, that is, closing down defense production capability through budget or regulatory controls, could become a massive problem. In other words, the defense base could collapse or compress to the point where diseconomies of scale take over, with the result that far less capability will be obtained for greater unit and total costs.

If this transition strategy and the fleet-in-being concept have value for the forces, they may have value for the industrial base. In this regard, as active-duty strength decreases, maintaining frontline, effective weapons of war should become more important. Thus, a substantial chunk of resources may best be invested in the industrial base to keep crucial capabilities open or "warm" on the thesis that it takes far longer to reopen production facilities and to manufacture weapon systems than it does to recruit and train active-duty personnel. This investment strategy also reduces the tension between budget outlays and authority as production can be spread out over many years. If such an investment strategy is adopted, however, it must be well spelled out because budgets will probably not be able to support halfway approaches. In the end, a halfway approach may do more damage by unduly crippling both the naval forces and the supporting defense base.

Lastly, given these enormous political, process, and fiscal pressures that will act to decalibrate any compass, the Navy must act to lessen their impact. One means is to alter the organization of the staff of the CNO to loosen the power and bureaucratic compromise mandated by the so-called platform barons for air, surface, and submarine warfare specialties. Each of these baronies is headed by a vice admiral who represents each warfare area. During times when difficult choices between competing programs could be made by "balancing" or not excessively gouging one area to favor the others, this system worked. In the environment of today and tomorrow, tough choices are going to mean that balance between the platforms will not be affordable or maintainable.

To ensure that tough choices can be made and then made to stick, a different organization is needed. Perhaps assigning the combined responsibilities of research, development, and acquisition to a single vice admiral with subordinate rear admirals for air, surface, and submarine warfare reporting directly to him would prove a satisfactory arrangement. If history is a guide, however, any attempts at reorganization will be exceedingly difficult to achieve. Despite the obstacles, the organizational structure must be revised because the current structure will not be able to meet the new and emerging needs of the changing environment in which reorientation of platform priorities will not only be essential from a military perspective but will be mandated by affordability criteria as well. To repeat, adopting this or any reorganization scheme may be the toughest assignment the Navy faces.

Finally, every effort must be made to streamline and repair the infrastructure, especially the defense industrial base and the acquisition process. Specific recommendations on that count have been made throughout this book. Unless there can be substantial, positive movement in this area, the procurement of ships, aircraft, weapons, and logistics items will continue in chaos. The principal if not only way to rationalize the Navy ship construction and aircraft procurement accounts is to overhaul the process. Otherwise, the turbulence of the system will overwhelm the brilliance or competence of any single program. This overhaul represents another vital cardinal point.

Thus, a strategic compass can be developed. Regardless of whether this is the best compass and whether it has been correctly calibrated to point to true north can be debated. Without a compass similar to this one, however, plotting the future course of the Navy will be a decidedly more difficult and dangerous task.

10

New Ways of Doing Old Business: Alternative Force Structures

THE DILEMMA

For any military service, examining alternative ways of carrying out roles and missions is extremely difficult, for several reasons. First, no analytical model or test is foolproof in determining in advance how well or how badly different force structures may or may not perform in action. Second, the military has a strong operational and tactical bias, based on experience and tradition, against departing from proven and effective force postures. Third, the technical-industrial reality of what can be produced and at what rate limits what technology can actually provide. Finally, the political reality is that new or different approaches require establishing both a consensus and a documented track record of some length to support making change. The result is volatility and vulnerability because technical risk requires exacting testing (especially for new concepts) that, in turn, can lead to dramatic failures and political catastrophe.

Reviewing the past 50 years of U.S. force structure (with the exceptions of nuclear weapons, nuclear power, and dramatic if not revolutionary improvements in virtually all types of weapons systems), U.S. forces today bear an interesting resemblance to the forces that won World War II. An exception to this is that the services now are extremely limited in the types of specific major platforms they can buy.[1] For example, the Navy can really argue only over the number rather than the type of basic platforms to be bought because the choices can be made from only one type of aircraft carrier, the *Nimitz*-class

---

1. Lower-cost alternatives to the SSN-21 and DDG-51 are now under active consideration and are called, respectively, the *Centurion* SSN and the *DDX* variant.

nuclear-propulsion aircraft carrier; one type of destroyer, the *Arleigh Burke*-class guided-missile destroyer; one type of submarine, the *Seawolf*; and one type of amphibious assault ship, the *Tarawa*. The aviation side, in 1991, is in equal turbulence and, for the first time in history, the Navy has no advanced aircraft under full-scale development. Designing alternative platforms and aircraft could take years. Thus, too often, force structure alternatives become exercises in downsizing or upsizing current force posture rather than deriving alternative types of capability and new ways of distributing power among various alternative platforms.

In any examination of alternative force posture, the tradeoffs among alternative political and strategic policies and objectives that are to be advanced (i.e., policy-driven models) and different means of applying power for projection and protection (i.e., distribution models) must be understood. From this interaction, alternative force postures and associated combat systems and technological capabilities can be derived and compared, assuming the same level of defense spending for each set of force structures. Through this process, alternative forms of projecting maritime power can be evaluated among sea-, land-, air-, and space-based elements.

Before moving to the policy-driven and force distribution model alternatives, a base case for future maritime force structure must be established. Although the level of future U.S. maritime power will be largely the function of budgetary actions (at least regarding numbers) in the 1992-1997 defense plan, the 600-ship, 15-CVBG Navy will be 20 to 25 percent smaller. The goal of 15 deployable carriers has been reduced to 12. The number of surface combatants will be reduced from 225 to about 130 to 140, and the number of SSNs will be reduced from 95 to between 70 and 75. Thus, barring some unforeseen crisis, the Navy of the 21st century will be at least one-quarter smaller than it is today. Such a compression is not trivial; it will require major restructuring of the Navy.

Any model for examining new choices must incorporate means of comparing the relative effectiveness of alternative force structures ultimately against the range of missions they will or may have to perform. One means of designing alternative force structures is through setting the policy objectives first (e.g., an anti-Soviet Navy, a SLOC-protection Navy, or a power-projection Navy). A second means is through the aggregation or disaggregation of capability between and among platforms, or a model of power distribution. The two extremes of the power distribution alternative could be a Navy made up of a few monster "floating islands" of 1 million tons or more displacement that carry many hundreds of aircraft and thousands of troops or a Navy made up of many small platforms that carry a handful of aircraft each. In between these two extremes, the notion of massive aircraft carriers that could carry 200 or 300 aircraft as single replacements for several current aircraft carriers should be reexamined closely. Obviously, reality and practical requirements imposed by economies of scale will set the balance in the direction of aggregation. Figure 14 shows this distribution model put in three dimensions.

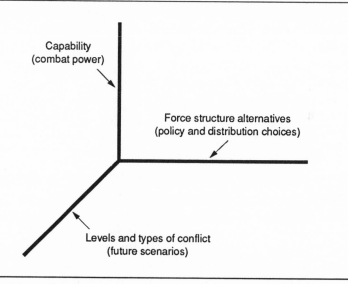

Figure 14. Three-dimensional representation of distribution model

Were it possible to use a fourth dimension, that dimension would flow from the force structure alternatives and incorporate the implications of each alternative for the defense industrial-technical base; the basing and shore establishment infrastructure; manning, retention, and training; supporting operational requirements and assumptions; and the necessary intelligence gathering and analysis.

ALTERNATIVE FORCE STRUCTURES

Four basic force structures flow from the policy-driven model. For ease of reference, these four force structures are called the Present as Future Navy, the Anti-Soviet Navy, the Three Navies, and the New World Order Navy. The Present as Future Navy is the base case. This Navy would be like today's Navy (i.e., patterned against a high-intensity Soviet threat). Strategic nuclear forces would be determined by START, which would set between 15 and 18 Trident SSBNs as the upper limit. The force structure would be more or less equally decremented to fit the budget and a 450- to 480-ship Navy with 12 CVBGs, 70 to 75 SSNs, and 130 to 140 surface combatants would result. Depending on future budgets, those numbers would be reduced further, more or less proportionally. The Anti-Soviet Navy force structure is tailored specifically for an anti-Soviet mission, assuming that other contingencies could be managed with these forces. Strategic forces would remain as dictated by START. This Navy would have two sub-options: (1) opposing the Soviet Navy through power projection directly and deeply into Soviet homewaters or (2) opposing it through containment, blockade, and sea control outside Soviet homewaters.

In the first sub-option, emphasis would be on standoff attack and SSNs that could operate forward. This sub-option would require cutting the CVBG force in favor of SSNs and relying on cruise missiles for power projection against the shore. This Navy, given top-line budget projections, would consist of perhaps 8 to 9 CVBGs, 85 to 90 SSNs and submarines carrying cruise missiles (SSGNs), and less than 1 MEF.

The sea-control or containment Navy sub-option would favor surface combatants and ASW aircraft. This Navy might consist of 10 to 12 CVBGs (some configured for ASW), perhaps

200 surface combatants, and 70 to 75 SSNs. Active sonar would become the principal ASW means of detection.

The Three Navies force structure is designed to provide specific capabilities tailored for nuclear deterrence, high-intensity conflict, and Third World intervention. This hierarchy conforms to the new force structure concept advanced by the Secretary of Defense and Chairman of the JCS and hedges a bit in shifting emphasis in principal power-projection instruments from strike to ground forces.

In this structure, nuclear deterrence would be provided by Trident SSBNs as determined by START. High-intensity conflict in the Pacific Force, Atlantic Force, and Contingency Force scenarios would be applicable to any advanced technology threat and based on the presumption that three CVBGs formed the critical battle-force mass necessary to operate in that environment. Presumably, one battle force would be stationed on each coast.

Third World or Contingency Force involvement would be dealt with using lesser amounts of force. Indeed, designing a CVBG equivalent, in which a certain percentage of a CVBG's combat power could be generated without the presence of an aircraft carrier, is an attractive idea. This force structure leads to the conclusion that perhaps a new class of ship may be needed that can perform a portion of the battle group and Marine expeditionary mission. Both the CVBG-equivalent concept and a new surface-combatant design will be discussed in this and later chapters.

The final force structure, the New World Order Navy, is designed to provide nuclear deterrence, residual capability against the long-term prospect of a rejuvenated Soviet threat, and capability for Third World involvement. This Navy should include the capability to conduct high-threat operations in which CVBGs provide support and ground forces are the preferred power-projection tool. This Navy would form the core or minimum-size Navy the nation would require and assumes a latent or even benign USSR. The basis for this Navy is being able to simultaneously deploy two battle forces of three CVBGs each in two separate regions to support the projection of a Marine force about the size of a MEB or other equivalent ground forces. The time to mount these operations would be measured in days or weeks and would not necessitate having battle forces ready around the clock from each coast.

For each of these four policy-derived force structures, nominal force structures should be designed and costed at different budget levels likely to represent the range of defense spending at the century's end. From these structures, both a capabilities and commitments evaluation can be performed.

The policy-derived force structures should be complemented by using the distribution model as a second basis for specific design of alternative forces. The distribution model encourages more imaginative uses of technology because it is system rather than threat biased. The distribution model assumes that a core force of 7 CVBGs will be retained in the future and that those forces will include 2 battleships, 50 surface combatants, 18 direct-support SSNs, and 2 MEBs of assault capability. The rest of the Navy's resources would be used in developing the alternative augmentation structure. The technical risk must be emphasized. Indeed, deploying any of these alternative distribution force structures by the year 2000 may be unrealistic; the year 2010 may be a more accurate estimate.

Six equal-cost distribution alternatives follow in which force projection and protection capabilities have been aggregated or disaggregated among various platforms.[1] The first is a distribution based on augmenting the core force with unmanned weaponry (table 12).

Manned aircraft and surface escorts for the five CVBGs were replaced with long-range, remotely targeted cruise missiles that rely on offboard sensors. Economies of scale would be achieved by using large, missile-carrying ships. Eight cruise missile battle groups (CBGs) formed around these large cruise-missile-carrying combatants with escorts would nominally replace the five CVBGs. The CBGs would carry hundreds or more of cruise missiles and remotely piloted surveillance vehicles.

In the second alternative (table 13), the five CVBGs groups are replaced with 30 cruise-missile-armed cruiser battle groups

---

1. These distribution models were derived by the author in 1985 and presented in similar form in the CSIS study entitled *U.S. Conventional Force Structure at a Crossroads*, Washington, D.C., 1986.

(CGVs) or through-deck cruisers (ships with a displacement of about 20,000 tons) and 60 patrol escorts (PCHs). These units would exploit long-range missiles, offboard targeting, advanced naval hull designs, and vertical lift aircraft (VSTOL) that enable greater distribution of firepower in more units. Although 30 CGVs may not be equivalent in firepower to 5 carriers, overall numbers permit more simultaneous deployments especially in lower threat areas.

Table 12. Unmanned weaponry case

Generic ship type	Core force	Augmentation force
Carriers	7	—
Battleships/CBGs	2	8 BBGs/CBGs[a]
Surface combatant escorts	50	32
Direct-support SSNs	18	16

a. A battleship battle group (BBG) or CGB substitutes an upgraded battleship or equivalent-sized cruise-missile-carrying ships, respectively, for the carrier.

Table 13. Distributed firepower case

Generic ship type	Core force	Augmentation force
Carriers	7	—
Battleships	2	—
Through-deck cruisers	—	30 CGVs
Surface-combatant escorts (conventional)	50	—
Direct-support SSNs	18	15
Small (sensor only) escorts	—	60 PCHs (hydrofoils)

Advanced naval hull designs, such as the small-water-area twin hull, surface effects ships, and hydrofoils, provide greater seaworthiness in smaller hulls, which saves on costs and permits greater use of distributed VSTOL aviation. The VSTOL would be used for surveillance, targeting, ASW, and conventional tactical air missions.

The third approach (table 14) can apply to any force structure. This alternative invests more on C^3I at the expense of actual force levels. The thesis is that increased surveillance, targeting, and C^3I require fewer weapons, as each weapon will have a much higher probability of success. Emphasis would be on increasing robust space-based sensors that permit nearly worldwide, real-time oceanic surveillance. This capability is estimated to cost the same as about one CVBG.

Table 14. Enhanced C^3I case

Generic ship type	Core force	Augmentation force
Carrier	7	–
Battleships	2	–
Through-deck cruisers	–	25 CGVs
Surface combatant escorts (conventional)	50	–
Direct-support SSNs	18	12
Small (sensor only) escorts	–	50 PCHs (high-capability space-based sensors)

The fourth alternative (table 15) assumes that stealth and reduced observables will increase naval effectiveness because of the difficulties in surveilling, detecting, and targeting the more stealthy force. Long-range missiles, the VSTOL, advanced naval vehicles, and offboard sensors are complemented by stealth and counter-C^3I capabilities. The costs of such an alternative are approximate at best.

In the fifth alternative (table 16), the Navy would be more formally divided into three functions: nuclear deterrence, conventional conflict, and nuclear war. The core force would be used for traditional roles and missions. The SSBNs would continue in the strategic deterrent role, but more SSNs would be procured—50 for the 5 CVBGs—for use in a variety of contingencies, including the possibility of nuclear war. Survivability of the SSNs is the key consideration. Given any greater emphasis on strategic defense, the Navy could absorb some of these missions. SSNs would also have a much larger strike mission against the shore using advanced conventional cruise missiles.

Table 15. Counter-C^3I case

Generic ship type	Core force	Augmentation force
Carriers	7	–
Battleships	2	–
Through-deck cruisers	–	20 stealthy CGVs
Surface combatant escorts (conventional)	50	–
Direct-support SSNs	18	12
Small (sensor only) escorts	–	40 stealthy PCHs
		(high-capability space-based radar/infrared (SBR/IR), many high-capability decoys, etc.)

Table 16. Three navies: the submarine variant

Generic ship type	Core force	Augmentation force
Carriers	7	–
Battleships	2	–
Surface combatant escorts	50	–
Direct-support SSNs	18	–
Strike submarines (other than SSBNs)	–	50 SSNs and SSBNs (high-capability SBR/IR)

In the sixth alternative (table 17), the same three roles apply except that long-range, long-endurance aircraft form the augmentation force. Given that long-range air may be more survivable than traditional surface forces, aircraft would be used to prosecute the strategic ASW mission.

Table 17. Three navies: the land-based air variant

Generic ship type	Core force	Augmentation force
Carriers	7	–
Battleships	2	–
Surface combatant escorts	50	–
Direct-support SSNs	18	–
Large multimission land-based naval aircraft	–	200 (high-capability SBR/IR)

These policy- and distribution-based force structure alternatives represent a range of choices to deal with uncertain futures and different spending levels. Each force structure has strengths and weaknesses. The value of this exercise, however, is to provide a broad and comprehensive means of comparing and evaluating the advantages and disadvantages of each in coming to grips with what the future Navy should be and what it should be able to do. Furthermore, when analysis is performed to evaluate the military capability and operational capacity of any of these alternatives, invariably the worst case is always the most likely—the equitably decremented Five-Year Defense Plan. Because of this, more serious attention must be placed on these alternatives should resource constraints occur as forecast.

To be sure, in several of these structures, the shift of CVBGs and their equivalents to supporting roles and of Marine Corps and ground forces to principal power-projection instruments would lead to the need for amphibious, ground attack, and minesweeping assets not currently on hand. Moreover, new and improved command-and-control systems would be essential in these and other options. It is also understood that a significant share of resources would automatically be shifted to conform with the change in the preferred and principal means of projecting power.

Finally, a wider range of alternative platforms needs to be investigated. Smaller and less costly SSNs and surface escorts are being examined. Revamped air wings and new follow-on aircraft, perhaps reflecting a requirement for less rather than more standoff range, are likely to be part of a future review. Unless there is a serious and rigorous attempt to design and evaluate truly alternative types of force structures and platforms, there will be no basis to reinforce whatever decisions the Navy and Marine Corps recommend to OSD and Congress.

11

Future Courses and Speeds

Fast forward: May 15, 2000. The president's decision to dispatch nearly 100,000 American fighting men and women into the joint U.S./USSR Peacekeeping Expeditionary Force was roundly criticized by both Congress and the media. Indeed, our NATO allies refused to permit either overflight rights or basing privileges to U.S. forces deploying to the crisis area, and the Organization of Petroleum Exporting Countries (OPEC) imposed an embargo on oil exports to the United States. Japan protested the decision to use force and announced it would take up its promise to reevaluate the Mutual Defense Treaty within the month.

The operational commander, in an unfortunate exchange with the media pool aboard his flagship, was openly critical of the nebulous rules of engagement and skeptical of how the U.S. and Soviet forces could indeed be integrated. No one had foreseen that such a requirement would ever emerge.

May 20, 2000. An American Aegis cruiser was struck by a torpedo fired from a coastal diesel submarine and put out of action for an indefinite period. The taking of heavy casualties was fortuitously and miraculously balanced by no accompanying loss of life. The international media satellite was stationed overhead providing instant reporting and automatic although inadvertent targeting. Public criticism in the United States was building explosively. Finally, after a nuclear weapon had been detonated in anger for the first time since August 1945, the world literally panicked.

* * *

The reader can finish this story according to his or her imagination. The conclusion, of course, depends on how the U.S. Navy and Marine Corps, along with their sister services, are designed, sized, structured, supported, and prepared for this uncertain future.

The broader national security framework that is emerging as the context and guidance for future maritime capabilities incorporates a much wider threat horizon and reflects the increasing importance of the domestic environment in influencing national security. As threats beyond that of Soviet political, military, and ideological hostility grow larger, they also are increasingly ambiguous and present us with more complicated problems that range beyond what military force alone can achieve. The notions of ensuring stability and a safe transition through this change in eras will become central tenets of this new security framework. To achieve these goals, the military instrument must be complemented with a larger variety of policy tools that address the expanding nature of the national security framework.

The Navy and the nation must answer four principal sets of questions in dealing with national security. The strategic answer rests in safely and securely redressing the Soviet threat at a time of profound uncertainty and transition and at a time when the spectrum of non-Soviet threats is broadening, becoming more complex, and not necessarily slackening in specific danger or risk for the nation.

The domestic environment will be more perplexing. Governance gives every sign of breaking down or choking in its own excess. Establishing and implementing priorities for national spending is illusive. De-politicizing issues and allowing some form of rationality to take hold is proving very difficult. In that regard, Congress deserves a great deal of blame and, unfortunately, chooses to accept little responsibility. Therefore, if current political trends are not immediately reversed, successfully negotiating this domestic decision-making-process quandary will loom as a far greater challenge in the future than defeating the Soviet Navy.

The operational answer rests in expanding the philosophy of maritime operations beyond planning for Soviet contingencies. Not only will most or all warfare assumptions be broadened to account for non-Soviet contingencies (especially in light of the Gulf War), but training, deployment, and doctrine also must be revised. This revision will apply to the design and capability of virtually all future combat and weapon systems and platforms.

The fourth set of answers rests in rationalizing the entire supporting defense infrastructure to meet the demands and realities of the 21st century. Old ways of doing business will not apply to a shrinking defense industrial base. The basing structure must be pared down to support the fleet and not vice versa. Manning and retaining the force will need new criteria and incentives. Finally, intelligence collection and analysis must be broadened to include and perhaps some day emphasize non-Soviet targets. Each of these quandaries is enormously complex and not easily resolvable.

THE STRATEGIC ANSWERS

For the U.S. Navy, geographic realities dictate that a substantial portion of U.S. forces must be flexible, readily projectable, and sustainable. Whether the United States is a maritime power in the classical sense or not, it will maintain interests overseas that must be provided some form of protection and defense. Especially in light of Operation Desert Storm, DON cannot assume that popular rationale and public consensus for the Navy's importance are likely to grow unless the Navy is able to demonstrate that it can provide superior and more affordable capabilities to project power than the other services. The strategic objectives for maintaining sufficiently strong and ready amounts of maritime power will include the traditional requirements of defending the United States and its allies from harm, protecting vital and important U.S. interests abroad, and responding as the nation's well-being and security demand. Besides these requirements, however, the Navy will also have two new and equally important roles.

The first role is to promote and protect stability. Stability does not mean protecting the status quo. It occurs when there is no disequilibria in international politics that could lead to a conflict in which the United States or its interests could be involved. Stability comes from reassurance, commitment, and combat capability. The presence of U.S. maritime assets (as well as other assets) reassures our friends and visibly reaffirms our commitments. Combat capability convinces would-be adversaries that taking on the United States is not a winning proposition. As the world continues to change dramatically and the old order disappears, maintaining stability grows more important. This need, however, does not lock the United States into a series of unbreakable deployments that cannot or should not be altered to reflect these changing times. The model is that of U.S. forces stationed in Europe—forces that, after 45 years of successful deployment, will now be reduced to match the fundamental changes that are reshaping Europe.

The Navy's second new role is to serve as a transition force providing, as it were, a national insurance policy in case things go wrong and as a force to influence and encourage the USSR to move to even lower levels of military capability. We know for certain that the future U.S. Navy is going to be much smaller. The strategic issue is to use this contraction to our advantage by inducing the USSR also to reduce its maritime forces in ways we see as less threatening.

Part of this new role can be filled through the concept of a fleet-in-being, that is, a fleet that can be regenerated and reconstituted relatively easily and quickly should maritime power be needed at a future date. The rest of this role can be pursued through aggressive arms control initiatives used strategically in which we challenge the USSR to move to far less threatening force postures as both navies are downsized. We need to declare what part of the Soviet Navy we find threatening and how we would like to see that threat reduced.

Thus far, the Navy has been adamantly opposed to naval arms control, and for good reason. The Navy, believing the USSR will reduce its naval forces unilaterally, sees no reason to bind future U.S. naval structure to Soviet actions. Such a linkage would be too restrictive. The Navy further argues that, because the Soviets will use arms negotiations as a means to constrain free use of the seas, the United States would be foolish to fall into that trap. Moreover, the ongoing START and CFE negotiations are already complicated enough without adding navies to an already full agenda.

Perhaps most significantly, the Navy is rightly fearful that arms negotiations on naval forces will remove the Navy's authority over its future, ceding control to another branch or agency that, by virtue of negotiations, could unduly influence the size, shape, and capability of U.S. maritime forces. This fear is absolutely justifiable; the Navy could lose control over its own destiny.

That the Navy has a good case is underscored by the refusal of the Bush administration, to date, to seek naval arms reductions other than for strategic forces. That view, however, is likely to change for three crucial reasons. First, when the other negotiations eventually come to an end, the USSR and Congress will be anxious to look to naval reductions as the next step. Furthermore, if Soviet actions continue on a benign path, there will be fewer reasons to avoid mutual reduction of all forces. Second, the defense budget has already imposed at least a 25-percent reduction in U.S. naval strength with no *quid pro quo* from the Soviet Union, and the Navy is losing control over its future. At least conceptually, using this decrease in size as a possible advantage in gaining influence over the direction of the Soviet Navy through mutual reductions is too valuable a concept to be dismissed out of hand. Third, provided no restrictions are placed on freedom of the seas, the U.S. public will increasingly question why naval arms reduction talks have not been pursued. The Navy must respond to these pressures.

However justified the Navy's concerns, taking the initiative in laying out what the U.S. position might be, what is acceptable, and what type of Soviet Navy we would like to see is a vital step in staking out lines of authority. Such an action does not commit the United States to anything, and, as we discovered over the Intermediate-Range Nuclear Forces (INF) Treaty, the Soviets may agree to terms previously held to be unthinkable. Recalibrating its attitude towards arms control at sea may be the most difficult yet important step the Navy takes this decade.

From the hierarchy of roles, missions, and uses, three specific missions for the Navy follow. The first is to deter war in which nuclear and other weapons of mass destruction could be used. The principal power to be deterred is the USSR. As other states who may not be well disposed towards the United States develop these weapons, however, the scope of the deterrent mission will expand, subtly or bluntly. This mission must be the bedrock of our strategy, and it must leave open the definition of what the specific next generation of threat will be.

The second mission of the Navy follows the U.S. legal code—namely, to be ready to conduct prompt, sustained combat operations at sea. In this case, the Navy must continue to operate on the principle of preparing to sail in harm's way and must have sufficient capability for high-threat, high-intensity conflict. Thus, until the Soviet Union can be reliably viewed as benign, the U.S. Navy must have the capability to defeat or neutralize Soviet maritime power wherever and whenever it may be present. Certainly, if Soviet maritime power lessens, U.S. power can also be reduced, provided it maintains this advantage.

The third mission of the Navy is to respond flexibly to contingencies, crises, and the demands of peacetime diplomacy. The Navy must have an intervention capability for high-threat conditions, which means that three to four CVBGs and a MEB must be available on a timely basis on both coasts as an absolute minimum.

Without an extraordinary future crisis to change U.S. priorities, the defense budget will be the largest single determinant of the Navy's future capability. Thus, determining what military capability can be obtained for given levels of defense spending and what that means for safeguarding national security is important. In other words, the questions of which commitments and roles can be undertaken and which will have to be either forgone or accepted with greater risk must be answered. The comparative evaluation in table 18 assumes a Navy in the year 2000 of similar design, of high readiness, and with numbers and capability determined by budgets.

Those who advocate large budget cuts need to understand the tradeoffs among capabilities, commitments, and spending before taking those actions. Although it is impossible to predict the specific ways in which the Navy will be used in the 21st century, it is virtually certain the Navy will be used in anger. It is also a virtual certainty that the range of uses will expand, reflecting the broader nature of the emerging national security environment.

Table 18. Cost, force, and capability tradeoffs

Annual budget (in 1991 dollars)	Force composition (shorthand)	Capabilities
$95 billion	Best-case Navy 14 CVBGs, 90 SSNs, 1+ MEF, 500 ships	• Very high confidence of destroying the Soviet Navy in conflict • Very high confidence of ensuring deterrence • In normal deployments, capable of keeping four CVBGs routinely on station; capable of surging to two or three battle forces • Capable of securing command of the seas anywhere on the globe
$85 billion	Core Navy with Soviet threat 10-11 CVBGs (12th carrier could be training ship), 450 ships	• Good confidence of defeating and containing the likely Soviet Navy of the year 2000 in conflict • Very high confidence of ensuring deterrence against non-Soviet threat; confidence vis-à-vis USSR is a function of the change in events and cannot be determined yet • In routine deployments, capable of keeping three carriers deployable, but deployments to the Indian Ocean would stress this posture. Could surge to two battle forces of two to three CVBGs each within days or weeks and to one more over time

(Continued on next page)

Table 18. (*Continued*)

Annual budget (in 1991 dollars)	Force composition (shorthand)	Capabilities
		• Capable of securing command of the seas against any non-Soviet threat
$75 billion	Core Navy without Soviet threat 8-9 CVBGs, 400 ships	• Fair confidence of defeating and containing the likely Soviet Navy of the year 2000
		• High confidence of ensuring deterrence against non-Soviet threat; as above, regarding USSR
		• In routine deployments, capable of keeping two and possibly three carriers deployable and surging to two battle forces or two CVBGs within days or weeks and to one more over time
		• Capable of securing command of the seas against any non-Soviet threat
$65 billion	6-7 CVBGs 350 ships	• Uncertain about defeating or containing the likely Soviet Navy of the year 2000 even though it is little or no threat
		• High confidence of ensuring deterrence against a non-Soviet threat; confidence vis-à-vis the USSR is indeterminate
		• In routine deployments, capable of keeping two carriers deployable; could surge to one battle force or more over time

(*Continued on next page*)

Table 18. (*Continued*)

Annual budget (in 1991 dollars)	Force composition (shorthand)	Capabilities
		● Capable of securing command of the seas against most likely future non-Soviet threats
$55 billion	5-6 CVBGs, 300 ships	● No confidence about defeating or containing the likely Soviet Navy of the year 2000
		● Medium confidence of ensuring deterrence against a non-Soviet threat; no confidence in deterring the USSR if it were to remain a threat
		● In routine deployments, capable of keeping one or two carriers deployable; could surge to one battle force over time
		● Capability to secure command of the seas against non-Soviet threats very uncertain
$45 billion	4-5 CVBGs, 250 ships	● No confidence about defeating or containing the likely Soviet Navy of the year 2000
		● Uncertain confidence of ensuring deterrence against a non-Soviet threat; no confidence in deterring the USSR
		● In routine deployment, capable of keeping one carrier deployable
		● Purely a defensive and reprisal force with little capacity or endurance for sustained, high-threat operations

Although the structure and size of the Navy in the 21st century will be largely a function of budget share and the time it takes to develop and implement new or advanced technology, at a minimum, that Navy should have at its core 8 to 9 CVBGs or their equivalents, about 350 ships, and a MEB assault capability on both coasts. This minimum or core force will enable the Navy to engage in high-threat operations whenever required. How the USSR evolves will determine whether this minimum force must be augmented to deal with the future Soviet threat. If there is little or no change, a 12-CVBG Navy will be absolutely essential. Depending on Soviet responses, either force is a navy that will prove responsive to popular support and will conform with the resources likely to be made available at the floor level of U.S. military capability mandated by the public.

OPERATIONAL ANSWERS

The operational answers are reflected in the growing requirements for non-Soviet contingencies. Not only are advanced weapons present worldwide, but chemical, biological and nuclear agents are finding their way into more inventories as well. This proliferation means that high-threat planning will be not only essential but made more complex by the reality that assumptions about standoff range for target detection, identification, and destruction may have to be brought down to minimum distances owing to the realities of geography and operational demands of non-Soviet contingencies. Imbuing the planning and designing process with this new philosophy is crucial.

As the Navy evolves and the actions of the Soviet Union provide the grounds for charting a future course (at least in terms of how the scope and pace of budget and force reductions are made), review of alternative force structures must be conducted along the lines outlined earlier. Even the discussion of a nuclear follow-on to SSN-21 caused great technical and emotional debate because of the concern that such a concession would be viewed as abandoning the *Seawolf* program in these difficult budget times. However, the Navy is now studying a less-expensive SSN class called *Centurion*.

One operational trend does appear to be emerging regarding surface combatants. Smaller ships, even 8- to 10,000-ton-displacement Aegis platforms, simply may not be large enough to accommodate the weapon systems likely to be needed in the future. (On the other hand, the DDX-variant is one excursion aimed at designing a smaller, 3- to 4,000-ton, less costly surface ship.) This size requirement particularly applies to sea-based tactical air whether manned or unmanned. Despite the economies of scale in the well-proven *Nimitz*-class nuclear carrier, carrier procurement costs for the current big-deck ships are so large that future carrier buys for that class of ship must be highly questionable on grounds of affordability.

One alternative could be a few "super-super" carriers displacing 300,000 tons or more and carrying 200 or 300 aircraft each. If Third World contingencies assumed greater significance in planning, these giant ships would literally serve as floating islands in terms of their capability. The costs for each monster ship could be two or more times greater than the current costs for a carrier and its air wing, or $15 to $20 billion if straight-line cost projections are used.[1]

The other alternative to a true super carrier could be a new class of ship design between the destroyer and the carrier, perhaps displacing 20,000 to 50,000 tons, that would replace the destroyer, carrier, and the amphibious assault ship. This ship would be a multipurpose surface combatant armed with long-range missiles, ASW systems, tactical aviation units of some type, and amphibious capability. Clearly, the ship would be configured to emphasize one or more of these combat roles, harkening back to the sea-control ship of an earlier era, and would include Aegis; long-range cruise missiles; some form of manned or unmanned aircraft for strike, ASW, and defense; and

---

1. Currently, a carrier and its air wing each cost about $3.5 billion, or $7 billion total. Assuming a 250,000-ton carrier at $6 billion and 250 aircraft at $10 billion, an approximate cost range is $15 to $20 billion.

a landing force that the ship could support. This new class would have excellent application to non-Soviet threat scenarios.

In considering a new multipurpose surface combatant, the Navy must evaluate how an alternative or equivalent in combat power to a CVBG can be configured. There may be no clear CVBG-equivalent without a carrier; however, there will probably be situations in which all the combat power of a CVBG is not needed and perhaps one-half or two-thirds of a battle group will suffice.

At the same time, new operational thinking can be extended to battle-force alternatives. A general rule of thumb has been that three or four carriers formed the critical mass needed in high-threat operations. With that number, large amounts of combat power for both strike and defense could be generated on an around-the-clock basis. Thus, a future battle-force equivalent might be constituted around only one or two, or even no, aircraft carriers, using instead a larger number of missile-armed large combatants supported by Aegis cruisers, destroyers, and SSNs. Furthermore, these equivalent forces could be used to carry out whatever forward deployments are deemed necessary.

DOMESTIC ENVIRONMENT ANSWERS

Of all the questions, the ones posed by the domestic environment may prove to be the most perplexing. In that regard, the Navy must learn to operate in a domestic environment perhaps untainted by fresh scent of Soviet threat and overloaded with new competing priorities for national security resources. Not only will new means of convincing the White House and OSD of maritime requirements be needed, but Congress and the American public are likely to respond more favorably to alternative strategies for making the maritime case.

The Navy has three broad options. First, it can stonewall, drawing arbitrary although well-thought-out lines and resisting any and all attempts to reduce maritime capability in the future, including arms control. Clearly, this position worked well over the past decade. If, as this writer believes, this option will not work in the next decade as receding threats and budgets drive force levels lower, another course must be taken.

A second approach is that of naval *glasnost*, making the strongest case possible but gracefully accepting the decision of *vox populi* as made by Congress. Although, in an era of declining budgets, this approach could maximize budget share of a smaller pie, it could dilute naval control over naval matters by relegating them to a highly amorphous Congress. That result could be undesirable.

The third approach is a combination of the previous two approaches. This strategy accepts the formulation that times have changed and the Navy is already changing in response. The Navy would not only be open to but would gently solicit all legitimate concepts for future direction. Moreover, it would make a good-faith effort to examine these directions. The Navy would define core forces, with and without a Soviet threat, and, after presenting a tradeoff analysis among costs, capabilities, and mission performance, would stand fast on those lower limits.

No matter which course the Navy chooses, however, the next version of the maritime strategy may best be designed with the domestic environment paramount.

DEFENSE INFRASTRUCTURE ANSWERS

Despite the rigors of dealing with the strategic, domestic, and operational quandaries, and despite how well or badly they are resolved, unless the infrastructure can be made to fit, we will be left with an anemic force at sea that cannot be adequately supported from the shore. The first order is for the Navy to assess how different resource strategies based on readiness and investment will affect the infrastructure and determine the likely consequences.

An ideal approach is to select a minimally acceptable force structure—say 12 CVBGs and 450 ships—and, after accounting for readiness, determine what portion of resources remained for research, development, modernization, and acquisition. The problem is that, in all likelihood, the future defense budget will not simultaneously support that size force structure and an investment strategy. Hence, if the Soviet Union can be induced to reduce its forces, the dilemma could be eased.

Interestingly, at the floor level of 8 to 9 CVBGs and a $70- to $75-billion-a-year budget, which assumes a minimal Soviet threat, both a readiness and investment strategy can be pursued. The issue rests with how to move from the uncertainties of today to a future steady and stable state.

The supporting basing infrastructure is supercharged by domestic politics. The Navy currently has over 500 bases, stations, facilities, and pieces of property in CONUS and nearly 90 overseas. At home, domestic politics make base closure enormously difficult at best. Overseas, symbolism and diplomatic reality are often obstacles to reducing those facilities as well. To respond to these pressures, the Navy must conduct a zero-based review of what basing and infrastructure are essential for given force levels. This review must be presented in a comprehensive package, along with future-force-level capability tradeoffs, to OSD and the White House and then to Congress and the public. From that package, a single series of decisions could be made to tie in the strategic and policy choices with tradeoff analyses of what those forces could and could not do and what supporting infrastructure is required. Without that degree of rigor and completeness, the results are likely to be chaotic.

The personnel quandary, like the others, is new. On the one hand, the major issues in manning the Navy may rest more in determining what and how personnel are turned away and may resort to other remedies for redress, rather than in the traditional concern of being able to recruit sufficient numbers of qualified people. This issue of excess supply applies to each of the services, and there well could be court cases, class action suits, and Congressional mandates for quotas to ensure equal opportunity.

These pressures from the personnel supply and quantity side will complicate the demand and quality side of recruitment and retention. As the service contracts, as weapon systems require greater technical skills, and as political reality dictates greater levels of competence in carrying out missions, higher quality personnel will naturally be required. Even though the manpower pool of 17- to 18-year-olds begins to increase after 1993, how well the services will be able to compete with the private sector for quality recruits is questionable.

On top of that, should large drawdowns in personnel be required, the services will have to have involuntary separations. Dealing with involuntary separation when service personnel have legal and binding contracts with the government could be immensely difficult, although this was done in the 1920s and 1930s as a result of the Depression. Thus, in addition to a comprehensive review of the other quandaries and the positing of options, these new, emerging personnel realities must be addressed.

Additionally, the Navy may resolve some future personnel problems by determining how its forces might be manned minimally in peace and filled out in war. A surface combatant could be appropriately designed and manned to fulfill its peacetime and contingency functions with 50 sailors and augmented in conflict for its wartime damage control, replenishment, and battle-station endurance needs with an additional 100 to 150 sailors.

The final infrastructure issue deals with the collection and analysis of intelligence. In the past, when the Soviet threat dominated our thinking and planning, highly covert, classified, and usually expensive means of reconnaissance and spying were used. Now that threats are becoming more diffuse, however, this general approach based on Soviet collection needs will be insufficient. Furthermore, because new threats may arise from the most unexpected sources, highly classified and expensive overhead collection means may be less important than regional experts who can assemble other forms of data, including personal knowledge of key leaderships and personalities, to assess a threat.

Interestingly, the solution is quite simple. The Navy should develop regional and functional expertise to deal with expanded collection and analysis needs. Rather than use a traditional approach of moving people in and out of these duties, however, which was the case when intelligence could focus on a single threat, expertise should be built and kept in that specialty with advancement and promotion inherent in regional or functional assignments.

In other words, if Latin or Central America were a region for this type of focus, a handful of aspiring specialists would be obtained and given those duties as their career. They would get to know the key officials in the region, the navies, and other services and would be able to provide accurate and up-to-date assessments as needed. In addition, some of these officers would be assigned, on a rotating basis, to operational staffs at sea.

CHARTING THE FUTURE

To summarize the results of using this strategic compass to chart future courses and speeds, the Navy needs to conduct a comprehensive review of how it will be used in the future, how that use matches national needs and national support, how alternative future budget levels will affect capability, how that capability tradeoff affects commitments, and how the supporting infrastructure can be made to fit the ultimate choices that are made about the future size and shape of the Navy.

12

Conclusion: Flying Four Battle Ensigns for the Future

For those who disbelieve that the ship of state has sailed into a minefield of change in which both safe navigation and sound damage-control practices are essential, consider what has transpired during the 12-month period from February 1990 to February 1991.[1] In 1990, debate over the state of the Cold War and the depth of the U.S.-Soviet rapprochement was still intense. Although the Berlin Wall had crumbled, there was no clear agreement over the future shape of a unified Germany, and Soviet actions and intent were partially, if not substantially, suspect. In the United States, the economy was not viewed as grievously ill, oil was about $20 a barrel, and the budget deficit projected for 1990 was less than $100 billion.

Despite America's 1989 Christmas intervention in Panama to remove Manuel Noriega, the combination of geography and common sense still suggested that maritime forces would emerge as the preferred national military instrument of policy in dealing with this changing world. Thus, the Navy and Marine Corps maintained serious aspirations for acquiring their 600 ships.

One year later, the strategic preference for maritime forces was receding and the argument for heavy, movable ground and air forces, transported in fast sealift and escorted by the Navy, seemed increasingly relevant. Although the Navy and Marine Corps are planning for 450 ships, short of war or crisis, the fiscal reality is that DON can only afford about 350 ships over the long term if they are postured similar to today's forces. Who knows what next year may bring.

In this environment, more than mere lip service in acknowledging the profoundness of these changing circumstances

---

1. That one-year periods are insufficient for determining change is obvious. The point is that 1990 became the outlet for these profound changes, many of which were decades in the making.

is needed. Indeed, even understanding the mechanisms and consequences of change will prove insufficient. Action is essential. Furthermore, these actions must include safe navigation and damage control, for, without them, the result will be a smaller, less capable, more inefficient force.[1] This is a risk the nation cannot accept.

Since the days of Sir Francis Drake, in time of war the Royal Navy has held to the tradition of flying several ensigns when sailing in harm's way so that, if one or more of the ensigns were carried away in battle, the enemy could never mistakenly assume British colors had been struck. As the 21st century approaches, this is a good tradition to follow in making the case for the Navy and Marine Corps and for U.S. maritime power. Four battle ensigns are needed.

One ensign must fly atop the roles and missions of the sea services and the public's understanding of what maritime forces can and must do to protect the nation's interests and well-being.

A second ensign must be broken over the analytical justification that shows the tradeoffs among various future maritime force structures driven by different levels of budgets and what those forces can and cannot achieve in carrying out the nation's maritime responsibilities.

A third ensign must fly over the mast that represents the domestic environment, an area that is becoming increasingly dominant in defining the limits and meaning of national security in terms of both process of government and the public's support for national defense.

The fourth ensign must sit atop the need for rationalizing the supporting infrastructure base on which maritime force rests. Both politically and bureaucratically, these ensigns will be holed and made bloody in the ensuing debates over defense.

---

1. Refer again to *Conventional Force Structure at a Crossroads*. In every case, when cuts were made more or less equally to preserve the current structure of forces and only to reduce them, the losses in aggregate capability were larger than when prioritization occurred. The flaw with the latter approach, however, is that a particular capability may be eliminated or reduced that is needed later. Unfortunately, we cannot have it both ways.

In raising these colors, the Secretary of Defense, the Secretary of the Navy, the CNO, and the Commandant of the Marine Corps should offer the following arguments and reasoning to underwrite the credibility and legitimacy of these metaphorical ensigns and to define the future course and speed of the service.

Our view of national security has been changed principally by the extraordinary diffusion of all forms of power that has diluted and weakened the authority, influence, and power of the United States and the Soviet Union. The principal result is that the focus of security is shifting from military and strategic terms towards economic factors. The most dramatic manifestation has been in the profound changes in the Soviet empire and the Soviet Union.

The United States, however, has also been swept by profound although less visible change. The clearest expression is in the diminution of U.S. economic strength, and the problem is brought home by our seeming ineptitude in dealing with the federal budget. An outcome of "Gorbaschina" and "budget malaise" will be less defense expenditure. Unfortunately, other persistent and dangerous threats have not been eliminated. Indeed, some are growing and others are ambiguous, difficult to predict, and, therefore, more treacherous to deal with in advance.

The strategic issue for the nation is dealing with this period of transition while the fading shadow of Soviet military power tends to obscure the damage it still can do. As a result, Soviet threat-based arguments to justify future levels of defense spending will become increasingly harder to support.

For the Navy and Marine Corps, the key challenge for this decade will be responding to these changes and to the strategic, domestic, operational, and infrastructure questions raised by this era of transition. The strategic rationale for the Navy and Marine Corps will fail if it rests exclusively on the basis that the public automatically and intuitively will accept the argument that our geography must favor maritime forces. The Navy will have to make a more compelling and plausible case. Budget realities will not help. As this decade progresses, budgets of $50 to $70 billion a year (in FY 1991 dollars) for the

Navy could represent the upper limits of national defense resource allocation.

One test will rest in determining whether any strategic
leverage can be gained from this inevitable and unavoidable
naval contraction and whether it can be used to obtain a satisfactory response from the USSR that leads to a less threatening Soviet posture. A less-threatening Soviet maritime posture
would be one that emphasizes direct defense of the homeland
and therefore requires far fewer forces. A capable nuclear
deterrent with a protective force of about 100 SSNs or less and
a modicum of surface ships and aviation units seems a stable
objective. This level also implies near numerical equality in
SSNs at least with U.S. goals and naturally flows from equal
levels of forces specified in the CFE Treaty. The maintenance
of a small amphibious capability is also in keeping with genuine Soviet interests. The question is whether the Soviet Union
will reduce its force levels on a unilateral or bilateral basis and
how the U.S. Navy and Marine Corps should be strategically
postured.

Clearly, given a realistic, if not highly optimistic, assessment of future defense spending, the best the Navy can hope
for is force levels based on 12 CVBGs and about 450 ships.
Against this ceiling, the Navy has to deal with Soviet and non-
Soviet contingencies. Regarding the latter, sizing of capability
can proceed either from prescient identification of future
threats, which is extremely difficult both to do and to sell, or
from establishing operational criteria that determine requisite
structure. It seems logical and plausible that the ability to respond simultaneously to a crisis in each hemisphere should
form the planning criterion; however, debate should focus on
the criterion from which forces flow and not on the forces
themselves.

As argued earlier, this leads to a core force of 8 to
9 CVBGs or their equivalents, 50 to 60 SSNs, 100 surface combatants, 2 MEBs, 10 Trident SSBNs, and a Navy of about
300 to 350 ships. This Navy and Marine Corps could be sustained at an annual outlay of about $70 billion. This force
would deal with non-Soviet contingencies and serve as a
residual in the event of a resurgence of the Soviet threat.

The delta (i.e., the 4- to 5-CVBG and 100-ship difference between today's force and the core force) would be used as the fleet-in-being to influence the transition of Soviet maritime power or to provide insurance until our perceptions change. Whether this force would be placed in cadre, reserve, or less active status is an important issue to be determined by subsequent study.

In designing the future core force, the issue of whether maritime forces are returning to the traditional support role for the battle ashore will be paramount. In 1991, that issue is not fully clear. In shifting to possible CVBG alternatives and a new class of combatant in the 20,000- to 50,000-ton-displacement range that can be modularized, however, sufficient flexibility should be maintained to cope with the huge uncertainties that lie ahead.

Thus, in addition to traditional roles of preventing war, projecting power, promoting peace, and protecting U.S. interests, the U.S. Navy must act as a force for stability and for ensuring a safe transition to this new era. A subset is the use of the Navy as a fleet-in-being to assist in filling these roles.

One other action the Navy should take beyond everything else is a root-and-branch review of future directions and options. This essential review must be predicated on the basis that, whatever Navy emerges, that Navy must be able and ready to sail in harm's way. Harm's way, too, must be redefined to account for these new operational realities and stringencies. Although, at present, this author is not certain how extensive the shift will be from CVBGs to ground- and land-based forces as the principal projection-of-power instrument, we must be prepared for this prospect. Therefore, most importantly, deriving tradeoffs that demonstrate what alternative navies can and cannot provide in defending the nation's interests becomes the overriding need in this uncertain new world. In addition, all this must be tied into the supporting infrastructure, because, unless that structure can be modernized and revitalized, any future Navy will not be able to guarantee carrying out its tasks effectively or successfully.

Part of this review must include the painful decisions required in changing decades of process and culture. In this regard, it is time that the powerful platform barons dominating the three warfare specialties be combined under a single platform sponsor whose principal function will be implementing the decisions and directions determined by the interaction of strategy, policy, budget, and warfare requirements. This change will not come easily, if at all. Despite the traditional and past usefulness of this platform-oriented organizational structure, however, the tough choices required by budget and operational realities will no longer permit balanced division of resources among air, surface, and subsurface warfare areas. To facilitate making these tough choices, the past authority and power of the platform sponsors will have to be limited. Otherwise, the future Navy may not be appropriately designed and structured to meet its requirements.

Never, in peacetime, have the challenges been more daunting. Never, in peacetime, have the opportunities been greater. The outcome—the course we set and the speed we take—is in our own hands, provided we are not overawed by the tasks ahead and not musclebound by past rationale and policies unsuited for this brave, new future world.

Postscript: Reflections on the Gulf War

The war in the Gulf is over, at least as far as Operation Desert Storm is concerned. The overwhelming and dazzling military victory of the U.S.-led allied coalition ejected Iraq from Kuwait in 100 hours of ground offensive and turned the fourth largest army in the world into a battered and beaten rabble. Most analysts were surprised by the lightning quickness of the campaign, the relatively tiny number of allied casualties suffered, and Iraq's failure to put up much of a fight. The American public was euphoric and many critics were disarmed by the exemplary performance of U.S. weapons systems and the senior officers commanding those forces.

Now, however, a difficult peace is at hand or, more correctly, a transition period is under way that will determine the future degree (or lack) of stability and security in the region. A very careful military lessons-learned process has been undertaken under the direct mandate of the Chairman of the JCS to ensure objectivity and comprehensiveness. As the public euphoria over the victory (and the extraordinary popularity of George Bush) recedes, the temptation to rush to judgment to deduce so-called military lessons while the memory of the war remains fresh will be difficult to resist. Indeed, within the Pentagon, there were early signs of maneuvering by the services either to exploit their particular contribution to the success or to block such attempts by others. Fortunately, Secretary Cheney and Chairman Powell have tried to exorcise these self-serving maneuvers. Time will tell how well they succeed.

There are, one expects, many points to be learned or relearned from the Gulf experience. To temper a premature rush to judgment, however, it is essential that certain warnings be posted and carefully heeded. Collectively, these warnings draw attention to an immediate danger and an opportunity, the extraordinary uniqueness of the region and the circumstances of this war, and the need for a comprehensive and ruthlessly objective analytical method in deriving any lessons. Put another way, without any of these admonishments, it would be simple, misleading, and irrelevant to use an unadulterated, first cut of the Gulf War as a test for validating virtually anything (including what has been argued for in this book about the future direction of the Navy and Marine Corps). Clearly, absent caveats and context, a grade of A+ could be assigned. Determining what grade is really justified in evaluating performance and lessons is a different and much more important matter. The fact is that virtually all U.S. systems seemed to perform well. Months of acclimation, preparation, training, and rehearsal took place without enemy inhibition or attack. Despite the heroism and conduct of allied forces, Iraq simply lacked the resolve and competence to resist. This failure to fight complicates analysis and derivation of meaningful lessons learned, especially in a world in which future defense budgets are not going to permit the acquisition of large numbers of different and expensive weapon systems regardless of their effectiveness. This somber assessment should condition us to look at the war with even greater intensity so that we derive all we can from a conflict in which rigorous, objective analysis may be hard to apply to the circumstances and available data.

That an immediate danger and an opportunity exist in the aftermath of the war is no surprise. The principal danger rests in the fact that Operations Desert Shield and Desert Storm provided a temporary fiscal balloon that kept force levels funded at current levels while long-term planning is headed towards at least a 25-percent cut. Now that the war and this special funding have ended, this bubble will burst and the forces must free-fall back to the planned and far lower levels that are affordable. Thus, the services will have to make dramatic cuts to account for this artificial boost of the war and to accommodate to the decline that was otherwise in train. In the case of the Army, for example, cuts of 50,000 personnel in both FYs 1991 and 1992 as well as the 30,000 troops added for the war must still take place. Although Congress will provide some relief, at the end of the day, the Army will have to slash about

150,000 personnel. These dislocations will be severe for each of the services. Furthermore, Congressionally approved relaxations in regulating endstrength were not matched by additional budget authority. Thus, to pay the costs for those service personnel, including separation, the services will have to cut from other programs.

The rare opportunity rests in exploiting the high regard the public and Congress currently hold for the forces and their performance in this war. Budgets will not benefit from this good will because the threat has passed and the government is already under too much debt to present any fiscal reward to DOD as a measure of national gratitude. The decision-making and acquisition processes, however, could be ripe for reform. Assuming this case for reform still can be made over the next months, the Navy would be wise to consider a dramatic plan to revitalize and streamline all aspects of the service in preparation for this turbulent and resource-limited future and use this opportunity to mount an assault on Congress to rectify many of the ills of the decision-making and acquisition processes that are so inefficient and wasteful. Clearly, this innovative and wide-ranging program can only be accomplished with and through the support of OSD and the administration. The recommendations made in earlier chapters, or ones like them, should form the basis for this comprehensive yet sweeping approach. The iron has never been hotter for striking. We may not have another opportunity for such sweeping reform in our lifetime.

Regarding the absolute uniqueness of the region, there is no other area in the world that combines the strategic, economic, and political importance, volatility, and dependencies of the Gulf. Inter-Arab conflict, fundamental Islam, advanced weapons (including agents of mass destruction), the Arab-Israeli-Palestinian impasse, and oil intersect with the most vital interests of East and West. Had Kuwait exported only bananas and not oil, it is doubtful that anyone would have acted forcibly to evict Iraq.

Second, the West had decades of intimate involvement in the region, dating back to the turn of this century. The United States has had a continuous naval presence in the Gulf since

1949. In 1961, shortly after Kuwait's independence, the British deterred Iraqi threats of annexation with a battalion of Royal Marines and an aircraft carrier that had been sent into the Gulf. Since then, few regions have had such extensive and on-going contingency planning thrust on them. In the 1970s, the Rapid Deployment Force was created to respond to Soviet aggression. In the 1980s, this force became U.S. Central Command, which added to its Soviet focus potential regional threats, specifically an expansionary Iran. An ambitious Iraq, however, was far from discounted. In fact, Central Command had just finished a planning exercise based on an Iraqi invasion of Kuwait days before Saddam Hussein actually struck.

Third, given the extensive infrastructure in Western Europe and Korea, there is no other region in the world that is as remotely conducive to the introduction of large numbers of U.S. ground and air forces as is Saudi Arabia. This infrastructure was the result of decades of smart, bipartisan U.S. policy and planning in the Gulf. Throughout much of the Cold War, policy was based on "two pillars"—Iran (in the days of the Shah) and Saudi Arabia—who received enormous amounts of U.S. arms and who were meant to preserve regional stability by counterbalancing other, would-be aspirants in the region, particularly the Soviets.

Even before the Shah fell in 1979, the United States had poured thousands of tons of concrete in Saudi Arabia for runways, revetments, and storage sites as a deterrent and safeguard against Soviet aggression. After Iran became actively hostile, the military infrastructure of Saudi Arabia was strengthened even more. Thus, the deploying forces of Desert Shield found that prepositioning and indigenous support in Saudi Arabia were advanced and accommodating and greatly eased the vast logistics burdens in transporting half a million troops and equipment. Indeed, the ability of Saudi facilities to absorb this buildup probably exceeded our ability to deploy troops into the region.

Finally, the Saudis operate advanced U.S. equipment, including F-15s and the Airborne Warning and Control System (AWACS), and many Saudis were trained in or by the United States. Thus, air operations were relatively easy to synchronize.

Moreover, the Saudis already owned large amounts of ordnance that was designed for and could be used by the United States. Deployment of vast numbers of U.S. forces anywhere else with such relative ease and speed would not be as easy or perhaps even possible. Hence, the use of land-based air and large numbers of ground forces cannot be replicated to a similar extent anywhere else in the world outside of Europe and Korea.

For these and other reasons, the Gulf is unique. This uniqueness that was translated into U.S. planning—area familiarity, access to forward basing and logistics support, and a largely U.S.-trained and -equipped host nation—made this operation far more practical and possible. As mentioned, allied forces had months to prepare, train, and rehearse. Without this access and local infrastructure, neither Operation Desert Shield nor Desert Storm would have been remotely as feasible and surely neither would have been as effective and cost free.

To address the above caveats and cautions, it is essential that a carefully planned and highly objective analytical methodology be put in place to assess the conduct, performance, and lessons of Desert Shield and Desert Storm across the relevant political, strategic, military, tactical, and operational boundaries. A chronological sequencing for this analysis is important and should be divided into three phases.

The first phase is the buildup period before the August 2nd invasion. The issues of deterring Saddam Hussein's ambitions, detecting and responding to Iraq's true intent, and the utility or disutility of actions that might have prevented the attack are central to this part of the analysis. The second phase should examine Desert Shield and Desert Storm along the lines of classical military and strategic analysis. Finally, the third and most difficult phase involves evaluation of the peace that follows. This final evaluation may take years before the reverberations settle out and yield adequate responses to the vital question of risk-reward and, in subsequent analysis, whether the fruits of a decisive military victory were sweetened or spoiled by the geo-strategic and political conditions that followed.

To complement this analysis, there needs to be a fourth category of what-ifs? (i.e., hypothetical questions with answers that could cause us to reinforce or revise any preliminary lessons learned). For example, what if Iraq had fought; what if U.S. war planners had used different operational assumptions and different strategies and tactics (e.g., beginning the bombing campaign in the south against Iraq's army first); and what if Iraq had had effective means such as cruise missiles to attack air bases in Saudi Arabia other than the ineffective Scuds? Although this list could be endless and perhaps dangerous if allowed to wander too far afield, this may be the most efficient means of assessing the real lessons to be learned. The best single model for assessing many of the military aspects of the war is perhaps the Strategic Bombing Survey that scrupulously dissected Germany and Japan after their defeats.

With these strictures, what can be said in the aftermath of the Gulf War that is relevant and scrupulously avoids the trap of instant and incorrect analysis (analysis like that following the October 1973 Arab-Israeli War which concluded the day of the tank was over)? The earlier framework of strategy, the domestic environment, defense infrastructure, and operations provide a basis for establishing some tentative conclusions about the war and the peace.

First, in terms of strategy, our long-term contingency planning in preparing for conflict in the Gulf was validated. Planning for the peace, however, poses a complex and highly demanding test. For better or worse, the United States will be consigned a much more visible and permanent presence as a guarantor of whatever passes for regional stability both in the Gulf and Middle East. The return of America's military forces home as quickly as possible following the successful resolution of the conflict will be an overriding priority. The nature of the peace and post-war settlement, however, particularly as a hostile Saddam Hussein remains in power and refuses to abdicate, could mandate permanent stationing of considerable numbers of forces on the ground and at sea to defend Kuwait and the Royal Kingdom from another round of aggression.

The embargo and blockade are directly related to Iraq's acceptance of the UN cease-fire agreement. Without the presence of sufficiently credible numbers of U.S. forces, a UN or Arab League peacekeeping mission could not absolutely ensure the peace. Although the rout of Iraq's army and the subsequent unrest in Iraq could depose Saddam Hussein, his successor would not automatically be better disposed to peace and stability in the Gulf, a lesson we learned after the overthrow of the Shah of Iran.

Meanwhile, having repelled Iraq's illegal occupation of Kuwait, the UN may no longer stand by indefinitely and take no steps whatsoever to deal with the Israeli occupation of the West Bank and Gaza, which has been in violation of UN Resolution 242 since 1967. Any attempt to negotiate or leverage a solution to the Arab-Israeli-Palestinian impasse will likely include stationing additional peacekeeping forces in the region, and it will be difficult to structure an effective peacekeeping force without U.S. support and participation.

Assuming events within the USSR do not rekindle fears of a Soviet military threat to Western Europe, it would not be implausible to see a shift in the United States' strategic-military centroid from Europe to the Persian Gulf and Middle East. Although the prospect of permanently stationing 300,000 U.S. troops (our past level in Europe) in that region appears negligible, there is little doubt that forces beyond the size and scope of the past peacetime U.S. naval presence in the Middle East Force will be needed. Saudi Arabia, not unlike Israel, has great sensitivity and ambivalence about any U.S. forces stationed within its borders. Certainly, the Royal Kingdom will not be as hospitable a host as Europe was for U.S. GIs. Perhaps Kuwait will be more welcoming, but the influence of a vehement Iran should not be underestimated in its opposition to a long-term U.S. Gulf presence on the ground.

The stationing of U.S. forces in the Gulf poses a further strategic dilemma. Although ground forces are militarily more relevant as a direct defense barrier against invasion, the logistical, support, infrastructure, and cultural costs of such a deployment are heavy and could be unaffordable. We may have no choice. On the other hand, maritime forces are self-contained and automatically transport a cultural and living environment over international waters that is not subject to the same thorny questions of sovereignty and access as bases ashore. There are clear political savings to this type of sea deployment.

One implication is that the international peacekeeping forces ashore could be relatively few in number (a tripwire force) and could rely on reinforcement, prepositioned equipment, and perhaps a strong air component supported by a continuously present afloat Navy-Marine Corps amphibious-strike force. This type of deployment could free up the bulk of U.S. ground and air forces for assignment elsewhere (although rapid reinforcement would remain a vital mission), but could restrict maritime flexibility by putting such an uneven operational load on maintaining deployments in this one region. The reverse configuration (i.e., larger ground and air forces with a smaller but reinforceable naval presence) would tie down the bulk of U.S. heavy forces in the region, limit flexibility elsewhere, and increase the economic cost. Perhaps most significantly, this configuration could impose enormous political and cultural costs that would have to be borne by the host nations.

Thus, the traditional strategic planning model for U.S. forces probably will be revised. The commitment in Europe will be considerably downgraded. Fewer forces will be stationed there and reinforcement and regeneration of capability for Europe will be based on long warning time scenarios. The Gulf will assume more importance as the rationale for U.S. force structure, replacing Europe in part but at much lower numbers of forces. Because, outside of Europe and Korea, there are no other comparable flash points on the globe where large-scale combat involving U.S. forces is plausible or likely, contingency requirements are likely to center on small wars and contingency crises of a local nature. These can be handled by relatively few U.S. forces as in the Grenada and Panama interventions.

This model can clarify the future rationale for maritime forces but will not establish the case for the necessary numbers and aggregate military capability that may be required. Along the lines of making a case for this force rationale, U.S. maritime forces will serve as an insurance policy to safeguard the transition period and the change in Soviet threat. Beyond the Soviet threat, and as a minimum, maritime force must be ready to respond to crises and contingencies elsewhere. This capability leads to fixing the numbers and capability needed. The criterion of responding to two simultaneous (non-Soviet) crises is recommended as the requirement to define the amount of future capability needed outside conflict with and deterrence of the USSR. The forces to meet these needs would have been sufficient to deal with the current Gulf War. In addition, maritime forces will no doubt be deployed as part of a Gulf peace settlement.

Two final strategic points: (1) in conditions where an external coalition of unified states is absolutely vital to a successful outcome, the performance of the Bush administration in fashioning such an alliance is textbook perfect, and (2) it will take time to determine whether the war ultimately was in our best strategic interests. The benefits of evicting Saddam Hussein and demonstrating the diplomatic and military power of the United States must be balanced against whatever costs and advantages accrue from the peace.

Domestically, there are certain lessons that are already visible. First, the fact that it took a prior UN resolution to authorize the use of force as a means of convincing a reluctant Congress to support the administration should not be overlooked. This suggests that executive-congressional relations will invariably be operating at cross-purposes and gives partial support to the argument that government is not getting any smoother in its operation. If a difficult peace follows, disharmony in government can only worsen.

More to the point, the so-called high-technology war, fought almost like a video game with the perception of antiseptic accuracy and virtually no bloodshed (at least in the air campaign to neutralize Iraq's strategic and tactical power), has created an unfortunate domestic impression that cost-free combat is indeed emerging, particularly in conditions of Third World conflict. The actual facts, namely, that the bulk of military technology was not "cutting edge," that the complete defeat of Iraq's air force, air defenses, and navy pitted virtually absolute U.S. and coalition superiority against the adversary's inferiority and that, budget-wise, little of this awesome striking power is inexpensive, will ultimately become more obvious and set the limits for defining the consequences for the debate over future force structure. The public, however, appears to have been conditioned to the prospect of war being decisive, quick, clean, efficient and, from our perspective, almost cost free. This is neither a correct nor a useful lesson.

The lesson to be drawn by the Navy is that a clear, objective, concise case must be made to the public that puts this conflict into the proper perspective. Ensuring this objectivity will be difficult because the justifiable pride and relief over the superior performance of our sailors and marines and their equipment can lead to a one-sided rendition of what happened. Imbalance in assessment is not in the Navy's interest because this could exacerbate interservice rivalry over who did best that is likely to harm rather than help DOD and reinforce the public attitude that modern war is only a giant Nintendo game.

The defense infrastructure is the most difficult category for which to draw immediate lessons with one exception: the intelligence base. Regarding intelligence, the arguments made for regional specialists have been validated. The allies lacked specific, advanced intelligence on Iraq. Although the overestimates of Iraqi military ability were prudent for planning, there needs to be a more accurate assessment mechanism, not only for that region but for other regions as well.

The largest potentially lasting lesson pertains to using whatever opportunity has been created by the enhanced trust and confidence of the public and Congress for the military to overhaul the decision-making and acquisition processes. Unless sufficient headway is made there, the nation will continue to suffer from enormous costs in time and money in acquiring the weapons of war.

It is the area of operations, however, that is likely to cause the greatest controversy. As is well understood, the combination of U.S. high performance and Iraqi capitulation is likely to distort lessons learned. For example, the F-117A stealth aircraft carried out its missions entirely undetected. This fact will be used to argue for the B-2. The Patriot antimissile missile was highly effective in hitting Scuds. That success will be used to justify continuing SDI. The same type of operationally derived arguments will apply across many new systems.

The fact of the matter is that the great success of both systems is largely irrelevant to the technical arguments for either the B-2 or SDI. All of our aircraft were able to penetrate Iraq's defenses and SDI was never meant to have capability against relatively low-flying ballistic missiles such as the Scud. Furthermore, given the overwhelming quality of U.S. systems, the key operational question may be whether the United States needs to move quite so quickly in upgrading its systems given the huge technical and operational edge held over likely Third World adversaries.

The most difficult task the services may have in any lessons-learned review is evaluating doctrine or service strategy. *Doctrine*—defined to mean the operational art of conducting battle—is holy writ because it is central to the systems the services obtain, to preparations and training for war, and to maintaining the professional ethos and self-confidence crucial to winning in war. The Army, for example, places its doctrine in terms of the air-land battle, that is, a coordinated air-ground combined-arms campaign that consists of firepower, mobility, and deception throughout the theater of operations. The Air Force believes in strategic bombing as the basis for breaking an adversary. The Navy's maritime superiority, while not as classical a doctrine as those of the other services because the Navy does not use the term similarly, likewise calls for commanding the seas in and around the theater to give the allies unimpeded access. In each case, the services should take a careful, agnostic look at the Gulf War, not so much to prove their doctrine's worth but to determine whether a fair test of doctrine really took place.

For the Navy and Marine Corps, there are several immediate lessons. First, contingency operations are likely to require doing the unimaginable: deploying four carriers in confined waters and using two Marine divisions as heavy ground forces without the benefit of an amphibious assault. This means there must be even more imaginative training and planning in the future to take on still other contingent possibilities.

Second, despite the assertions to the contrary about the war being a combined-arms victory, in fact, ground-based forces no doubt could have prevailed by themselves once they arrived in sufficient numbers. Moreover, had ground bases not been as readily available, there is every likelihood that sea forces could have prevailed (certainly in winning the air campaign and possibly in retaking Kuwait) because Iraq probably would have still declined to fight. The uniqueness of the region and the nature of this conflict must be fully understood and incorporated into the lessons-learned analysis that will follow.

Third, in these circumstances, not only will obvious gaps in mine countermeasures need to be addressed yet again, but shallow-water ASW and defense against cruise missiles will become reinforced operational needs. Clearly, had Iraq possessed diesel submarines and a large number of relatively stealthy cruise missiles, the war at sea could have been a very bloody one. Making progress in changing budget and program priorities to accommodate these needs, however, will still be difficult.

The war is over. As ships and forces return home, the Navy and Marine Corps find that they were well prepared to sail into harm's way. Fortunately, this latest instance was less dangerous and costly than most rightly feared. Although it may be true that this war was the harbinger of a return to the prenuclear age in which projection of forces and units ashore becomes the Navy's central role again, it will take some time and study to draw this conclusion.

On the other hand, in this first crisis of the post-Cold War era (or of the New World Order), it was clear beyond doubt that sailing into harm's way continues to require capable, ready, and deployable forces that are highly trained and well led. The Gulf War has unequivocally supported and demonstrated the validity of those obvious and long-standing naval maxims that produce victory. In this new world, however, where fundamental change collides with fiscal imperatives and a domestic environment that will hold increasing if not dominant sway over the future of the Navy and Marine Corps, it would be a gross disservice to the nation's well-being to permit this broader planning reality and necessity to be obscured by overstating or misinterpreting what can and should be learned from the marvelously decisive victory in the Gulf.

There will always be a harm's way. Whether we will be as ready and able to respond remain the burning questions that must be effectively and affordably answered.

Appendix: Selected Military Capabilities of Selected States

Tables A-1 through A-5 summarize the general capabilities of selected Third World regional and local powers for combined operations (primarily ground and air) and air, land, and sea operations. The nuclear, chemical-biological, and ballistic and cruise missile capabilities (primarily surface-to-surface capabilities, but also including other offensive capabilities such as air-to-surface and ship-to-surface missiles) of these states are also shown. The tables demonstrate the range of capabilities that are present in the Third World and for which U.S. forces

Table A-1. Summary of military capabilities of selected regional and local powers in Southwest Asia

Nation	Capabilities						
	Combined	Air	Land	Sea	Nuclear	CBW	Missile
India	B	B	B	B	Y	U	CM, BM
Pakistan	B	E	B	E	Y/P	U	CM, BM
Afghanistan	B	E	B	N	N	U	BM

NOTES:
B = Battle capable (has the ability to conduct operations from days to weeks)
E = Engagement capable (has the ability to conduct operations for several days, at most)
S = Skirmishes only
Y = Yes
C = Capable
P = Potential
U = Unknown
N = No capability
CM = Cruise missile
BM = Ballistic missile.

Table A-2. Summary of military capabilities of selected regional and local powers in the Middle East

Nation	Capabilities						
	Combined	Air	Land	Sea	Nuclear	CBW	Missile
Israel	B	B	B	E	Y/C	Y/C	CM, BM
Syria	B	B/E	B	S	N	Y/C	CM, BM
Egypt	B	B	B	E	Y/P	Y/C	CM, BM
Libya	B/E	E	E	E/S	N	Y/P	CM, BM
Iran	B	S	B	E	Y/P	Y/P	CM, BM
Iraq[a]	B	B	S	S	Y/P	Y/C	CM, BM
Saudi Arabia	E	E	E	E/S	N	U	CM, BM
Jordan	B	E	B	N	N	N	N
Kuwait	E	S	E	S	N	N	CM, BM
Bahrain	S	S	S	S	N	N	N
Oman	S	S	S	S	N	N	N
Qatar	S	S	S	S	N	N	N
United Arab Emirates	S	S	S	S	N	N	N
North Yemen	E	S	E	S	N	U	BM
South Yemen	E	S	E/S	S	N	U	CM, BM

NOTES:

B = Battle capable (has the ability to conduct operations from days to weeks)
E = Engagement capable (has the ability to conduct operations for several days at most)
S = Skirmishes only
Y = Yes
C = Capable
P = Potential
U = Unknown
N = No capability
CM = Cruise missile
BM = Ballistic missile.

a. Iraq's military capabilities must be reassessed after the decisive defeat it suffered destroyed much or most of its equipment.

Table A-3. Summary of military capabilities of selected regional and local powers in Asia

Nation	Capabilities						
	Combined	Air	Land	Sea	Nuclear	CBW	Missile
Burma	S	S	E	S	N	Y/P	N
Indonesia	S/E	E	E	E	N	U	Y/P
Kampuchea	E	S	E	S	N	U	N
North Korea	B	B	B	E	Y/P	Y/C	CM, BM
South Korea	B	B	B	E	Y/P	Y/P	CM, BM
Laos	E	S	E	N	N	N	N
Philippines	E/S	S	S/E	S/E	N	N	N
Singapore	S	S	S	S	N	N	N
Taiwan	S	S	S	S	N	N	N
Thailand	E	E	E	E/S	N	U	CM, BM
Vietnam	B	B/E	B	S	N	Y/C	CM, BM

NOTES:

B	=	Battle capable (has the ability to conduct operations from days to weeks)
E	=	Engagement capable (has the ability to conduct operations for several days at most)
S	=	Skirmishes only
Y	=	Yes
C	=	Capable
P	=	Potential
U	=	Unknown
N	=	No capability
CM	=	Cruise missile
BM	=	Ballistic missile.

Table A-4. Summary of military capabilities of selected regional and local powers in Central and South America

Nation	Capabilities						
	Combined	Air	Land	Sea	Nuclear	CBW	Missile
Argentina	B	B/E	B	E	Y/P	U	CM, BM
Brazil	B	B	B	E	Y/P	U	CM, BM
Mexico	E	E	E	E	Y/P	U	N
Cuba	B	E	B	B/E	N	Y/C	CM, BM
Chile	E	E	E	E/S	N	U	N
Nicaragua	E	E	E	S/E	N	N	N
El Salvador	E	E	E	S	N	N	N
Guatemala	S	S	S/E	S	N	N	N
Honduras	S	S	E	S	N	N	N
Peru	E	E	E	E	N	N	N
Colombia	S	S	S	S	N	N	N
Venezuela	E	S/E	E	E	N	N	N
Panama	S	S	S	S	N	N	N

NOTES:
B   =   Battle capable (has the ability to conduct operations from days to weeks)
E   =   Engagement capable (has the ability to conduct operations for several days at most)
S   =   Skirmishes only
Y   =   Yes
C   =   Capable
P   =   Potential
U   =   Unknown
N   =   No capability
CM =   Cruise missile
BM =   Ballistic missile.

Table A-5. Summary of military capabilities of selected regional and local powers in Africa

Nation	Capabilities						
	Combined	Air	Land	Sea	Nuclear	CBW	Missile
Angola	B/E	E	E	E	N	N	N
South Africa	B	B	B	E	Y/C	U	U
Ethiopia	E	E	E	E	N	Y/P	CM, BM
Somalia	S/E	S	E	S	N	U	N
Algeria	E	E	E	E	N	U	CM, BM
Tunisia	E	S	E	E	N	N	N
Morocco	E	E	E	E	N	U	N
Chad	S	S	S	N	N	U	N
Sudan	S/E	S	E	S	N	N	N
Kenya	S	S	E	S	N	N	N
Congo	S	S	S	S	N	N	N
Nigeria	E	E	E	E	N	N	N
Zaire	S	S	S	N	N	N	N

NOTES:
B = Battle capable (has the ability to conduct operations from days to weeks)
E = Engagement capable (has the ability to conduct operations for several days at most)
S = Skirmishes only
Y = Yes
C = Capable
P = Potential
U = Unknown
N = No capability
CM = Cruise missile
BM = Ballistic missile.

must be prepared. The capabilities of these states to conduct combined operations is growing. Many of these states either have local arms industries or increasingly purchase weapons from other Third World suppliers.

The ability of a growing number of Third World states to use what are commonly termed *weapons of mass destruction* (namely, chemical and biological agents and, to a lesser extent, nuclear weapons) poses threats to U.S. interests. As these ominous capabilities grow, so too does the ability of an increasing number of Third World states to strike over greater distances. The spread of cruise and ballistic missiles adds another menacing dimension to the proliferation of chemical and biological warfare (CBW) and nuclear weapons.

CHEMICAL THREATS

Chemical weapons are used to cause casualties; decrease an opponent's effectiveness; restrict and channel the use of terrain; delay an opponent's advance; attack hardened targets; deny to the enemy the use of structures, material, and equipment; and attack an opponent's reserves, fire support, and logistical train. Because these weapons are cheap and effective (especially against an unwarned and unprepared enemy), they are attractive to some Third World states. In addition, delivery systems are available to many states, in the form of either artillery shells or spray mechanisms. The agents themselves can be, for the most part, manufactured from chemicals that are used in relatively common industrial processes, such as the manufacture of insecticides and pharmaceuticals.

There is a clear and actual threat of chemical warfare in the Third World. The Iran-Iraq war, as well as events in Southeast Asia and the Horn of Africa, prove both the capability and the willingness of nations to use chemical weapons. There are strong indications that other nations are contemplating such uses as well. Although there have been sporadic reports of chemical-weapon use over the last 25 years, inept use and a lack of coordinated operations are the principal reasons why these weapons have not had greater effect. Table A-6 lists instances of chemical-weapon use that have been confirmed by the U.S. government.

Table A-6. Use of chemical weapons

Country attacked	Time period	Description
Yemen	1963-67	Egypt is confirmed to have used chemical bombs (mustard gas) against Yemenese tribesmen.
Laos	1975-83	The Vietnamese used Soviet chemical and toxin weapons against the rebellious Hmong tribe, killing from 700 to 1,000 persons. Yellow rain, mycotoxins, became known when the U.S. State Department reported that samples of various agents and weapons were used in both Laos and Cambodia.
Kampuchea	1978-83	The U.S. government confirmed the use of chemical weapons by the Vietnamese against the Kampuchean resistance.
Afghanistan	1979-88	The Soviets and the Afghan army used a variety of chemical weapons against the Mujahedin guerrillas.
Iraq/Iran	1982-88	Iraq has developed production facilities for chemical weapons and has used chemical bombs against both Iran and the Kurds in Iraq. In early February 1986, an Iraqi attack resulted in the treatment of about 8,500 persons who suffered from sulfur mustard, nerve (tabun), and blood (cyanide) agents. The use of agents in Halabja focused world attention on this issue. UN teams verified the use of chemical weapons from 1984 to 1988.
Angola	1984-88	Cuban forces used mixes of mustard gas and nerve gas against UNITA (National Union for the Complete Independence of Angola).
Ethiopia	1975-?	Chemical weapons were used by Ethiopia against the Eritrean- and Somalia-backed rebels.
China/Vietnam	1978	Chemical weapons were used during the Sino-Vietnamese war.
Vietnam	1975-88	Chemical weapons were believed to have been used against Montagnard resistance forces.

Table A-7 lists the states possessing chemical weapons; however, the ease with which most of the agents can be manufactured in industrial plants involved in insecticide and other chemical production makes any list almost irrelevant. In short, any nation determined to equip its armed forces with a chemical capability can easily obtain the means to do so. The challenge for the U.S. military is (1) at the intelligence level, to know which states have chemical and biological weapons so that, if U.S. forces are to be used in the vicinity, they can be prepared, and (2) at the force structure level, to ensure that our troops are adequately protected, able to decontaminate themselves and their equipment, and able to receive proper, prompt medical attention. A competent chemical-biological defense capability must also include training.

Table A-7. States possessing chemical weapons

Known to possess	Reported to possess	Reported making progress
United States	Libya	Iran
USSR	Ethiopia	South Korea
France	Burma	
Iraq[a]	Thailand	
Egypt	China	
Syria	Taiwan	
Israel		
Vietnam		
North Korea		
Cuba		

a. Current Iraqi capabilities following the Gulf War must be categorized as uncertain.

TYPES OF CHEMICAL-BIOLOGICAL WEAPONS

More countries have chemical-weapon capabilities now than at any time in the past. This analysis will focus on identifying the agents and delivery systems available in most

Third World states. The following are the six classes of chemical agents:[1]

- *Casualty agents*—these chemical compounds are used in military operations to kill, incapacitate, or seriously injure personnel. The principal types that would be deployed in combat are blister, blood, choking, and nerve agents.

- *Incapacitating agents*—these compounds produce physiological or mental effects that make the enemy cease fighting without producing death or injury. These effects may persist for hours or days.

- *Vomiting agents*—vomiting agents are solid, arsenic-based chemicals that vaporize and condense when heated to form aerosols. These chemicals, although generally obsolete in the West (having been superseded by tear gas), are used for riot control and cause rapid vomiting.

- *Tear-gas agents*—these compounds cause transient flow of tears and irritation of the skin.

- *Biotoxins*—biotoxins are a class of agents between biological and chemical agents that are made from the poisonous by-products of microorganisms, plants, and animals. They are more stable than microorganisms because they are not living and are relatively easy to manufacture. The Soviet Union considers biotoxins the third generation of chemical weapons.

- *Biological agents*—biological agents are living organisms that attack the human body, disrupting its processes and endangering its health and well-being. These agents cause deliberate epidemics. The principal types are bacterial, fungal, rickettsial, and viral.

Tables A-8 through A-13 list chemical and biological agents according to the above distinctions and provide their symptoms

---

1. Herbicides will not be discussed.

Table A-8. Common casualty agents[a]

Category/designation	LCT_{50}	ICT_{50}	Symptoms/effects
Blister agents			
Mustard			
HD	10,000	200 eye	Inflammation, redness, blisters, permanent
	1,500	2,000 skin	damage to respiratory passages; symptoms occur in several hours to days
Arsenicals			
MD	3,000	25	Rapid rate of action; attacks blood, endocrine system and respiratory tract
PD	2,600 inhale	1,800 inhale	Induces vomiting in 1-2 minutes; immediate effect on eyes, toxic to skin in 30 minutes
		633 eyes	
		16 vomit	
ED	3,000 inhale	5-10 inhale	Immediate irritation, blistering delayed 2-4 hours; attacks lungs and eyes and causes extreme pain
(Lewisite)	1,200 inhale	300 eyes	Very toxic; attacks tissues, causes blood
	100,000 skin	1,500 skin	poisoning, rapidly destroys lungs
Nitrogen mustards			
HN1	1,500 inhale	200 eyes	Rare, but deadly and easy to make; delayed
	20,000 skin	9,000 skin	effects, 12 or more hours for blisters
HN2	3,000 inhale	100 eyes	Irritates eyes and throat, damages blood;
	9,500 skin		delayed effects, 12 or more hours for blisters
HN3	1,500 inhale	200 eyes	Same as above
	10,000 skin	10,000 skin	
Oximes			
CX (phosgene)			Instantaneous effects, systemic poison over a period as long as 1 year; attacks whatever tissue it comes in contact with; causes neuro-destruction, hardens tissue, and causes intense pain; Soviet invention, used in Southeast Asia (Laos)

(Continued on next page)

Table A-8. (*Continued*)

Category/designation	LCT$_{50}$	ICT$_{50}$	Symptoms/effects
Mixes			
HL	1,500 inhale	200 eyes 1,700 skin	63% Lewisites, 37% mustard; very toxic; subcutaneous damage, dry-land drowning, destruction of bone marrow
HT			60% mustard, 40% T; obsolete
Not in production			
Q		300 eyes	Obsolete
T		400 eyes	Obsolete
<u>Blood agents</u>			
Cyanide compounds			Nonpersistent asphyxiating agents; any nation with ammonia and cyanide production can make these agents; common assassin's weapon
AC	2,000 to 4,500 in open, 300 enclosed	150	Rapid rate of action, death within 15 minutes; effects vary according to concentrations; irritates eyes and upper respiratory tract and inactivates enzymes; explosive hazard, therefore common in mines and booby traps
CK	11,000	7,000	Same as above; attacks hemoglobin
Hydrate of Arsenic			
SA (Arsine)	5,000	2,500	Delayed action, from 2 hours to 11 days; accumulates in body and replaces calcium
<u>Choking agents</u>[b]			
Chlorine gas	19,000	1,800	Immediate effects; very corrosive, destroys tissue by replacing hydrogen bonding, dry-land drowning
Phosgene			
CG	3,200	1,600	Easy to make, many legitimate uses; immediate effects, extremely fatal

(Continued on next page)

Table A-8. (*Continued*)

Category/ designation	LCT_{50}	ICT_{50}	Symptoms/effects
Diphosgene CP	3,200	1,600	Phosgene and chloroform; effects same as above
Nerve agents[c]			
General			
GA (Tabun)	400	300	Very rapid effects, death in 10 to 20 minutes; skin absorption greatest risk; stimulates nervous system to destroy itself by congestion of enzymes in fluids; symptoms include sweat, blurred vision, nausea, difficult breathing, and loss of control over body functions
GB (Sarin)	100	75	Death in 1 to 10 minutes; penetrates skin; symptoms same as above
GD (Soman)	100	35	Death in 1 to 15 minutes; penetrates skin; symptoms same as above
VX	100	50	Death in 1 to 15 minutes; penetrates skin; symptoms same as above
Bicyclophosphonates			New developments that are toxic Trojan horses; toxic peptides are inserted in amino acids

a. Casualty agents are pre-nerve-agent technology. Any nation with a pesticide or basic pharmacological industry can make these agents.
b. These agents are erratic because of their gaseous form and have been superseded by nerve agents. They are very easy to make, however, because they are agents in organic chemical manufacturing.
c. These agents require sophisticated manufacturing. They have common ancestry in the German and Czech insecticide industry and attack the nervous system, specifically enzyme cholinesterase.

Table A-9. Common incapacitating agents[a]

Category/designation	LCT$_{50}$	ICT$_{50}$	Symptoms/effects
Central nervous system stimulants[b]			
Cocaine	.5 to 2 gm	20 mg	Mimics actions of noradrenaline, increases muscle activity and interferes with other enzymes that break down noradrendyme; causes hallucinations, hypertension, hyperventilation, chills, fever, headaches, failure of muscle control, and weakness
Amphetamines	.5 to 2 gm	100 mg	Same as above
Dexamphetamine	.5 to 2 gm	100 mg	Same as above
Methamphetamine	.5 to 2 gm	100 mg	Same as above
Central nervous system depressants			
Morphine	200 mg to 2 gm	20 mg	Predominantly causes depression or blocks the central nervous system, which interferes with the transmission of impulses across neural synapses; high dosages produce delirium; possible uses in riot control
Opiate derivatives	200 mg to 2 gm	20 mg	Same as above
Heroin	200 mg to 2 gm	20 mg	Same as above
Methadone	200 mg to 2 gm	20 mg	Same as above
Codeine	200 mg to 2 gm	20 mg	Same as above
Darvon	200 mg to 2 gm	20 mg	Same as above
Demerol	200 mg to 2 gm	20 mg	Same as above

(Continued on next page)

Table A-9. (*Continued*)

Category/ designation	LCT_{50}	ICT_{50}	Symptoms/effects
Psychedelic drugs			Becoming more usable with the development of microencapsulation and skin-penetrating solvents; induce visual, auditory, or other hallucinations that separate victims from reality; may also induce disturbances in cognition and perceptions, and in some instances produce psychotic behavioral patterns; wide range of effects, many related formulations of each
BZ	Unknown	Unknown	Central nervous system depressant that blocks action of acetylcholine (lessens degree and extent of impulse transmission); effect is toxic delirium
Mescaline	Unknown	400-700 mg	Similar to amphetamines; immediate threat is extreme distraction through vivid auditory and visual manifestations; hazard to others, especially when operating equipment or doing dangerous tasks; produces strong fright/flight/fight syndrome
Psilocybin	Unknown	6-16 mg	Stimulant that acts on neurotransmitter serotonin; victims unable to perform complex tasks that require hand-eye coordination; second most powerful hallucinogen to LSD
LSD		1-4 micrograms	Extremely strong central nervous system stimulant and hallucinogen that causes severe behavioral modifications and psychological effects; in 30 to 60 minutes causes profound intoxication; cannot perform even simple tasks or make rational decisions

(Continued on next page)

Table A-9. (*Continued*)

Category/ designation	LCT_{50}	ICT_{50}	Symptoms/effects
PCP		.2 micro- grams	Hallucinogenic anesthetic; produces amnesia through dissociation; acts on brain to separate victim from objective awareness, victim remains conscious; effects are bellicosity, violence, no sensitivity to pain, cardiovascular and lung spasms, coma, and confusion and dissociation for up to two months
Cannabis			Central nervous system depressant
Methaqualone			Central nervous system depressant; similar to morphine
Nitrazepan			Hypnotic, sleep-inducing substance
DMSO (dimethylsulfoxide)			Organic solvent capable of skin penetration that has a drug chain attached to it

a. These agents have been unsuccessful so far. To be successful, they must produce effects that endure for hours or days and must not endanger life or cause permanent injury. In addition, recovery from these agents must require no medical treatment or aid, and the agents themselves must be potent and easy to store.
b. These stimulants cause excessive nervous activity by boosting or facilitating impulses to the brain. They flood the brain with too much sensory information, making concentration difficult and causing indecisiveness and inability to act in a sustained, purposeful manner.

Table A-10. Common vomiting agents[a]

Designation	LCT_{50}	ICT_{50}	Symptoms/effects
DA	15,000	12	Rapid rate of action, vomiting within 3 minutes; severe irritant to eyes, nose, and throat
DC	15,000	8-22	Same as above
DM (Adamsite)	10,000	20-30	Same as above

a. These agents are not toxic enough for battle, but have been used for riot control. They have been superseded in the West by tear gas.

Table A-11. Common tear-gas agents[a]

Category	LCT_{50}	ICT_{50}	Symptoms/effects
CA	8,000	30	Causes immediate flow of tears and irritation of skin; obsolete
CN (Mace)	7,000	80	Civilian agent that causes immediate flow of tears and irritation of skin
CNB	11,000	80	Causes immediate flow of tears and irritation of skin; obsolete
CNC	11,000	80	Causes immediate flow of tears and irritation of skin; semi-obsolete
CNS	11,400	60	Causes immediate flow of tears and irritation of skin; obsolete
CS	61,000	10-20	Standard NATO riot control agents; effects are immediate; extreme irritant to nose and respiratory system.

a. These agents cause transient casualties.

Table A-12. Common biotoxins[a]

Category	Symptoms/effects
Botulinus	Neuropoison produced by bacteria that effect the release of acetylcholine in a manner similar to nerve agents; works in 12 hours to 8 days; hazard to public water and food supplies; causes cramps, constipation, vomiting, nausea, and blurred vision; affects muscle coordination and strength, respiratory tract, and heart
Ricin	1,000 times deadlier than VX; rapidly penetrates the blood/brain barrier to suppress heart functions; death occurs within minutes; favorite assassin's weapon, umbrella with platinum iridium pellet containing Ricin responsible for the deaths of several prominent people
Tricothecene Myotoxins	Yellow rain; derived from toxic contamination of grain; caused Soviet crop blight during the 1930s
Nivalenol	Strong hemorrhagic; causes immediate tissue necrosis, blisters, nausea, dizziness, and vomiting
T-2	Caustic skin irritant and hemorrhagic; other effects and symptoms same as above

a. All of these agents can be laboratory cultured. Biotoxins are classified as agents between biological and chemical agents. They are poisonous by-products of microorganisms, plants, and animals. Terrorists have cultivated these agents for their potential use against populations and food supplies.

Table A-13. Common biological agents

Category	Symptoms/effects
Bacterial	
Plague	Bubonic plague is a bloodborne disease from the bite of infected animals or their fleas; common in urban areas; symptoms include chills, fever, swelling of lymph nodes, bursting of sores, and complications, including pneumonia, meningitis, shock, and heart attack
Salmonella Typhimurium	Causes diarrhea and other gastrointestinal disorders; commonly associated with food poisoning
Tularemia	Rabbit fever; symptoms occur in two days to one week; symptoms include fever, chills, headache, acute pneumonia, lesions in intestines, and infections around the eye
Typhoid Fever	Endemic to Third World; symptoms occur in 1-4 weeks; symptoms include fever, headache, pain, nausea, vomiting, loss of appetite, nose bleeds, pneumonia, rosy spots, abscesses on buttocks, and marked decline in metabolism
Fungi[a]	
Caccidiodmycosis	Desert rheumatism; pulmonary symptoms include fever, lung congestion, and aches; disseminated symptoms include fever, rash, and meninges and bone lesions
Anti-plant fungi	
Agent C	Soya bean, sugar beet, potato, cotton, and tobacco blight
Agent E	Rice blight
Agent IE	Rice blight
Agent LO	Potato blight

(Continued on next page)

Table A-13. (*Continued*)

Category	Symptoms/effects
Rickettsia	
Q Fever	Group of microorganisms with limited metabolism that live in the body of insects and spiders; a common mode of transmittal is body lice; symptoms include constipation and diarrhea; inflammation of the heart, brain, liver, and kidneys; severe fever; intense pain; and loss of appetite; fatal 20 percent of the time
Rocky Mountain Spotted Fever	Carried by ticks; symptoms include headache, loss appetite, stupor, delirium, coma, liver and spleen enlargement, blood congestion, and circulatory collapse; many other strains of spotted fever
Typhus	Symptoms include fever, chills, headache, muscle pain, weakening, constipation, flushed skin, rash, and lesions; attacks central nervous system; causes liver and spleen damage, secondary pneumonia, and personality changes
Epidemic Typhus	Endemic to Third World; carried by human lice; rapid onset of above symptoms
Murine Typhus	Carried by fleas of rats; causes above symptoms
Brill-Zinsser Disease	Does not involve whole-body spotting; symptoms take from months to decades to develop; less violent symptoms than Epidemic Typhus
Rickettsial Pox	Carried by a mouse mite; does not involve whole-body spotting; white blood cell matter and tissues are expelled through cutaneous eruptions; symptoms include fever, loss of appetite, headache, malaise, and rash
Scrub Typhus	Carried by chiggers; common in Asia and in Pacific Islands; does not involve whole-body spotting

(Continued on next page)

Table A-13. (*Continued*)

Category	Symptoms/effects
Viruses[b]	
Dengue Fever	Carried by mosquitoes; causes fever, sore throat, skin eruptions, and pain and inflammation of the nose and throat
Encephalitis	Carried by ticks; attacks the brain and spreads through the central nervous system causing severe damage within a week; degenerates body organs and causes severe mental changes
Influenza	Spread person to person, often pandemic or epidemic; causes weakness, inflammation of respiratory tract, muscle pain and insomnia, and opportunity for other infections
Meningitis	Condition brought on by mumps, measles, herpes, and other viruses; inflames meninges around the brain and neck; can cause personality changes
Yellow Fever	Carried by mosquitoes; attacks liver and digestive tract; three stages: fever and pain, false remission, and profuse sweating with yellow skin
Smallpox	Spread person to person; symptoms include severe chills, headache, pain, skin eruptions, and pustules
Rift Valley Fever	Carried by mosquitoes; common in East Africa; symptoms include fever, diarrhea, liver damage, inflammation of retina, and altered state of consciousness
Psittacosis	Carried by poultry; common in tropical areas; symptoms include nausea, diarrhea, chills, fever, and pneumonia; fatal 20 percent of the time

a. Single-cell vegetable organism that cannot metabolize certain proteins and enzymes without a living organism.
b. Viruses are the smallest and simplest life form and consist of a protein jacket around a core of nucleic acid. A virus is attracted to and attaches to specific areas in a host where it redirects host cells to its own end. Bioengineered viruses attack specific areas or bodily functions. Viruses are very durable and difficult to detect.

and effects. The tables of chemical agents (tables A-8 through A-11) also include two measures of toxicity—LCT_{50} and ICT_{50}. The toxicity, or dosage, of a chemical warfare agent is a function of its concentration and the time the victim is exposed. When an agent is lethal, the lethal dosage that will kill 50 percent of the population is expressed as LD_{50}, and the lethal concentration/ time that will kill 50 percent of the exposed population is expressed as LCT_{50}. The lower the LCT, the greater the toxicity. Units are measured in $mg/m^3/min$. The ICT_{50} is the dosage of a chemical warfare agent that will incapacitate 50 percent of the exposed population by interfering with normal duties.

Selected Third World Examples

Several Third World nations have advanced CBW capabilities. Those addressed here are Syria, Libya, North Korea, and Angola.

Syria possesses the most advanced CBW capability in the Arab world. The Syrians reportedly have a facility that can produce nerve agents. Early in 1988, reports surfaced that Israel was "extremely likely" to attack the nerve-gas plant in Syria, which is located north of Damascus. This highlights one of the dangers of chemical and biological agent proliferation and proliferation of advanced weapons in general: the military pressure to preempt before the possessor uses the weapons.

The problems over the Libyan chemical plant began to intensify in 1987 when the United States sent 2,000 gas masks to Chad in anticipation that Libya might use chemical weapons. This concern came to light when U.S. intelligence discovered that Libya had struck a deal to supply Iran with advanced mines in return for chemical weapons.

North Korea possesses the world's third largest CBW force, which includes sophisticated means of delivery [artillery and rocket systems, tactical missiles (Frog-7 and Scud-B), mortar shells, aerial bombs, spray tanks, and mines] and local production of agents (at least eight plants). Although not self-sufficient, North Korea still imports significant quantities of chemicals from Japan, providing a good example of how an underdeveloped country can build a substantial chemical warfare force. The most disconcerting aspect of North Korea's chemical-biological capability may be the North Korean Government's willingness to assist other countries in the production and employment of these weapons. North Korea is believed to have provided Iran with Scud-B chemical warheads and is apparently cooperating with Syria in biological warfare research. In the case of Libya, a similar pattern was attempted—first importing agro-chemicals, then obtaining training and technical assistance to build (dual-use) production facilities, and finally producing the agents.

In the event of a North Korean invasion of South Korea, U.S. troops would be in serious trouble because the South Koreans lack retaliatory means and U.S. capabilities are not present. North Korea's inventory includes Sarin (GB), Tabun (GA), Phosgene (CX), Adamsite (DM), various mustard gases, and blood agents. In addition, North Korea has had biological warfare capabilities since the early 1980s, including such strains of bacteria as anthrax, cholera, bubonic plague, smallpox, and yellow fever.

In an operational sense, perhaps the most ominous implication is the growing use of chemical agent mixtures to achieve breakthrough. Gas, formerly a useful but annoying backup to conventional operations, is now used as a strategic weapon. In addition, gas has been shown to be useful in guerrilla warfare, wiping out the villages that the insurgents rely on for support. The Soviet Union appears to have used this technique quite effectively in Afghanistan and has supplied Cuba and Ethiopia with the means to do the same.

The use of lethal mixtures could become standard practice in the Third World, as well as by communist armies. The mixes in Angola were used by Cubans and dropped from Hind helicopters to flush out UNITA rebels from strongholds in remote areas and to deny them the support of the local population. In this case, the Cubans used chemical weapons just after the FAPLA, the military wing of the ruling Popular Movement for the Liberation of Angola, suffered its most decisive defeats of the 12-year civil war. In addition, nations do not have to rely on the traditional CBW agents such as Sarin or mustard to develop their arsenals. Third World states seeking to develop a

CBW capability surreptitiously may also use nontraditional chemicals as weapons to retain the element of surprise.

Effect on U.S. Forces

For LIC scenarios, the ease with which chemical agents and simple delivery means can be obtained or even produced, coupled with their devastating and dramatic effect, makes chemical weapons ideal for terrorists. Barring the use of a nuclear device, no other weapon can achieve the havoc, attention, and effect of a simple chemical weapon in a crowd or facility.

This assessment is probably on the conservative side, because the full extent of the chemical threat in the world is not fully known. Production is simple; possession is not easily detected; and latent capabilities exist almost everywhere. Many of the precursor chemicals and most of the processing equipment required for the production of lethal agents have numerous legitimate industrial applications.

Historically, the greatest leverage for the United States over the direction and outcome of Third World wars comes from resupply efforts. The teeth of Third World armies far outstrip their tails. Besides, many states are tempted to invest in visible and high-prestige items such as aircraft and tanks and find, in warfare, that they are suddenly dependent on external sources for resupply, spare parts, and, often, the technicians to install them. When resupply ceases, there is a military collapse or a halt in fighting. This pattern may not continue as Third World states stockpile ammunition and many spare parts of the material needed to sustain operations. For now, however, the effectiveness of the majority of major advanced weapon systems depends on such intangibles as organization.

U.S. forces are vulnerable to CBW. The normal, initial defensive role of U.S. troops makes them known targets subject to surprise attacks. The tactical advantages of chemical and biological weapons favor offensive forces because they choose the time, location, and persistency of the attack. Chemical and biological weapons are unique in action and offer advantages unparalleled by conventional ordnance. Furthermore, they cause no collateral damage to equipment or facilities. Varied and intense climates exacerbate the problems and highlight shortfalls in the U.S. chemical-biological defensive equipment inventory. Protective clothing has a debilitating effect on operational effectiveness, and, in some areas (such as Southwest Asia), high temperatures will require more frequent doses of antibodies and preventative chemicals.

In addition, naval forces operating within the range of shore-based delivery systems are also vulnerable. Alarm systems and air-filtration devices should be required on all naval vessels, especially those to be deployed in a task force. Numerous studies have shown how degrading a chemical or biological weapon attack would be to naval forces.

If U.S. or allied forces become involved in a crisis area, or in other nations that have such capabilities but have not used them yet, chemical-biological protection is vital. Rear-area operations, such as airlift and sealift, face the prospect of landing in areas subject to chemical-biological attacks. These forces do not typically train for this environment.

Above all, given the dangerous Third World environment and the relaxation of constraints, the United States should proceed with a chemical deterrence and retaliatory capability. In addition, the availability of such a capability must be ensured. This will lessen the asymmetries of force effectiveness that historically provide an incentive for chemical use. Weapons like Bigeye would play important roles in deterrence and retaliation in the Third World because they can be carried on board naval vessels and can be delivered by naval aircraft.

As for the very real potential of chemical and biological weapon use by terrorists, the problems for overseas forces are compounded. Terrorist use of these types of weapons may well be under way: 400 kilograms of organo-phosphorous compounds were seized in Germany; a cell of the Bader-Meinhof gang was apprehended in the process of manufacturing botulism toxin in Paris; and do-it-yourself CBW handbooks for terrorists have been confiscated. This threat extends to vulnerable government installations, which are grossly unprepared physically and psychologically for such an attack. Chemical and biological weapons could be an attractive alternative to defeat current physical security measures. Deterrence, in this case, is a matter of defense means, measures, and readiness. Terrorists do not usually provide targets for retaliation. In the case of state-sponsored terrorism, such organizations could have access to chemical and biological resources; therefore, protective systems and intelligence systems must be in place, first, to provide warning and, second, to defend against chemical and biological weapon use.

NUCLEAR WEAPONS

The mechanisms in place to control the proliferation of nuclear technology have been relatively successful. Since the Chinese conducted their test in 1964, no state has officially joined the nuclear club, although certain states have made progress in obtaining nuclear weapons. Specifically, these states are Israel (late 1960s), India (1974; has since suspended its program, although recent reports indicate that it could build a thermonuclear device), South Africa (early 1980s), and Pakistan, which is at the threshold. Argentina, Brazil, Iran, Iraq, and Libya, although they lack the ability to manufacture nuclear weapons, have taken active steps towards that end. Progress has been slow for several reasons. The pressures of major powers (for instance, the Soviets are closely scrutinizing Libyan efforts) and the great lag between initiating a program and actually developing the capability to build a nuclear weapon are the primary reasons for the restraint on nuclear aspirations of Third World states thus far. Table A-14 lists those countries that possess nuclear weapons and those that could construct them in the future.

Several dangers are obvious. First, Third World states may upset the relatively stable and predictable balance that has developed among the five nuclear powers. Unpredictability is added: many of the states that are close to possessing nuclear devices are in unstable regions with a history of recent conflict. Second, the weapons may fall into the hands of terrorists, either by deliberate state support or via internal instability. When radical leaders come to power, restraints are often swept away and any action that furthers the revolution is justified. Third, the risk of war by preemption is increased.

Table A-14. Nuclear-weapon-capable states

	Date of first fission explosion	Date of first thermonuclear explosion
States with confirmed capability		
United States	1945	1952
Soviet Union	1949	1952
China	1964	1967
United Kingdom	1952	1957
France	1960	1968
India	1974	–

States that have a high probability of possession

Israel (since 1960s)
Argentina
Taiwan
South Africa (since late 1970s)
Canada

States capable of building within 1 to 3 years

Japan (possesses reprocessing plants)
Pakistan
Italy
Sweden
Iraq[a]
Germany (possesses reprocessing plants)
Spain
Iran

(Continued on next page)

Table A-14. (*Continued*)

	Date of first fission explosion	Date of first thermonuclear explosion

States capable of building within 7 to 10 years

Austria
Egypt
Mexico
Romania
Yugoslavia
Denmark
Finland
Portugal
Turkey

States capable of building within 4 to 6 years

Belgium
Czechoslovakia
South Korea
Poland
North Korea
Brazil
Netherlands
Switzerland

a. Current Iraqi capabilities following the Gulf War must be categorized as uncertain.

SHORT- AND MEDIUM-RANGE BALLISTIC AND CRUISE MISSILES

Tables A-15 and A-16 list Soviet missile systems for which chemical warheads are known to exist. Because these systems are found in the armies of many of the nations identified above, it would be prudent to assume that, in a worst case, they could be used to deliver chemical munitions. Table A-17 presents a breakdown of known missile capabilities by country.

Table A-15. Soviet chemical delivery systems

Weapon	Range	Projectile weight	Unit deploying	Number of weapons in unit
122 mm	12 km	25.8 kg	Regiment	6 (36 MRDs[a]; 60 TDs[b])
130 mm	27 km	33.5 kg	Army	36
152 mm	17 km	43.6 kg	Division	18
BM-21	15 km	45.9 kg	Division	18
Frog-7 540 mm	70 km	436 kg 216 kg agent	Division	4
Scud-A	90 km	~ 680 kg	Army	3
Scud-B 884 mm	280 km	985 kg 555 kg agent	Army	3

a. Motor rifle divisions.
b. Tank divisions.

Table A-16. Soviet/Warsaw Treaty Organization multiple rocket launchers

Weapon	Caliber	Range	Number of tubes
RM-71	122 mm	20.5 km	40 (x2)
WP-8	140 mm	9.8 km	8
RPU-14	140 mm	9.8 km	16
BM-14-17	140 mm	9.8 km	17
BM-14-16	140 mm	9.8 km	16
BM-27	120 mm	9.8 km	16
M-51	130 mm	8.2 km	32

Table A-17. Third World short- and medium-range ballistic and cruise missile capabilities

Country	Missile	Range	Warhead	Notes
Afghanistan	Scud-B	300 km	2,000-kg HE	Ballistic missile; chemical and nuclear-capable, truck-mounted
	Saqr-80	80 km	–	Egyptian ballistic missile
Algeria	Frog-7	70 km	700-kg HE	Ballistic missile; chemical and nuclear capable; launched from a wheeled transporter
	SS-N-2B Styx	80 km	400-kg HE	Shipborne cruise missile
Argentina	Condor-1	150 km	–	Ballistic missile
	Condor-2	800 km	1,500-kg HE	Ballistic missile; in development
	MM-40 Exocet	70+ km	105-kg HE	Naval surface-to-surface cruise missile
	MM-38 Exocet	50+ km	HE	Naval surface-to-surface cruise missile
	ASM-2	–	–	Air-to-surface cruise missile
	AM-39 E/H Exocet	50-70 km	165-kg HE	Air-to-surface cruise missile
Bahrain	MM-40 Exocet	38 miles	HE	Naval surface-to-surface cruise missile
Brazil	Astros-2	68 km	–	Ballistic surface-to-surface missile
	SS-300	~300 km	–	In development
	EE-150	~150 km	–	In development
	Sonda-4	~300 km	–	In development
	EE-600	~375 km	–	Negotiations with Libya
	MM-38 Exocet	42 km	165-kg HE	Naval surface-to-surface cruise missile
	SM-70	–	–	Antiship cruise missile

(Continued on next page)

Table A-17. (*Continued*)

Country	Missile	Range	Warhead	Notes
Cuba	Frog-7	70 km	700-kg HE	Ballistic missile; chemical and nuclear capable, launched from a wheeled transporter
	SS-N-2 Styx	80 km	400-kg HE	Shipborne cruise missile
Egypt	Frog-7	70 km	700-kg HE	Ballistic missile; chemical and nuclear capable, launched from a wheeled transporter
	Saqr-80	80 km	–	–
	SS-1C Scud-B	300 km	2,000-kg HE	Ballistic missile; chemical and nuclear capable
	Badr-2000	1,000 km	–	Ballistic missile; chemical and nuclear capable; working with Iraq and Argentina from Condor-II
	SS-N-2A Styx	80 km	400-kg HE	Shipborne cruise missile
	AS-30	12 km	240-kg HE	Air-to-surface cruise missile
	AS-7 Kerry	10 km	100-kg HE	Air-to-surface cruise missile
	Otomat SSM	180 km	210-kg HE	Naval surface-to-surface cruise missile
	AS-1 Kennel	90 km	HE	Air-to-surface cruise missile
	AS-5 Kelt	180 km	1,600-kg HE	Air-to-surface cruise missile
	AGM-65 Maverick	–	59-kg HE	Air-to-surface cruise missile
India	Prithvi	240 km	–	One-stage ballistic missile
	Agni	2,400 km	–	Two-stage ballistic missile
	SS-N-2/C Styx	80 km	450-kg HE	Shipborne cruise missile
	SS-45	40-50 km	HE	Multiple launch rocket system, in development

(Continued on next page)

Table A-17. (*Continued*)

Country	Missile	Range	Warhead	Notes
India (cont.)	Trishul	–	HE	Antiship cruise missile; in development
Indonesia	RX-250	~250 km	HE	In development
	RGM-84A Harpoon	90+ km	HE, nuclear	Naval cruise missile
	MM-38 Exocet	50+ km	HE	Naval cruise missile
Iran	Oghab	40 km	About 700 kg	Ballistic missile; local production version of the Frog
	Shahin-2	125 km	HE	Ballistic missile
	Nazeat	125 km	HE	Ballistic missile
	SS-1C Scud-B	300 km	2,000-kg HE	Ballistic missile; chemical and nuclear capable
	SM-1	–	–	Naval ballistic missile
	Sea Killer	25 km	70-kg HE	Naval cruise missile
	AS-12	800 m	28-kg HE	Air-to-surface cruise missile
Iraq[a]	Frog-7	70 km	700-kg HE	Ballistic missile; chemical and nuclear capable, launched from a wheeled transporter
	SS-1C Scud-B	300 km	2,000-kg HE	Ballistic missile; chemical and nuclear capable
	Astros	68 km	–	Ballistic missile
	al-Hussayn	600 km	HE	Modified Scud ballistic missile
	al-Abbas	900 km	HE	Ballistic missile, in development
	MGM-52 Lance	110 km	225-kg HE	Ballistic missile
	Otomat	180 km	210-kg HE	Naval surface-to-surface cruise missile

a. Current Iraqi capabilities following the Gulf War must be categorized as uncertain.

(*Continued on next page*)

Table A-17. (*Continued*)

Country	Missile	Range	Warhead	Notes
Iraq (cont.)	SS-N-2 Styx	80 km	400-kg HE	Shipborne cruise missile
	AS-30 Laser	10 km	240-kg HE	Air-to-surface cruise missile
	Armat	–	–	Air-to-surface cruise missile
	AS-5 Kelt	180 km	160 kg	Air-to-surface cruise missile
	AM-39 Exocet	50-70 km	165-kg HE	Air-to-surface cruise missile
	AS-4 Kitchen	300-800 km	Nuclear or HE	Air-to-surface cruise missile
Israel	Jerico-1	450-650 km	500-kg HE	Ballistic missile; chemical and nuclear capable
	Jerico-2	1,450 km	500-kg HE	Ballistic missile; chemical and nuclear capable; in development
	Gabriel	60+ km	HE	Ship-to-surface cruise missile
	RGM-84A Harpoon	90+ km	HE, nuclear	Ship-to-surface cruise missile
	Gabriel II	36 km	100-kg HE	Air-to-surface cruise missile
	Luz	–	–	Air-to-surface cruise missile
	AGM-65 Maverick	–	59-kg HE	Air-to-surface cruise missile
	AGM-45 Shrike	16 km	HE	Air-to-surface cruise missile
	AGM-12 Bullpup	17 km	454-kg HE	Air-to-surface ballistic missile
North Korea	Frog-7	70 km	700-kg HE	Ballistic missile; chemical and nuclear capable, launched from a wheeled transporter

(Continued on next page)

Table A-17. (*Continued*)

Country	Missile	Range	Warhead	Notes
North Korea (cont.)	SS-1C Scud-B	300 km	2,000-kg HE	Ballistic missile; chemical and nuclear capable
	SS-N-2 Styx	80 km	400-kg HE	Shipborne cruise missile
South Korea	Honest John	33 km	HE, nuclear	Surface-to-surface ballistic missile
	RGM-84A Harpoon	90+ km	HE, nuclear	Ship-to-surface cruise missile
	MM-38 Exocet	50+ km	HE	Ship-to-surface cruise missile
	AGM-65A Maverick	–	59-kg HE	Air-to-surface cruise missile
Kuwait	Frog-7	70 km	700-kg HE	Ballistic missile; chemical and nuclear capable; launched from a wheeled transporter
	MM-40 Exocet	70+ km	165-kg HE	Ship-to-surface cruise missile
	AM-39 Exocet	50-70 km	165-kg HE	Air-to-surface cruise missile
Libya	Frog-7	70 km	700-kg HE	Ballistic missile; chemical and nuclear capable, launched from a wheeled transporter
	SS-1C Scud-B	300 km	2,000-kg HE	Ballistic missile; chemical and nuclear capable
	SS-N-2C Styx	80 km	400-kg HE	Shipborne cruise missile
	Otomat	180 km	210-kg HE	Naval surface-to-surface cruise missile
	SS-12M	–	–	Naval surface-to-surface cruise missile
Pakistan	Haft-2	80 km	–	In development
	RGM-84A Harpoon	90+ km	HE, nuclear	Ship-to-surface cruise missile
	AM-39 Exocet	50-70 km	165-kg HE	Air-to-surface cruise missile

(*Continued on next page*)

Table A-17. (*Continued*)

Country	Missile	Range	Warhead	Notes
Saudi Arabia	Astros-2	68 km	–	Ballistic missile
	CSS-2	2,500 km	2,045-kg HE	Chinese DFA-3; ballistic missile; chemical and nuclear (1.3 megaton) capable; inaccurate
	AGM-65 Maverick	–	59-kg HE	Air-to-surface cruise missile
	Otomat-2	180 km	210-kg HE	Naval surface-to-surface cruise missile
	RGM-84A Harpoon	90+ km	HE, nuclear	Ship-to-surface cruise missile
Syria	SS-21 Scarab	150 km	2,000-kg HE	Ballistic missile; Syria reportedly possesses 36 SS-21 missiles; chemical and nuclear capable
	Frog-7	70 km	700-kg HE	Ballistic missile; chemical and nuclear capable, launched from a wheeled transporter
	SS-1C Scud-B	300 km	2,000-kg HE	Ballistic missile; chemical and nuclear capable
	SS-C-1B Sepal	300 km	750-kg HE	Mobile cruise missile for coastal defense
	SS-N-2 Styx	80 km	400-kg HE	Shipborne cruise missile
Taiwan	Honest John	33 km	HE	Ballistic missile
	Hsiung Feng	18 km	100-kg HE	Modified Gabriel cruise missile for coastal defense
	HF-2	–	–	Modified Gabriel naval surface-to-surface cruise missile
	AGM-12 Bullpup	17 km	454-kg HE	Radio-commanded anti-ship missile
	AGM-65A Maverick	–	59-kg HE	Air-to-surface cruise missile

(*Continued on next page*)

Table A-17. (*Continued*)

Country	Missile	Range	Warhead	Notes
Thailand	MM-40 Exocet	70+ km	165-kg HE	Ship-to-surface cruise missile
	Gabriel	60+ km	HE	Ship-to-surface cruise missile
Vietnam	SS-N-2 Styx	80 km	HE	Shipborne cruise missile
North Yemen	SS-21 Scarab	120 km	3,000-kg HE	Ballistic missile; chemical and nuclear capable
South Yemen	Frog-7	70 km	700-kg HE	Ballistic missile; chemical and nuclear capable, launched from a wheeled transporter
	SS-1C Scud-B	300 km	2,000-kg HE	Ballistic missile; chemical and nuclear capable
	SS-21 Scarab	120 km	3,000-kg HE	Ballistic missile; chemical and nuclear capable

The data in this appendix were taken from *The Military Balance 1989-1990,* published by the International Institute for Strategic Studies, and *The Jane's* series on *Fighting Ships, All the World's Aircraft, Weapons Systems,* and *EW and Electronics Systems.*

About the Author

Dr. Harlan K. Ullman wrote *In Harm's Way* as part of the Center for Naval Analyses Senior Fellows Program. In addition to his duties as a CNA Senior Fellow, he serves as a Senior Associate at the Center for Strategic and International Studies in Washington, D.C., Counselor at the Atlantic Council in Washington, D.C., and Chairman of the South Pacific-USA Group as well as on several boards of directors.

He received his bachelor's degree from the U.S. Naval Academy and his Ph.D. in Political Science and International Economics from the Fletcher School of Law and Diplomacy, a joint program of Tufts and Harvard Universities. In addition, he was a visiting fellow at the Naval War College and at the International Institute for Strategic Studies in London, England, from 1972 to 1973. During 20 years of naval service, he was posted to a variety of command, operational, and staff assignments, including a tour as commanding officer of a destroyer that deployed to the Persian Gulf during the Iran-Iraq war, Professor of Military Strategy at the National War College in Washington, D.C., two years with the Royal Navy at sea, and a tour in Vietnam in Swift Boats.

He is widely published in the fields of defense and national security and is a frequent commentator on U.S., Japanese, and British television. He is working on his next book, tentatively titled *America Strikes Out*, about the United States in the new century. This book is scheduled for completion in 1992.